Food, Family and Tradition

Hungarian Kosher Family Recipes and Remembrances

For information, write to:
Lynn Kirsche Shapiro
The Cherry Press, LLC
4020 West Oakton Street
Skokie, Illinois 60076
lynn.thecherrypress@gmail.com

Printed in Canada by Friesens Corporation

Editor: Nancy Ross Ryan
Literary Consultant: Lisa Ekus
Book design: Anda Reuben, anda.reuben@gmail.com

Publisher: The Cherry Press, LLC
ISBN 978-0-9898479-0-2

Food, Family and Tradition

Hungarian Kosher Family Recipes and Remembrances

....

Lynn Kirsche Shapiro

"As my parents have planted for me, so too I plant for my children."
(Talmud Ta'anit 23a)

DEDICATION

To those who planted:

This book is dedicated to my parents, Sandor *z"l* and Margit Kirsche, who cherished and nurtured their parents' faith and traditions, passing them on to future generations.

And to the memory of my grandparents *hy"d*, who were murdered in the Holocaust; and my aunt, Goldie Weinberger *z"l*, who survived and remained true to the Jewish faith even in the Soviet Union.

Acknowledgements

Special thanks to the following without whom this book would never be:

Irv Shapiro, my "extra ordinary" husband,
for supporting me in every aspect of this project while encouraging me to persevere

My mom, Margit Kirsche, for reliving painful and joyful memories,
for remaining, at 90, the expert, the cook, the inspiration

My father, Sandor Kirsche ז״ל, for teaching me the power and meaning
of telling the story of my heritage, for remaining ever hopeful and always kind

My daughter, Tova, for being my on-site food styling and presentation coach
and for walking through the glitches with me

My daughter, Rocky, for giving her heart and soul and countless hours,
listening, writing, editing, recipe testing, and for her passion for telling this story

My son, Sammy, for his optimism and encouragement, for his listening ear
and above all, for sharing my vision from the first moment

My son, Aaron, for his talents in writing, storytelling, and cooking,
bringing clarity of vision and confidence when I needed it most

My sons-in-law, Mikey and Myles, and my daughter-in-law, Debbie,
for their support and for sharing this family experience

All my grandchildren, the next generation of "Kirsche family chefs,"
for giving me the reason to write this book

My brother, Ira Kirsche, for our unique bond as siblings
and his commitment to the legacy of this book

My niece, Alisa, the nutritionist, for her fresh perspective on traditional food,
and my nephew, Daniel, for his expertise in kosher wines

My cousin, Ibi Gelb, for launching this project with me
and contributing with recipes and stories

My cousins, Irving and Sonia Weinberger,
for major remembrances, hours of sharing and telling the story of Munkács

Rabbi Moshe Soloveichik and Rabbi Harvey Well
for their religious advice and steadfast friendship

Veronica Sporia for cooking and sharing stories with me,
Caryn Bean for her unfailing organizational talents,
and Matt Levy for his guidance in kosher wines

For remembrances, recipes, and testing:
Rabbi Nachum Muschel, Rachel Grossman, Moshe Moskovics, Apfeldorf Family,
Brindy Cziment, Elsa Ickovic, Alex Zelczer, Beatrice Zivic, Joe Mauer,
Ellena Maghanoy and Maria Fratila,
United States Holocaust Memorial Museum for finding family documents and history
and Steven Vitto for his patience and perseverance with the research

Nick Ulivieri, my amazing photographer, for bringing the food to life·

Anda Reuben, my brilliant designer, for magically transforming my vision into reality,
and Yoraan Rafael Reuben for his photographic contributions

Nancy Ross Ryan, my editor, for her partnership and reassurance
and for taking the journey over endless hours with me

Lisa Ekus, my publishing consultant, for believing in me and my book from Day One

Contents

Part II
Recipes

Foreword

Mesorah

Mesorah—a special word that is loosely translated as tradition, in reality means so much more. Indeed Mesorah is, in many ways, the very foundation of our people, the Jewish people, and the reason that we have survived for all of these years as a nation.

The root word of Mesorah is *masar*, to hand over, to pass from one generation to another. It is far more encompassing than the laws of honoring one's parents because it teaches us how to keep our parents' lessons and their examples both relevant and alive.

My dear friend, Lynn Shapiro has authored a book on Mesorah, on tradition. The casual reader may think that it is a cookbook, but they would be mistaken. Indeed the very recipes that are included in this book are part of Lynn's traditions, the lessons that she learned from her parents, the legacy that she carries within her.

My wife Vivien and I have a marked and important advantage over most people reading this book. We were adopted by Lynn's parents who took us on a trip to their hometowns in Eastern Europe. We had the *zechus* (privilege) of being with them for over a week, of visiting their *shtetlach* (villages) in Europe and of seeing the very homes in which they grew up, and especially of being included in the Kirsche Mesorah, a Mesorah that continued after the trip when we returned to Chicago. Mr. Sandor Kirsche, of blessed memory, a Holocaust survivor, taught us how to be forgiving, how to always be optimistic in life, how to be industrious and how to build for the future. And Mrs. Margit Kirsche, may she be blessed with years and health, became blind at the age of 75, yet taught us how to see through the darkness and how to face each challenge with courage.

Their daughter Lynn has faithfully continued in their ways. Her book is divided into two parts. The first is a reflection of the Kirsche family and their amazing story of survival and success. It brings vividly to life their *shtetlach*, and their daily lives there. Their story is not theirs alone, because it mirrors the stories of so many Holocaust survivors. The second part of the book is a cookbook and the family recipes that made Hungarian Kosher, the store that they built, into a landmark institution. Lynn has preserved the Mesorah of her parents and more importantly, she has passed it on, together with her husband, Irvin, to their children. And now she shares it with us.

I congratulate Lynn on this remarkable achievement with the full knowledge that anyone who reads this book will be doubly rewarded. First they will benefit virtually from reading and preparing the wonderful recipes. Second they will benefit spiritually, knowing that they have shared in an important aspect of the Mesorah of our people.

Rabbi Harvey Weil

The Jew of Erev Shabbos

Since its inception, Jewish tradition has been perpetuated by the Mesorah, which is the linkage of its generations. Jewish history has been stained by calamitous events that have not only resulted in the genocide of a large number of our brethren, but threatened to break the golden chain that linked the generations of the Jewish people: the exile of the Jewish people from their land, the Crusades, Spanish Inquisition, and the Nazis' methodical campaign to destroy the Jewish nation. The Nazis not only eliminated organized Jewish life and most of the communities of Europe, but also created perhaps the greatest challenge to the continuation of the Mesorah. However, as a result of a strong educational, religious, institutional involvement through Synagogues, *Yeshivas*, etc, the intellectual Mesorah of Torah, learning and observance has been revived.

While the intellectual Mesorah as well as the Mesorah of compliance with Jewish law and customs has successfully been revived, I believe that the Mesorah of feeling, emotion and spirit remains dormant. Before World War II, the home and family were the base for transmission of Mesorah; today it has become the religious institutions.

My uncle, "The Rav," Rabbi Joseph B. Soloveitchik, z"l, spoke about the "Jew of Shabbos" and the "Jew of Erev Shabbos." During the years after World War II, we have produced generations of Shabbos-observing Jews who adhere to the *halachos* (laws) concerning Shabbos, but not the "Jew of Erev Shabbos." Erev Shabbos has few *halachos* (laws) associated with it; but it has feelings and emotion of the anticipation of the coming of Shabbos associated with its preparation.

The Kirsche family not only educated their children in Jewish schools, but, like their ancestors, built a home that perpetuated Jewish tradition. This was coupled with a strong emphasis on giving over the religious feeling and emotions that were shared by their parents and grandparents pre-World War II. Their home was one that had its foundation in *chesed* (kindness), respect for all human beings, love of Torah as well as love and concern for Jews everywhere especially in the State of Israel. There was also an unparalleled work ethic with a rigorous attitude of honesty. The major attribute of the Kirsche family was giving over these Jewish values to future generations.

Mr. Sandor Kirsche z"l, and his wife, Mrs. Margit Kirsche, endured and survived the worst of the hell of the Shoah (Holocaust). To all those who have known them, they were not just survivors, but builders and perpetuators of our full Mesorah. Their children, grandchildren and now, even great-grandchildren, each in their own way, continue in their path in perpetuating the Jewish tradition.

The spirit of Erev Shabbos in the Kirsche home also became visible in their business. When customers come to Hungarian Kosher Foods to acquire food for Shabbos, they leave with a spirit and feeling of anticipation for Shabbos that was a pre-World War II phenomenon.

This book is not just a compilation of recipes, but a book that perpetuates the feeling and emotions of the Jewish home. Its publication will, I hope, contribute to strengthening the idea that even post-World War II, the Jew can be both a "Jew of Shabbos" as well as a "Jew of Erev Shabbos."

Rabbi Moshe Soloveichik

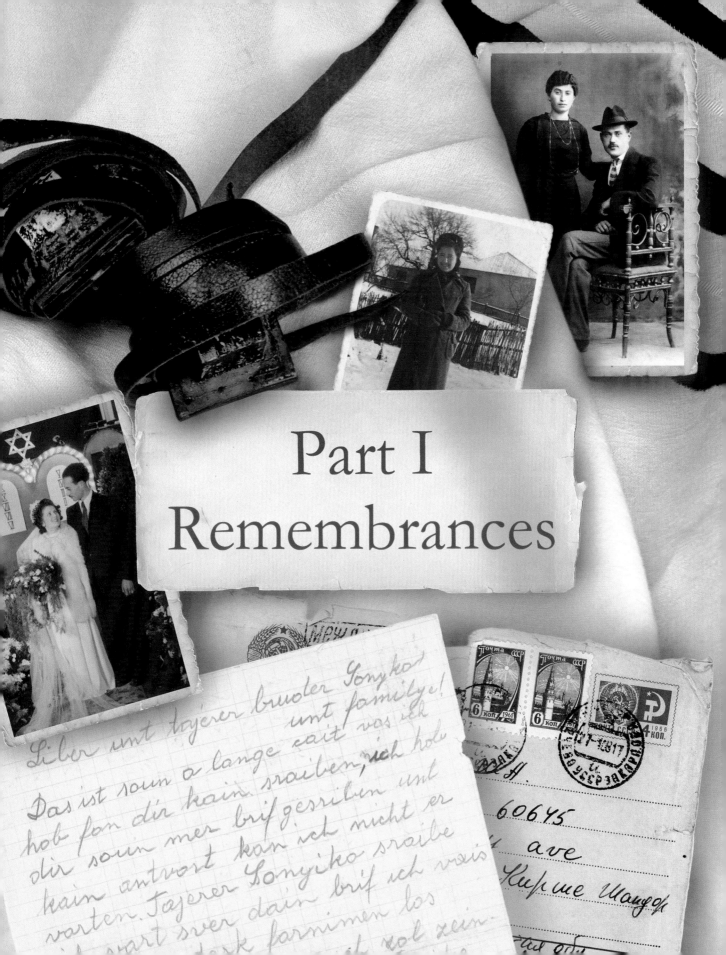

Part I
Remembrances

Introduction
Lynn Kirsche Shapiro

Sandor and Margit Kirsche, 1948

This cookbook began as my way to complete two unfinished legacies: my mother's recipes and my father's autobiography. I wanted to write down my mother's recipes—for her and for me. For her, because at 75 this active, fiercely independent woman became, in the blink of an eye, blind from ischemic optic neuropathy. By writing down her recipes I hoped to let her see some small part of her contribution to our lives and the lives of others. I wanted to write the recipes down for myself so they would not be lost to future generations.

While compiling these recipes my father had begun his autobiography together with my daughter Rocky. He wanted not only to tell his life story but also to "bear witness" to all the lives that had touched his and that had been lost in the Holocaust. His project was cut short by his death at the age of 81.

After beginning the book I understood that my family's recipes and history were part of a larger world: the traditional Jewish life in Czechoslovakia and Hungary before the Holocaust. Many books have been written to educate others, to bear witness to the events and atrocities of the Holocaust. My book also attempts to give a picture of the richness of Jewish life in Eastern Europe prior to the Holocaust. Strong family traditions were the bedrock on which our parents, and so many of the Holocaust survivors, were raised. It is because of this strong family bond, deep tradition and unwavering faith that our parents were able to live again, to build a family, and to contribute to the future.

I am no historian, but my hope is that through my family's stories you will see a picture of the community that was suddenly and brutally extinguished, the dedication to Jewish law that was solid and resilient, and the warmth of the Jewish community. I hope that through these centuries-old recipes you will get a taste of the culinary tradition of the Jews in Hungary and Czechoslovakia. Finally, I hope that you will feel the dedication of the Holocaust survivors—those who remained in Europe, those who went to Israel and those who came to the States.

Synagogue in Ungvár (Uzhgorod), 2001

Cooking and sharing food have been central to our family life. Through the daily and special holiday meals that our parents cooked, we were able to visualize our grandparents and their daily life, immersed as it was in Jewish tradition and observance. As children of Holocaust survivors, whose families had been mostly wiped out, the preparations as well as the meals were replete with tales and stories that filled me with a sense of and longing for the large loving family that my parents so vividly described. Cooking with my parents connected me with their family and filled the void.

Each year in preparation for Pesach, my mother would bake sponge cakes: plain sponge cakes, chocolate sponge cakes, frosted sponge cakes, sponge cakes with nuts, and more. A few nights before the Seder, my mother would prepare about six cakes at a time, using huge dishpans as mixing bowls. Baking these sponge cakes was much easier with two people. While baking together, she recalled her childhood memories, preparing and celebrating Pesach with her large family. Even though our family during those years consisted only of my mother, my father, my brother and myself, our Pesach was shared with the grandparents, aunts and uncles who were no longer with us.

My father, Sandor Kirsche, survived the Holocaust at the age of 19, having lost most of his family. He told stories at the family dinner table, while he was cooking at Hungarian Kosher Foods, and even to customers in the store. Stories of my father's childhood and of the Holocaust were my bedtime stories. So readers should not be surprised or dismayed to find, alongside the recipes, both happy stories and horrendous tales. For example, his memory of community matza-making in his family's home, alongside the tale of returning home from Budapest in March of 1944 just before Pesach to find his father had been taken by the Nazis—and yet, the family still made the matza.

Just as the stories in this book are their stories, the recipes are their recipes. These recipes reflect a Jewish culture that was cut off by the Holocaust, but whose tradition lived on even after the destruction of six million Jews. I share with you, as they have shared with us—their children, grandchildren and great-grandchildren—their food, their faith and their tradition, through their cooking "at home."

"At home" is a common phrase that my parents used to refer to the homes where they grew up

Kirschenbaum family home in Hluboka

and spent their childhood years, before the Holocaust. For my mother, this meant her home in Vásárosnamény, Hungary. For my father, as well as my aunt, Goldie Weinberger, home refers to Hluboka, Czechoslovakia; for my cousin, Ibi Gelb, home refers to Munkács, after the Holocaust. The one place that "home" never meant was Chicago, where they all ultimately lived and made their home.

Writing about the journey of my family, has been a journey for me. I thought my journey would be simple: retelling their stories and writing down their recipes. But the book took on a life of its own. I connected with relatives and friends both here and in Israel who told me stories about my parents that I had never known. Through gathering recipes I connected with other children of survivors and met landsmen with whom my mother had lost touch. I was enriched and given a deeper understanding of the strength and optimism of Holocaust survivors and was determined to share their stories as well.

What began as a personal tribute to my parents became a way to pay tribute to all Holocaust survivors. The collection of recipes and remembrances that have enriched my family will, hopefully, enrich your family, as well.

Margit Kirsche and grandson Sammy at Weisz home, Vásárosnamény, 2001

A family stroll on Kirschenbaum lands, 2001

Note: All Yiddish terms for foods and holidays are expressed in the vernacular used by the Jews of the pre-Holocaust Hungarian-Czech region.

Our Family Tree
Lynn Kirsche Shapiro

Road sign entering Hluboka

I have done my best to chronicle the history of my parents' families starting with my father Sandor Kirsche (Kirschenbaum) z"l and my mother Margit (Weisz) Kirsche. Many of their ancestors were born in countries with names and borders that have changed. So I listed their place of birth geographically to correspond with Holocaust era maps. There are branches of both families whose details I have been unable to reconstruct, mainly as a consequence of the casualties and disrupted lives from the Holocaust. The Nazis had not began evacuating the Jews of Hungary and Czechoslovakia until the spring of 1944 and within a few months, they managed to achieve JudenRein, to "clean out all the Jews".

This family tree only encompasses the immediate family and does not note the hundreds of extended family members on both my mother's and my father's side who were killed by the Nazis. Our family tree was broken and burned by the Holocaust, its many branches cut off and with them all their future fruit. But its roots were strong, and today the branches that were left have blossomed in the new generations.

Shalom Kirschenbaum
b. Czechoslovakia
d. 1919

Golda Kirschenbaum
b. Czechoslovakia
d. 1915

Moshe Moskovics
b. Czechoslovakia, 1871
d. Hluboka, Czechoslovakia, 1938

Rivka (Auslander) Moskovics
b. Czechoslovakia, 1874
d. gas chamber, Auschwitz,
28/5/1944 (6 Sivan 5704)

Yitzchak Kirschenbaum
b. Nagy Láz, Czechoslovakia, 16/6/1895
d. Magdeburg, 16/8/1944 (27 Av 5704)

Chaya Zisel (Moskovics) Kirschenbaum
b. Hluboka, Czechoslovakia, 1895
d. gas chamber, Auschwitz,
28/5/1944 (6 Sivan 5704)

(3) Sara Moskovics
⚭ Eliyahu
b. Hluboka, Czechoslovakia, 1897
d. Holocaust, 1944

Beryl Leib Ben Kirshenbaum
⚭ Mary Schechter
b. Czechoslovakia c. 1890
d. Chicago, Ill. 12/1947

(4) Chaim Hersch Kirshenbaum
⚭ Shoshi
b. Czechoslovakia c. 1890
d. Holocaust 1944-1945
2 of 4 children survived Holocaust,
married and had children

Rachel Moskovics
⚭ Tzvi
b. Hluboka, Czechoslovakia, 1900
d. Dachau, 1944

(6) Frima (Moskovics) Rosenbaum
⚭ David HaCohen
b. Hluboka, Czechoslovakia, 1902
d. Holocaust, 1944

(4) Esther (Moskovics) Grossman
⚭ David
b. Hluboka, Czechoslovakia, 1904
d. gas chamber, Auschwitz,
28/5/1944 (6 Sivan 5704)

(3) Yitzchak Moskovics
⚭ Sarale Cohen
b. Hluboka, Czechoslovakia, 1907
d. Netanya, Israel, 1970
Yitzchak survived Holocaust,
but his wife, daughter and son were killed.
He remarried, had 2 children & grandchildren

(5) Freida (Moskovics) Lenerovic
b. Hluboka, Czechoslovakia, 1910
d. gas chamber, Auschwitz,
28/5/1944 (6 Sivan 5704)

Efraim Moskovics
b. Hluboka, Czechoslovakia, 1912
d. Holocaust, 1944

(3) Chana (Moskovics) Horn
b. Hluboka, Czechoslovakia, 1915
d. gas chamber, Auschwitz,
28/5/1944 (6 Sivan 5704)

Golda Moskovics
⚭ Eliezer
b. Hluboka, Czechoslovakia, 1918
d. Israel, 3/5/2001 (10 Iyar 5761)
survived Holocaust; had 3 children, many
grandchildren and great-grandchildren

Yisrael Menachem Mendel Weiss
b. Hluboka, Czechoslovakia, 1915
d. Holocaust, 1944 -1945

Meir Weiss
b. Hluboka, Czechoslovakia, 1917
d. Holocaust, 1944-1945

Goldie (Kirschenbaum) Weinberger
⚭ Leib
b. Hluboka, Czechoslovakia, 6/1921
d. Chicago, Ill., 7/7/1980 (23 Tammuz 5740)
survived Auschwitz
married, had 3 children, grandchildren
and great-grandchildren

Chana (Kirschenbaum) Goldberger
⚭ Joseph
b. Hluboka, Czechoslovakia, 1/8/1923
d. Chicago, Ill., 3/5/2001 (10 Iyar 5761)
survived Auschwitz, had 2 sons, 1 grandson

Chaim Kirschenbaum
b. Hluboka, Czechoslovakia, 21/7/1928
d. Buchenwald, 12/1944

Sandor Kirsche [Kirschenbaum]
b. Hluboka, Czechoslovakia, 24/1/1926
d. Chicago, Ill., 27/4/2007 (9 Iyar 5767)
survived the Holocaust

Ira Kirsche
⚭ Judy

6 grandchil
11 great-

⚭ indicates the married relationship

The direct family lineage is marked by the double line frame;
siblings are marked with a dotted line frame

Yosef Weisz
b. Munkács, c. 1860
d. Munkács, late 1930s (19 Adar)

⊗

Rivka (Apfeldorfer) Weisz
b. c. 1860
d. Munkács 1893

Yaakov Yehuda Hacohen Cheimovics
b. Czechoslovakia, c. 1872
d. gas chamber, Auschwitz,
25/5/1944 (3 Sivan 5704)

⊗

Chava (Schechter) Cheimovics
b. Czechoslovakia, c. 1872
d. gas chamber, Auschwitz,
25/5/1944 (3 Sivan 5704)

Shmuel Tzvi Weisz
b. Munkacs, 1892
d. shot in concentration camp
20/2/1945 (7 Adar 5705)

⊗

Leah Lanka (Cheimovics) Weisz
b. Czechoslovakia, 3/1894
d. gas chamber, Auschwitz,
25/5/1944 (3 Sivan 5704)

---

(4) Sheindel (Weisz) Beinhorn
⊗ **Yechiel Mechel**
b. Nizni Verecky, Czechoslovakia, 1885
d. Auschwitz, 18/5/1944 (25 Iyar 5704)
5 of her 8 children
(including Sarah Muschel
and Piri Apfeldorf)
survived the Holocaust,
married and had children

(4) Cipra (Weisz) Simsovitz
⊗ **Avrum Simcha**
b. c. 1890
d. Holocaust, 1944
3 of her 5 children survived,
married and had families

Miriam Weisz
d. Holocaust 1944

Yitzchak Isaac Weisz
d. Holocaust 1944

Esther Malka Weisz
⊗ **Moshe**
b. Czechoslovakia, c. early 1900s
d. Israel, 1988
survived the Holocaust
had 3 children

(8) Rivkah Yachat (Weisz) Beinhorn
⊗ **Yehoshua**
b. c. 1910
d. gas chamber, Auschwitz,
25/5/1944 (3 Sivan 5704)
with 4 daughters and 1 son,
her mother and father-in-law.
Yehoshua survived,
along with daughter
Blanche (Brindy) Cziment,
who married and had children

---

(5) Aaron Hacohen Cheimovics
⊗ **Esther**
b. Czechoslovakia, 1892
d. Holocaust, 1944

(5) Chaim Hacohen Cheimovics
⊗ **Brandel**
b. Czechoslovakia, 1896
d. Holocaust, 1944

(7) Tzvi Elimelech Hacohen Hersh Meilech Cheimovics
⊗ **Yulanka**
b. Czechoslovakia, 1898
d. Holocaust, 1944

Margit (Weisz) Kirsche
b. Gergely, Hungary 5/1/1923
survived the Holocaust

Morton Elimelech Chaim Weisz
⊗ **Magda**
b. Gergely, Hungary, 1/6/1920
d. Miami Beach, Fla., 20/5/1992, (17 Iyar 5752)
survived Buchenwald, married
and had 2 sons, 3 grandchildren

Yitzchak Isaac Weisz
b. Vásárosnamény, Hungary, 1933
d. gas chamber, Auschwitz,
25/5/1944 (3 Sivan 5704)

Isser Meir Weisz
b. Gergely, Hungary, 1930
d. gas chamber, Auschwitz,
25/5/1944 (3 Sivan 5704)

Dov Beirish Weisz
b. Vásárosnamény, Hungary, 1934
d. gas chamber, Auschwitz,
25/5/1944 (3 Sivan 5704)

Lynn Kirsche - Shapiro
⊗ Irv

and to date,
lchildren

All family members whose name is written in black
were murdered in the Holocaust.
The number (3, 4, 5, etc.) at the beginning of each entry
indicates how many people died, if there were more than one

Note: The dates are formatted according to the European
date format DD/MM/YEAR. In the case when only the
month and year are known it is MM/YEAR.
The Hebrew calendar date of death is included in parentheses.

Part I - Remembrances: Our Family Tree

Czechoslovakia (highlighted in orange) declared independence from the Austro-Hungarian Empire at the end of WWI in 1918 and remained a democratic nation until 1938. In 1939, Czechoslovakia was invaded by Nazi Germany, and the area known as Subcarpathian Rus, or Carpatho-Ukraine (lighter orange) where Ungvar, Munkács and Hluboka are situated, was dominated by Hungary. After WWII, Czechoslovakia was controlled by the Communist regime of the Soviet Union until 1989. In 1945, Czechoslovakia signed a treaty with the Soviet Union, incorporating Carpatho-Ukraine into the Soviet Union. In 1993, Czechoslovakia divided into the present-day Czech Republic and Slovakia, while Carpatho-Ukraine has remained within the borders of the Ukraine.

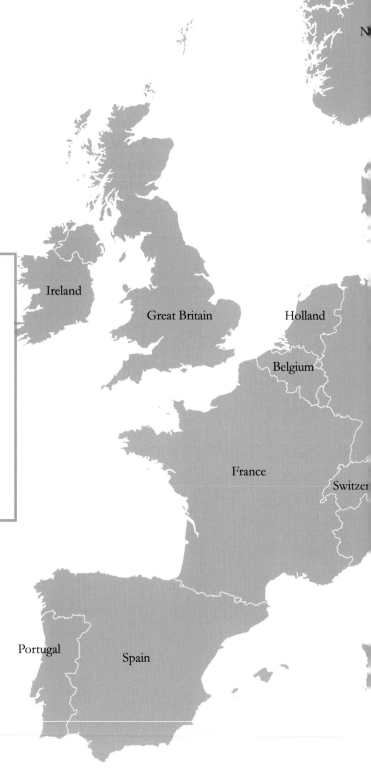

Sandor Kirsche (Shalom Kirschenbaum)

Lynn Kirsche Shapiro

My father, Sandor Kirsche, was affectionately called "Mr. Kirsche" by customers and "Sanyi" by close friends. Underneath his outer charm and sensitivity was a will of iron. Guests in my parents' home or customers in the store, all remember his conversation, his stories and his advice. He was a businessman, with a thirst for knowledge, realistic yet optimistic. He was a visionary whose values were formed in childhood—a bridge from the past to the future.

My father was born Shalom (Alexander) Kirschenbaum in 1926 in Hluboka, a small village in Czechoslovakia, in the Carpathian region. Living across the street from his maternal grandparents, Moshe and Rivka Moskovics, he grew up embraced by his close-knit family. As a small boy, "Shulemku" (his nickname) was completely attached and devoted to his *Zaidie*, his grandfather, a "tall man with a long white beard." He would sit and learn Torah with him, hold his hand while walking to shul, and bask in the warmth of his *Zaidie*'s love. His grandfather was highly respected in that region as a *Dayan*, a religious advisor, answering Jewish questions pertaining to religious law. Additionally, his grandparents supplemented their income selling dry groceries from a "small grocery store" which was set up in their home.

My father's mother, Chaya Zisel Moskovics, was the oldest of ten siblings, eight sisters and two brothers. All but the two youngest were married and had children prior to the Holocaust. Of the ten Moskovics siblings and their families, about thirty-eight family members, the only survivors were five: my father and his two sisters Goldie and Chana; his aunt Golda, and his uncle Yitzchak.

Shalom Kirschenbaum, age 16

Chaya Zisel, born in 1895, had married at the very young age of sixteen to David Weiss and had two sons, Meir and Yisrael Menachem Mendel. David Weiss was killed, fighting in WWI. (This was confirmed through his dental records). After WWI, Chaya Zisel married Yitzchak Kirschenbaum in 1919. Yitzchak Kirschenbaum, a "spinka chasid" (follower of the Spinka Rebbe) was the youngest of three sons born to Golda and Shalom Kirschenbaum in 1895 in the Ungvár region. He was a proud soldier who fought in WWI in the Czech army, and returned home as a decorated soldier with war medals for bravery. (The family hid the medals underground when they were taken to the ghetto, but they were never found).

Yitzchak and Chaya Zisel Kirschenbaum lived in a large home in the center of Hluboka on a sizeable lot of land with acres of plum and other fruit trees. They lived a religious Chassidic life, dedicated to Jewish observance and the Jewish community. For Pesach my grandmother cleaned the entire house, and the family baked matza in their big kitchen for all the Jews in their town.

Kirschenbaum Family Life

The Kirschenbaums owned farm machinery; renting it out to the farms in the surrounding area. They raised six children: Meir and Yisrael Menachem Mendel Weiss (from her previous marriage) and their own four children, Goldie, Chana, Shalom (my father) and Chaim. When my father was a baby, Hanya, a girl from one of the large peasant families in the area came to live with the Kirschenbaum family. Hanya was born to a poor family with twelve children, whose parents literally could not afford to feed her. She was just twelve years old when she

Chaya Zisel and Yitzchak Kirschenbaum

came to help with the daily chores. Hanya learned to speak fluent Yiddish (to the extent that she taught my father his very first morning prayers when he was two years old), and although she retained her Catholic religion, she was considered as a family member. After the War my father and his sister Goldie remained close to Hanya, helping her family in many ways.

As a young boy, my father went to a one-room school in Hluboka until the age of ten. Beginning at three years old, Monday through Friday, he began his day at 6 a.m. at *Cheder* (Jewish school), where he *davened* (prayed) and learned Hebrew and Torah. Then, at 8 a.m., he went to public school until 4 p.m., with a one-hour lunch break. After school, he returned to *Cheder* to continue learning Torah until 8 p.m. On Sundays, he studied in *Cheder* all day.

At the age of eleven, he went to study in Serednye, a larger, neighboring town, where he could continue both his secular studies as well as his Jewish studies. Except for the hours he spent in public school, he learned in a Talmud Torah (Yeshiva for ages ten to thirteen), studying Talmud as well as Halacha (Jewish law). During the week he stayed with his aunt and uncle, Frima and David Rosenbaum (Frimit and Dovid) and their family, going home every second Shabbos. He continued this until after his bar mitzvah in January 1939.

Life Changes

On March 15, 1939, as the Hungarians took control of Czechoslovakia, they marched into Hluboka. The Hungarians introduced new laws. Life was getting difficult for the Jews, so at the age of fifteen, my father left his small town and traveled to Budapest, looking for work. He found a place to live with a religious Jewish family, as well as work at a Jewish company that manufactured caps.

In mid-March 1944, the Nazis marched into Budapest. My father was just eighteen, frightened and worried about his family. He, along with three friends, secretly crossed the borders, in fear of being identified as Jews and arrested by the Nazis, and arrived home two weeks before Pesach. His family still baked the matza for everyone, but in "a small, hidden way." The last day of Pesach, 1944, the Jews of Hluboka were taken from their homes by the Hungarian police to a ghetto outside of Uzhgorod (Ungvár). His father, who had been set up as part of the "Jewish committee" because of his honor as a Czech soldier, was brought to the ghetto a few weeks later. There they remained until the third and final transport from the ghetto to Auschwitz.

My father and his family, including his grandmother, parents, sisters, younger brother Chaim, many aunts, uncles and cousins, arrived in Auschwitz on the first night of Shavuos. They were separated. His mother, grandmother, and most of his family were taken straight to the gas chambers. He remained at Auschwitz with his father, brother Chaim, Uncle Dovid and his uncle's son, Aaron. Within a week they were sent to Buchenwald. While in Buchenwald, his uncle and cousin Aaron were sent somewhere else and never returned. After three weeks, my father, his father, his sixteen-year-old brother Chaim, and the other inmates were taken to the German prison work camp at Magdeburg. On August 16, 1944, the Allies (458th Bombardment group) bombed Magdeburg, killing my grandfather, and my father was left with only his brother, Chaim. In December 1944, Chaim's feet froze and he was killed by the Nazis. Now my father was truly alone, and, in

Official document certifying that Sandor Kirschenbaum was imprisoned in Nazi Death Camps

January 1945, taken back to Buchenwald. On April 8, 1945, with a group of 2,000 men, he began the Death March from Buchenwald. (Knowing that the war was ending, the Nazis wanted to "clear out" the camps, and they forced many groups on the long march with no destination except death.) He and my mother's brother, Morton, were among the few hundred who survived. He landed in a hospital in Freising, Germany, weighing seventy pounds. He was almost six feet tall. There he fell into a coma. A few weeks later, he was nourished back to life. His health was never the same.

Life Begins Anew

He made his way back home to Hluboka where he found his two sisters Goldie and Chana. He stayed home until December 1945 (for Goldie's wedding), leaving the day before the borders were closed and sealed. He journeyed back to Freising, hoping to be able to leave Europe from there. Originally,

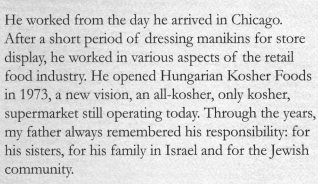

Sandor and Margit,
Freising, Germany, 1947

he planned to go to Palestine (Israel) but the boat he had signed up for was cancelled. Then he met my mother, and they married in October 1947. In February 1948, they boarded the SS Marine Tiger in Bremen, Germany, traveled to the States, and came to Chicago, sponsored by my father's Uncle Ben.

He worked from the day he arrived in Chicago. After a short period of dressing manikins for store display, he worked in various aspects of the retail food industry. He opened Hungarian Kosher Foods in 1973, a new vision, an all-kosher, only kosher, supermarket still operating today. Through the years, my father always remembered his responsibility: for his sisters, for his family in Israel and for the Jewish community.

My father, Sandor Kirsche, loved life and he loved people. He is not here today to see this book that I hope fulfills part of his wish "to instill the truth

of what took place in those years—lives that were conducted as a religious people—the atrocities of gassing people who were conducting a normal life."

I hope that as you read the stories throughout the book that give tribute to the courage and determination of survivors and victims of the Holocaust, you

Uncle Ben and
Aunt Mary Kirschenbaum

may learn that truth of which he spoke. My father was, in the words of the song my son, his youngest grandson, Aaron wrote "a collector of memories… a teacher with a golden heart."

Mr. and Mrs. Kirsche, c. 1990

Margit (Weisz) Kirsche
Lynn Kirsche Shapiro

When I first proposed the idea of this cookbook to my mother, her response was, "After all that I have lived through, I never imagined that what I would write would be a cookbook!" And yet, traditional kosher food from "home" has inspired and sustained her through all the chapters in her life: in the warm, close, Chassidic Jewish family of her childhood, in the Hungarian Beregszász Ghetto, in Auschwitz and Torgau, the concentration camps in which she was imprisoned during the Holocaust, in Germany during the first years after the Holocaust, and then in the United States, as she built a new life together with my father, Sandor Kirsche.

Margit Weisz with her three brothers, Hungary, 1940

Only a Dream

My mother, Margit Weisz, was born on January 5, 1923, in her maternal grandparents' home, in the small town of Gergely, Hungary. Her Yiddish nickname Rivcsu was derived from her Hebrew name Rivka Mirl. My mother's mother Leah had been born in Czechoslovakia, and moved to Gergely with her family, traveling by train through the mountains, when she was eleven years old, because her father, my mother's grandfather, was offered the position of rabbinic advisor for the *Kehilla* (Jewish community) in Gergely, Hungary. My mother's parents met when her mother, Leah, went to visit an uncle in Munkács, where Samuel (Shmuel Tzvi) Weisz lived. The shidduch (match) was arranged between them and they were married in 1919. During the next few years, Samuel Weisz, a Chassidic man and a professional watchmaker, had a jewelry store that also sold and fixed watches. When his store was robbed, my grandparents realized, as my mother says, "there was not too much future for the Jewish people in Hungary. It was difficult for Jewish people to go to school. There was six percent

Jews in the entire population, so only six percent of the students in higher education were allowed to be Jewish."

Dreaming of a Better Life

In 1923 my mother's father, Samuel Weisz, who wanted to give his family a better, safer life, tried to go to America, and, once there, bring his family. Because he was unable to obtain the necessary papers, he went instead to Havana, Cuba, and worked as a watchmaker. He ate rice and vegetables during the week to keep kosher, and went to a Jewish family for Shabbos. For the next five years, he sent money home to support the family, which my grandmother supplemented with money she made by sewing custom dresses for women. He left when my mother was five months old and returned in 1928 when she was five years old.

My mother recalls, "I remember, even today, going to the station (to meet my father) with my grandfather, who had a long beard, and every time another man with a long beard walked down from the train, I asked, 'Is that my daddy?' " Her parents had considered moving to Cuba (then a safe haven), but decided against it, as there was not a Yeshiva where my mother's brother, Morton, would be able to learn Torah and study Talmud. The only option would have been to leave him in Hungary to be raised by the grandparents, and her mother, Leah, would not consider leaving her son. So the family remained in Gergely.

Shortly after my mother's father returned to Hungary, he opened a store in the central square in Vásárosnamény, a much bigger town than Gergely. Vásárosnamény was equidistant, approximately 30 kilometers, from the borders of Romania and Czechoslovakia. Vásárosnamény was two kilometers from Gergely, so my mother's family moved to Vásárosnamény to live close to their work. However, each week, on Shabbos, my mother walked the two kilometers to visit her grandparents in Gergely.

Life in Vásárosnamény

Their life in Vásárosnamény was dedicated to family and to living an observant Jewish life. Her father, a watchmaker, opened a store together with his brother-in-law, that sold watches, eyeglasses, rings on one side, and yard goods on the other. Her mother designed and sewed shirts for men and dresses for women, which were sold in the store. The store was in the center of town, a five-minute walk from the shul (synagogue) and also from their house. In 1930, 1933 and 1934, my mother's three younger brothers were born: Isser Meir, Yitzchak Isaac, and Dov Beirish. The Weisz family lived across the street from the shul, and down the block from the public school, which all the town's children, including my mother, attended.

A Good Life

My mother attended public school through sixth grade. Once or twice a week there was a religious hour during which the children went to learn with the leaders of their religion—priests for the Catholic, the ministers for the Protestants, and their local rabbi, Rabbi Eliyahu Cohen, for the Jewish children. After the fourth grade, students could either stay in public school through sixth grade, or go to *polgari*, a four-year high school. My mother wanted to continue learning in *polgari* but her grandfather would not allow it for religious reasons. After sixth grade, my mother went to public school twice a week for two more years, where they reviewed what they

Leah and Shmuel Tzvi Weisz

had previously learned. My mother learned basic reading of Hebrew with a few other girls from a private teacher. Jewish law, the laws about kashrus, the holidays and the prayers—these she learned from living a Jewish Chassidic life, from helping her mother with kashering meat, baking for Purim, cleaning and preparing for Pesach, and cooking and preparing for Shabbos. Even though the family ate their meals together during the week, their house had a special ambiance on Shabbos. On Shabbos, she would get together with her friends in the afternoon, and walk to her grandparents' house in Gergely. She was deeply attached to her maternal grandfather, and simply loved spending time with him.

In those days, everything had to be done by hand and from scratch—including washing clothes with a washboard, sewing clothes, baking bread, cooking and cleaning. Beyond cooking and baking, beginning at the age of nine, my mother learned to sew professionally from her mother. Using remnants from the yard goods store, she sewed dresses.

My mother loved sewing. At the age of 18, she traveled to Beregszász to learn sewing and custom designing from a professional seamstress. My mother became so proficient so quickly that she was taken along on jobs with the seamstress who hired out my mother's services as well. My mother's youthful days were full.

Dark Days Begin

In the spring of 1944, on the last day of Pesach, her uncle Hersh Meilech came from shul to her parents' house. She was so glad to see him, but then she noticed that he was crying. He said that the Nazis were coming the next day to take all the Jews away. Both her family and his family hired non-Jews with wagons to drive them away that night. Her family was caught after they had gone thirty kilometers and brought back. The next day, the day after Pesach, they were taken along with all the other Jews from Vásárosnamény to the Beregszás Ghetto. Her uncle's family was never seen again.

Margit Weisz, Freising, Germany, 1946

When they arrived at the ghetto, her youngest brother, Dov Beirish, had the measles and was taken to a special infirmary building. So when the Nazis asked for volunteer nurses who would stay in the infirmary, my mother volunteered, although she had no prior training in nursing. She wanted to be with her brother to be able to help him. She cooked together with the others who were volunteer nurses.

After six weeks my mother was taken on the second transport from the ghetto, with her entire family—including her grandparents—to the death camp of Auschwitz. In Auschwitz, the War was nearing an end, the Russians were coming close and the Nazis were in a hurry to kill as many Jews as they could, so she did not get the customary tattoo, only a number on a wristband. She was separated from her family and put in Barrack No. 7. Her mother, her three younger brothers and her grandparents were sent directly to the gas chambers. After six months my mother was transferred to the work camp in Torgau, Germany. Torgau, a subcamp of Buchenwald, was a small work camp where 250 women lived in three rooms and worked repairing wooden crates and making ammunitions. Throughout this time, while other women despaired of ever being freed or living, my mother was "certain that I would not die in the camps," but felt that she would somehow survive. On April 27, 1945, she was liberated by the Americans.

Morton Weisz, Margit's brother, Freising, 1946

She went home to Vásárosnamény, not knowing if her older brother Morton, her father or any other family members had survived. Finally after six months she found out that her father had been killed, but her older brother Morton survived. He smuggled her across six borders from Hungary to Freising, Germany, where he had been living since surviving the Death March from Buchenwald.

She met my father in Freising, Germany, in December of 1945, and they were married on October 21, 1947. They arrived in Chicago in February 1948 with the clothes on their back.

Margit and Sandor Kirsche, Freising, Germany, 1947

After living on the South Side for one month, they moved to Humboldt Park and then to the North Side in 1961. Originally, my mother worked as a professional seamstress (sewing clothes for herself from the remnants) and considered a career in professional designing. But after two children, she joined my father in his food business, using her culinary talents, as well as her business skills. They worked together in the retail food industry, and ultimately started the business that is now Hungarian Kosher Foods.

Throughout her life, her home has always been open and inviting to family, friends and anyone needing advice, the comfort of a warm meal and compassion of a warm heart. She has been the rock and inspiration of our family. The cooking that she took so much for granted has provided us with nourishment for body and soul.

Margit, at home, with (l. to r.) Lynn and Ibi

Bubbie's Gift
Rocky Shapiro Brody

Ten years ago, in honor of my Bubbie's eightieth birthday, we compiled the first version of this cookbook. In truth, we were creating a gift for Bubbie to give to us. The family project aimed to capture the essence of Bubbie's recipes, so that we could replicate them for weekday, Shabbos or holiday meals.

Photo: David Y. Lee for U.S. Holocaust Memorial Museum

Favorite Foods and Stories

With the delicious aromas of my Bubbie's home, and the constant variety of freshly cooked meals on her table, she created a meeting place for the cousins (me, Tova, Sammy and Aaron and our first cousins Alisa and Daniel). She always welcomed us, no matter what time of day, or how much notice we gave her before our arrival at her apartment.

Each of the cousins had a favorite dish and knew each other's favorites: *nakidlach* (dumplings) for a special family dinner; chicken soup on Friday night; green bean soup on Friday afternoon, and jelly sweet

bread kugel for a light snack. We laugh together as Bubbie tells her favorite stories. "When Alisa was a little girl," recalls Bubbie, "she used to get up on a stool and wash 'didish' which I figured out meant 'the dishes'." As the Pesach season approached each year at Hungarian Kosher Foods, we grandchildren took our responsibility seriously, helping out at this busiest of seasons. While I think that we actually did assist my grandparents at unpacking the groceries onto the shelves, peeling hundreds of hard-boiled eggs for Seder orders, preparing *charoses* (a mixture of apples, nuts and wine for the Seder), gefilte fish, and matza balls, bagging groceries, etc., we also approached the season with a hidden incentive. We simply loved the 3 a.m. chicken soup breaks, fresh-grilled chicken livers, the arguments over who got to use the pricing gun, and most of all, the family bonding experience.

Traditions Grow Stronger

As time passed between the original family cookbook project in 2003 and today, the recipes picked up

"Hungarian Kosher Foods," Jerusalem, Purim, 2009

new memories along the way. Today, the traditions continue within our growing family, to our spouses, Avi, Mikey, Cat, Myles and Debbie, and to our children.

Raising my children in Israel across the ocean from Hungarian Kosher Foods (HKF), I did not want them to miss out on the childhood experiences that I treasure so dearly. I decided to build a mini model of HKF in our own Israeli home. We converted our entire living room into a kids' supermarket, dressed up as workers at the store, brought in all of the HKF paraphernalia (plastic bags, containers, labels, hats, etc.), printed up fake money, and invited our friends to come shop at the first annual opening of HKF in Jerusalem, Israel. Our kids and friends had such a fabulous time that we recreated the store for two more years, and were fortunate to have my parents and in-laws join in the endeavor. Of course, my mother's recipe for the traditional potato kugel, which you will find in this cookbook, flew off the shelves!

The spark of HKF permeates our lives beyond the holidays, to our everyday routine. I love our family tradition of baking *kakaós* (chocolate yeast cake) for Shabbos with my children. My son, Shalom Amichai, shared the recipe when he was in preschool, and the children baked it for the end-of-the-year party to give to their parents. Many parents emailed me for the dough recipe, saying that they had tried similar recipes and never tasted such great dough. Even my three-year-old daughter, Maayan, has taken over the rolling pin. I videoed her at the age of two, telling her older sister Gila, "No, Maayan bake it *kakaós*!" Every time that we bake *kakaós* for company, or to bring to friends, people are just amazed at the taste of the rich cocoa oozing out of the light pastry dough.

How a "Real" Chef Braids Challah

My children take great pride in their legacy from their great-grandparents. My daughter Gila tells all of her friends that her great-grandparents are real chefs, from a real store. "My Bubbie taught us how to braid challah in six, even after she lost her eyesight. And next time that she comes to Israel she is going to teach us how to braid in eight, or maybe even twelve!" exclaimed Gila at a recent Shabbos meal conversation. When Gila had a cooking contest-themed birthday party for her seventh birthday, she insisted that her *savta* (grandmother) be in town,

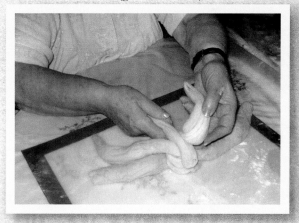

Bubbie braiding challah (after losing eyesight)

because her *savta* (my mother Lynn) "is a real chef, who learned from Bubbie and Papa Sanyi." I see the smile on her face when she brags about her family legacy, and I recall my own happiness when I would visit my grandparents' store with my friends. As my grandfather pointed my friends to the candy aisle to choose their favorite treat, their faces lit up, as did my grandfather's eyes. I felt so special that I was my Papa Sanyi's granddaughter.

My Cooking Hotline

I, like my children, also love boasting of my Bubbie's talents. I love sharing my secret solution to all cooking crises. I start by frantically calling my Bubbie just when I think that I ruined a dish, and she calms me with such ease, by quickly advising me how to fix up the dinner. Yes, we live in Israel, but my friends and neighbors all know about our packed freezer of meats that we bring from Chicago.

We take great pleasure in sharing these meats with friends and family, on holidays and special occasions, obviously because they are so tasty, but also on a personal note because they afford us the opportunity to talk about HKF and my grandparents.

Even while cooking alone in my kitchen, I picture the cooking-related conversations that resurfaced periodically in my Bubbie's and Grandpa's home. As I put a pot on the stove I recall asking Bubbie during one phone conversation, "So who's the better cook, you or Grandpa?" "I think I'm still better," she responded. "When he makes *chulent* for Shabbos and I tell him to measure it comes out good, but one time he didn't measure and it didn't come out good." Grandpa, or Papa Sanyi, however, disagreed. When I asked him who was the better cook, he once responded jokingly, "Bubbie may have taught me how to cook, but you know what they say: the student is sometimes better than the teacher." While daydreaming about these conversations, I suddenly awake from my stories, and realize that I need to pay attention to my pot boiling on the stovetop, even if I, like my Bubbie, am not following an exact recipe.

It's a What recipe?

The first time that my Bubbie gave me a cooking lesson in my own home was about nine years ago, when my grandparents came to visit me on Israel's Independence Day, *Yom Haatzmaut*. I had asked my Bubbie to teach me how to make *nakidlach*, one of my all-time favorites. When we began discussing the recipe for the dumpling dough she explained, "It's a *schit* recipe." Not believing my ears, I asked, "Bubbie, what did you say?" After repeating herself, she clarified, "You know, I don't have an exact recipe, I just "*schit arain*," meaning I pour a little of this and a little of that until it comes out the right consistency." (*Mir schit arain* means "we just throw in.") We were both laughing hysterically, another trait that I must have inherited from my Bubbie.

A Handful of Sugar

While writing the first edition of this cookbook, ten years ago, we had little vision of the shape that this book would take—the endless hours of recipe testing and memoir editing that would be required to translate it to a wider audience. The process challenged each of us in our own way. When cooking, I am a perfectionist, paying attention to each detail of the preparation without ever looking at the clock. However, in editing the manuscript and testing recipes I was forced to meet deadlines regardless of the demands of children, family and life. I am in awe of my mother's persistence in translating my Bubbie's "*schit* recipes" into ones with defined universal measurements.

The fact that my Bubbie never recorded or followed standard measurements does not indicate any less precision in her replications. Each time that my Bubbie kneads dough, for example, she judges the amount of flour necessary based on the feel and consistency of the dough, until she obtains the exact consistency. In order to formulate the recipes, my mother, Lynn, and Bubbie measured out each handful or pinch into a measuring cup before adding it to the mix.

One time, Bubbie told my mother to take "a handful of sugar", but then upon feeling how much sugar was in my mother's hand, she exclaimed, "That's not a handful! Let me show you what a handful really is." Bubbie cupped her hand tightly and demonstrated to my mother the true quantity of "a handful".

These recipes play an integral role in my everyday life, in the twinkle that I carry from my grandfather, and in the bond that I treasure with my Bubbie. When preparing meal after meal starts feeling mundane, I know that I can turn to these recipes as a source of inspiration and passion for my dinner preparation—and for my life.

Bubbie with Lynn's family, Jerusalem, Pesach, 2013

Goldie (Kirschenbaum) Weinberger
Lynn Kirsche Shapiro with Ibi Gelb and Irving Weinberger

Goldie (Aranka) Weinberger devoted her life to her family and the Jewish faith and tradition in which she was raised. She was committed to holding the remnants of her family together over the years of their lives, the miles that separated them, and the tragedies that beset them. Although she was physically weakened by her time in Auschwitz and the eventually fatal hepatitis that she contracted there, she was emotionally strong, and worked tirelessly in the service of others.

The Eldest Child

Chana, Goldie and cousin, c. 1942

Goldie, named after her paternal grandmother, was the eldest child of Yitzchak and Chaya Zisel Kirschenbaum. Born in 1921 in Hluboka, Czechoslovakia, a small village in the Carpathian Region, she lived most of her life in this area, first in Hluboka, then after the War, in Kalnik, and then in Munkács, until 1973. Goldie attended the small, local one-room school in Hluboka until fifth grade. She was tutored in reading and writing Hebrew and Yiddish, along with other Jewish girls. From her mother, she learned the Jewish laws of homemaking, Kashrus, Shabbos and the holidays. As the eldest daughter, Goldie was always at her mother's side, cooking, baking and sewing. She learned to cook and bake without recipes; to sew without patterns. Additionally, she formed a very protective relationship with her younger sister, Chana, and a close bond with her younger brothers, especially my father Sanyi (Sandor).

Hanya Joins the Family

When Goldie was a young girl, her family took in Hanya, a young gentile Czech girl whose family was too poor to provide for her. Hanya lived with the Kirschenbaums, both as helpmate and as part of the family (although retaining her own religion) until her marriage in 1939. When the Nazis marched into Hluboka on the last day of Pesach in 1944, the Jewish families were forced to leave their homes the very next day and to live within a sealed-in ghetto, a former brick factory. Hanya and her husband Andre risked their lives to smuggle food to the Kirschenbaums. After the Holocaust when Goldie returned home, Hanya returned to her the family's Pesach dishes and other keepsakes that she had been able to hide when the Nazis drove the Jews from their homes.

Goldie and Cousin Chani, c. 1942

Life in Auschwitz

Goldie and her entire extended family lived in the ghetto for about six weeks before they were taken to Auschwitz, arriving on the evening of May 27, 1944, the first night of Shavuos. Goldie and her sister Chana were separated from most of their family, including their mother, who was taken immediately to the gas chamber. During their time in Auschwitz, Goldie and Chana worked in a munitions factory making bullets. The food they were given was barely enough to sustain life, but Goldie often shared her food with her sister.

Goldie and her three children, Soviet Union, 1954

The Move to Munkács

Goldie and Chana were liberated in the spring of 1945 and returned home to Hluboka looking for any remaining relatives. In December of that year she married Leib Weinberger. The day after their wedding the borders were sealed and they were only able to move within a specified region. They moved to Leib Weinberger's hometown, Kalnik, Czechoslovakia, (to his father's home), where their three children were born. In the early 1950s they moved to Munkács near the main train station where they lived and raised their children. Their relatively large home in Munkács had a summer kitchen, extensive acreage and a hundred fruit trees, but they had no indoor bathroom, only an outhouse. They went to public shower houses to shower or washed in a basin in the house. Despite living under oppressive Communist rule, Goldie sent her two sons to Soviet schools wearing *yarmulkes* and *peyos* (Jewish skullcap and sidelocks). To say that her dedication to her faith was strong is an understatement.

Keeping Kosher

There were no kosher stores in the town, forcing the Jews who adhered to the laws of kashrus to prepare everything from scratch. When Goldie wanted to cook chicken, she bought a chicken from the market and took it to the *Shecht Shteibel* (small slaughterhouse which was allowed by the communist government, only in Munkács) to be slaughtered. Then she would start the kashering process and carry it through, step by step, salting the chicken, removing the feathers, and cleaning the chicken. With that one chicken, she was able to prepare at least three delicious meals for her family.

In the Weinberger home, there was only kosher food, and the laws of Shabbos were followed strictly. And she was dedicated to the community through her service and generosity. There was no catering service and certainly no "kosher catering" in the Soviet Union. Goldie was known within the circle of her friends and family as a master chef and baker.

So, together with other women in the community they prepared delicacies and pastries for the Jewish holidays and events. This was not a "business"; there was no charge, this was done as a *chesed*, a kindness, a labor of love.

Relocating to the States

For 25 years Goldie and her family tried to leave the Soviet Union. Finally in April 1973, they were granted permission to leave with only very few possessions. They were originally allowed to leave to immigrate to Israel but Goldie wanted to live near her brother, in the States, and my father who had petitioned for many years to sponsor them in the States was thrilled. On route, they stopped in Vienna for one month, living in a small hotel and eating in a kitchen supported by the HIAS (Hebrew Immigrant Aid Society). After Vienna, they traveled to Rome, living for six months in a small hotel, whose other tenants included Jews from the Soviet Union as well as priests and monks, and Mama Agatha (who took care of the priests). Aided by the HIAS, the family bought a couple of pots and found kosher food. Even in Rome, Goldie cooked for her family as well as other Jewish families who came over on Shabbos. And even Mama Agatha asked Goldie to cook or bake for her. Finally in the fall of 1973, they immigrated to Chicago and reunited with her brother, my father, and his family.

When they arrived in Chicago, Goldie used her natural talents and began to work in the kitchen of Hungarian Kosher, alongside my mother. My mother has often remarked that she loved cooking with Goldie; their recipes from "home" were very similar. Goldie was a magnificent baker, and together they developed many recipes, and gave new life to the timeless traditional recipes from "home."

Goldie Weinberger died in Chicago on July 7, 1980 (23 Tammuz 5740) at the young age of fifty-nine, a direct result of the hepatits contracted at Auschwitz. She was surrounded by her siblings and children and lived to see a new generation, her grandchildren. She died knowing that her children, her future, remained dedicated to the Jewish faith and tradition of her family.

Her recipes in this book are a tribute to the strength and courage with which she clung to her faith. As you read through the recipes, it is my heartfelt wish that you will share the bond I feel with Goldie Weinberger as well as with the Jewish mothers through the generations. And as you prepare the food for your holidays and *smachot* (happy times), I know you will appreciate the devotion to family, which Goldie expressed through the tradition of her cooking.

A Little Town Called Munkács

Irving Weinberger and Sonia Weinberger

A little town, called Munkács during the Austro-Hungarian Empire, 1867-1919, and Mukatchevo during the Soviet regime (1945 on) could be claimed by many nationals. Among them were Ukrainians, Hungarians, Czechs, Slovaks, and Russians, depending on the times, who was in control, and the level of loyalty to the Motherland. But no folks claimed it with such pride throughout the centuries as did the Jewish population of Munkács.

Shteible in Munkács

For the Jews, this was the city of the Munkács Yeshiva, or Jewish school, known for its sages, religious philosophers and *Talmidei Chachamim*, or Talmudic scholars. Munkács was a city so rich with Jewishness, the only city in Hungary with almost 50% Jewish population, that neither the anti-semitism of the Austro-Hungarian Empire, nor the death camps, concentration camps, and slave-labor camps of World War II, nor even the Soviet Union's post-War enforcement of atheism and assimilation could erase it.

Our generation, born to Holocaust survivors in the Soviet Union, grew up with Jewish pride, which had been transferred from generation to generation, although without the presence of our grandparents, most of whom did not return home from the lagers or concentration camps. Most of our family members had been killed in the Holocaust. We grew up well familiar with tattooed concentration camp ID numbers on the forearms of our parents. We grew up with personal stories of big losses and small victories. We, the children born to Holocaust survivors, knew well which relative, who perished in the War, we were named after and why it was so important.

Growing up in post-World War II Munkács under Soviet rule, we attended Soviet schools. Our parents, Holocaust survivors, some of whom may have become Komsomol or Party members to survive politically and to provide food for their family, named their children Kolya, Misha and Tanya specifically for attending Soviet school. But at home their children were called Itzhak, Chaim, and Toby. At home, the Jews of Munkács, kept the traditions and strictly followed Jewish law. I remember, for example, that we even had the *shoichet* come to our yard to kill the cow according to Jewish law to provide meat for many families. At home we celebrated religious observances such as Brit Mila, Bar Mitzva, and Chupa. Because the Communist rule did not allow religious observance or ceremony, these Jewish religious ceremonies were performed in secret, but nevertheless with pride and knowledge of *Halacha*, or Jewish Law. They were performed by rabbis who had been educated in pre-Holocaust Munkács Yeshiva.

*Chana with nephew, Irving Weinberger,
Munkács, c. 1968*

The entertainment—the music and dancing—
following these ceremonies was unique to the
Munkács Jewish community. The food preparation
was often a business of neighbors, relatives, and
friends. Whenever there was an event the community
cooked together.

Because Jewish education was officially forbidden
under Communist rule, none of us had formal
Hebrew education. However, we all had private
Hebrew studies from rabbis who came to our
homes for two to three years to prepare us for our
bar mitzvah. Additionally, many of us as teenagers
gathered in each other's homes in small groups to
learn Hebrew. Waiting anxiously for the day that we
would be permitted to leave the Soviet Union and to
live as free Jews.

Each neighborhood had its own prayer houses
located in private homes, or *shteiblach*, and all of us
teenagers were coming together for morning and
evening prayers. Of course, a lot of talking and
horsing around was going on as well.

The community worked together as well, helping
each other during all the Jewish holidays. Preparation
was especially difficult before Pesach (Passover).
Throughout my childhood in Munkács (after the
Holocaust and under the Soviet regime), in spite
of the oppression and difficulty in observing the
Jewish tradition, I remember that I had the greatest
time helping out in the preparation for the holidays.
For me, Passover was the favorite. I remember
bringing the Passover dishes down from the attic
where they were stored during the year, only to be
used on Passover. These dishes were beautifully
designed, handmade from red clay. Hidden during
the Holocaust, they were a treasure to my mother
(Goldie Weinberger) and to all of us, containing
within them the memories of our grandmother, who
had died in the gas chamber. These dishes as well as
other religious articles hidden during the Holocaust
reminded us of the richness of the Jewish life prior
to the Holocaust.

We could not simply walk into a store and purchase
matza and other kosher specialties during the year
and certainly not for Pesach. But somehow we
managed to bake matza in the Jewish community

oven located in one of the home *shteiblach*. Matza baking was preserved by the entire *Kehilla* or community. It was preserved as a symbol that the Jewish Community is alive and well in the here and now, as it had always been in the little town of Munkács.

Later on, in the late 1960s and 70s, when we were in our early twenties, came the fever of emigration to Israel, the States or wherever possible. That era was a story in itself. To those of us who had been locked in the Soviet Union, the excitement of leaving, being able to go, do and travel and live as a free people, is indescribable.

Jewish wedding in Munkács, 1972

The Jews who have called Munkács home over the centuries, have always created a rich culture that, at its heart, harbored a unique devotion to their faith and religious practices. Today, Jews of Munkács, no matter were they live now, be it in Tel Aviv, Brooklyn or Paris, can proudly insist they never lost touch with their Jewish self.

The History of Hungarian Kosher Foods

Lynn Kirsche Shapiro

When my father and mother, Sandor and Margit Kirsche, first came to Chicago, my mother worked as a seamstress, and my father worked for his cousin, in the "manikin business," for less than minimum wage. My parents needed more income to survive, even though my parents were renting just one bedroom with kitchen privileges within someone's apartment. In his next job, as a wholesale grocery salesman, my father learned the grocery business. In the years that followed, my parents worked together, acquired and sold, several small grocery stores.

Tradition Discovered

When I researched the family history, I learned that my parents' families had been in the "business of food," for a few generations. In the years prior to the Holocaust, because there was no refrigeration, the local grocery stores in the small towns throughout Eastern Europe sold only non-perishable items, dry goods, such as flour, sugar, spices and perhaps some vinegar, or coconut shortening. One of my mother's maternal uncles, Chaim Cheimovics, owned two grocery stores in Vásárosnamény. My father's maternal grandparents also owned such a grocery store. They sold flour, sugar, and other dry goods from the first floor of their home. And each year for Pesach, the Kirschenbaum family prepared and baked matza in the large kitchen of their home, providing the matza for the entire Jewish community of Hluboka.

Given this background—business, commitment to the community, providing food and groceries—the creation and establishment of Hungarian Kosher Foods was inevitable.

The First All-Kosher Store

In 1973, my parents bought a small kosher meat market on Devon Avenue in Chicago, Illinois, with the dream of providing the Chicago Jewish community an all-kosher, only-kosher supermarket. This was a unique concept at that time, especially in the Midwest United States. They began working, integrating my father's knowledge of the grocery business with his skill in kosher meats and my mother's talents in cooking and baking. In the beginning and up until a few weeks before his death, my father worked in every aspect of the business. He served the customers, ordered groceries, produce and meats, cut and kashered meats, cooked the foods, worked behind the deli counter, and filled huge orders for caterers and hotels. In addition, he donated food to those in need, both organizations and individuals. My mother worked by his side in everything except the meats. And many of today's best-selling recipes are hers. A few months after my parents had purchased

Sandor Kirsche works in the kitchen at Hungarian Kosher Foods

Hungarian Kosher, surviving members of my father's family were finally granted permission to leave the Soviet Union, and when they came to Chicago, his sister, Goldie, began to work in the kitchen alongside my mother. Together, they created authentic recipes from "at home," recipes they had learned from their mothers in Hungary and Czechoslovakia.

A Family Enterprise

Everyone in our family has worked in the business at some time, from my parents, and my father's sisters, to the grandchildren. Over the years as Hungarian remodeled and expanded, kosher groceries and dairy products were added. Ultimately, Hungarian outgrew its space on Devon Avenue. In April of 1986, Hungarian Kosher Foods opened its doors at its new location on Oakton Street in Skokie, Illinois. The dream of a "One Stop Kosher Shop", completely under rabbinic supervision, finally came true.

More than a Store

Hungarian Kosher Foods became more than a store, for the employees, who are like family, as well as for the customers, who are like friends. It evolved into a kosher shopping experience that was many things to many people. It was and still is a meeting place. Friends meet there on certain days to shop. Families gather on Friday mornings and before the holidays. Customers come for cooking advice, recipes and kashrus questions. The Israeli community comes to shop for familiar products, read their news and greet their friends. Survivors find long lost landsmen and are reunited. Sometimes even "matches" have been made. All generations are served. School children have come for hands-on lessons in the laws of kashrus. My parents have had a special affection for children and always showered them with attention. When customers were too frail or elderly, they could call in orders and have them delivered. They still can and they still do. In 1993, Hungarian Kosher Foods added a wine store stocking kosher wines and liquors from all over the world.

My parents had a vision, and their vision was realized. This vision encompassed not only the store, which served the Jewish community, but also our family who served the store. It was and is so successful because of my parents' commitment, which they have instilled in us. As you read our family history and the recipes in the cookbook, it will take you full circle: back to the beginning, the roots, and forward into the future.

ONE STOP HUNGARIAN KOSHER FOODS KOSHER SHOP

HUNGARIANKOSHER.COM

Friends of Refugees
of Eastern Europe

and the entire Russian Jewish community

acknowledge and express
their deep appreciation to

Mr. Sandor Kirsche

of

Hungarian Kosher Foods, Inc.

'020 W. Oakton Street/Skokie, IL

for his continuous support of Soviet Jewry

Special Thanks!!
for sponsoring the two Pesach sedarim
for the 700 newly arrived Soviet Jews.

*"May G-d repay you
with the best of health, wealth and
nachas from your family."*

Going Forward

Ira Kirsche

"You've got to keep going forward. You can't look back. You made a decision; even if it was a mistake; don't look back." That's what my dad told me when I worked with him at Hungarian Kosher Foods. When I believed I had made mistakes I would get upset; my dad lived by his words: "You either go forward or you are going backward."

Getting Started

My mom and dad came to this country after the War. They "got off the boat," and the next day they were working, my mom as a seamstress and my father for a relative (making minimal pay). He passed his GED right away, and he was planning on college. But their basic needs forced him to look for a better-paying job, which he found in the grocery business, my mother working at his side. I worked in the store on my days off of school, among other things, sorting and recycling empty pop bottles in the days before plastic bottles and aluminum cans.

Hungarian Kosher Meat Market

In 1973, my parents bought Hungarian Kosher Meat Market on West Devon Avenue in Chicago. I was graduating college and joined them. The front of the store held a fresh meat counter, a case for sausages and cold cuts, and a case for traditional homemade carryout, including our own pickles. In the back were two distinct rooms: a room for meat preparation and sausage manufacturing, and behind that a kitchen with a smokehouse. My mother and my father's sisters, Goldie and Chana, my cousins and my sister Lynn worked there as well.

We got in forequarters, *trebured* (de-veined) the meat, kashered and custom-cut the meat. We also aged certain cuts, and we manufactured sausages. My father was the sausage maker while I stuffed the sausages. In those days, to smoke meat we walked into the smokehouse, took the temperature, adjusted the smokers, did everything by hand. Today, I roll a wagon of meat into the computerized smoke house and press a button. Hungarian Kosher Meat Market was 300 square feet when they bought it and by the time we left it had expanded to 5,000 square feet—and we were out of room.

Hungarian Kosher Foods: One-Stop Shop

In 1985, my father needed a new location that would take the store to the next level. I found the store we are in now—previously a large supermarket. After extensive renovations (including an expanded meat market with a computerized smokehouse, and a commercial kitchen with separate facilities for meat, dairy and parve), my parents, my cousin Irving Weinberger, and I, opened Hungarian Kosher Foods on Oakton Street in Skokie on April 1, 1986. My father was then 60 years old. Our format was and is an all-kosher supermarket, I believe the first store of its kind in the country: produce, bakery, meats, deli, grocery and frozen foods—25,000 square feet—entirely under orthodox kosher supervision. After a few years, we acquired a liquor license and began selling kosher wine and spirits.

Food, Family and Tradition

April 27, 2007

My father worked steadily—14 hours a day—until right before his death on April 27, 2007. In 2007, our Passover season was from April 3 until April 10. Pesach was and is the busiest time of the year, and we came into the store at three or four in the morning to start making trays. That year winter lasted into spring: cold, snowy and slushy. My dad said, "Call me, I want to go in with you." The weather was so terrible I did not call, and for the very first time he did not make it in to work.

The Future

As I write this I am sixty-two years old. I don't know what the future holds, but as long as I am physically able I will keep on going. Listen, my dad worked until his eighties, and if God gives me the years, I may do the same!

The Tradition of Eating Well

Alisa Kirsche Oler, MS, RD, CNSC, LDN

Food has always played an important role in my life. I identify the celebration of each of the Jewish holidays with the foods we prepare. I have fond memories of working in the kitchen at Hungarian Kosher Foods with my grandparents, brother and cousins, preparing gefilte fish and matza balls for Pesach. I studied nutrition in college, not only because of my family's food business, but because I was fascinated with the idea of food as medicine.

A Labor of Love

As a dietitian I know that a diet rich in plant-based foods and foods with bright colors is highly nutritious. In contrast, I think about some of my favorite dishes from my grandparents—*nakidlach* with chicken *paprikás*, *chulent* and *kishke*—and I wonder how my grandparents survived on such beige foods! However, in reality, those dishes were not eaten every day, rather in combination with healthy fruits and vegetables as well as an active lifestyle beyond today's norms. Exercise was not a choice but a necessity in daily activities from transportation to food preparation. There was more to my grandparents' way of eating than the traditional favorites I associate with them.

"Life was not easy in Europe," my grandmother, Margit Kirsche, often tells me. Everything my grandparents ate was made from scratch, from the hand-churned butter to the home-cooked and preserved tomato sauce. All of their foodstuff was free of artificial preservatives and additives. The concerns about trans-fats and artificial sweeteners did not even exist.

Fruits and vegetables were either grown on their own land or purchased from the local farmer's market.

My grandparents' families made their own dairy products with milk fresh from a cow. My grandmother's grandparents grew a variety of fruits and vegetables in their yard, including corn as well as a sour cherry tree, from which they made sour cherry soup. My grandfather's family had an abundance of plum trees on their property. When he was hungry he would go outside and eat the plums he picked off the tree. Eating foods locally improves the freshness and therefore the nutritional quality. This concept may have recently become a trend in urban areas but was the way of life for my grandparents in Europe.

Nature's Medicine

Supplements are commonly used today. While they do have their benefits, it is important to remember that nothing is better than obtaining nutrients from foods. Foods are packed with more than vitamins and minerals. They also include fiber and phytochemicals. Phytochemicals are compounds found in plant foods, such as fruits and vegetables, that have powerful effects on health and disease prevention. They are much more potent when consumed directly from the food. Some of my grandparents' often-eaten foods are powerhouses of nutrition.

Onions are probably the most commonly used vegetable in the family recipes. They are a rich source of quercetin, which is a type of flavanoid phytochemical. Quercetin is a powerful antioxidant that may have benefits in the prevention of cancer and heart disease. As an antioxidant, it can eliminate free radicals (which can damage cells in our body) and prevent low-density lipoprotein (LDL cholesterol) from oxidizing. This oxidation may lead to plaque build up and coronary heart disease. The strong smell in onions comes from sulfur-containing phytochemicals. These compounds are known for its detoxifying powers, which work by stimulating enzymes in the digestive tract to eliminate toxins. The phytochemicals in onions also have anti-inflammatory, antibacterial and antiviral properties.

Cabbage is another vegetable that takes center stage in recipes such as soups, stuffed cabbage and cabbage with noodles. This cruciferous vegetable gets its bitter taste from phytochemicals called glucosinolates. These particular phytochemicals stimulate enzymes in our body that prevent cancer, and may alter the activity of hormones, thereby decreasing the risk of hormone-related cancers such as breast cancer. Chopping cruciferous vegetables like cabbage (as in Cabbage with Noodles) will activate the glucosinolates. Stir-frying and light steaming will maintain the glucosinolate concentration while prolonged cooking will decrease it.

Cooked tomatoes, rich in the phytochemical lycopene, form the sauce for stuffed cabbage. They are also used in *lecsó*, a familiar traditional vegetable relish that could be thought of as Hungarian ratatouille. Some studies found lycopene to decrease the risk of some cancers, including prostate cancer, as well as lung and stomach cancers. As a powerful antioxidant, lycopene also plays a role in prevention of heart disease.

Deep red and blue fruits and vegetables get their coloring from flavanoid phytochemicals known as anthocyanins. I think of cherry soup, beet borscht, red cabbage and the juicy blackberries my grandmother picked as a child along the banks of the Tisza River as examples of these foods. The anthocyanins may contribute to lower risk of certain cancers, urinary tract health, memory function, and healthy aging.

Diet and Lifestyle

As you prepare the recipes in this cookbook I hope you will remember how my grandparents cooked and ate and lived and take their tradition to heart: choose the freshest ingredients to ensure the best flavor and the highest nutritional value. Most importantly, color your plate with plenty of vibrant and varied fruits and vegetables.

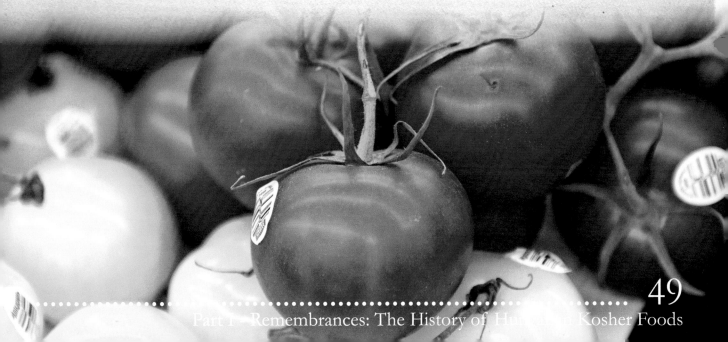

The Wide World of Kosher Wines

Lynn Kirsche Shapiro with Matt Levy

"Yayin yesamach l'vav enosh."
(Wine gladdens one's heart.) Psalms 104:15

Kosher wine has become an integral part of the wine world, as well as the Jewish community worldwide. What used to be prepared at home solely for religious use, is now produced and sold around the globe, competing in quality with the best wines, both kosher and non-kosher. Wine that used to be reserved for traditional purposes has evolved into something greater, wine that not only satisfies those traditions but enhances them.

In Biblical times, Jews were prohibited from drinking any wine that could have been used for idolatrous or non-Jewish religious rituals. Because of the social implications and consequences, the Rabbis extended this prohibition to include any wine where a non-Jew was involved in the process of making, moving (handling) or drinking the wine.

The new definition of kosher wine emerged, (or *yayin kasher*): wine that has only been touched by Jewish hands from the beginning of the process of making the wine and including moving (or serving) the wine, and drinking the wine. In order to stay within the framework of the Jewish law, the concept of wine that is *mevushal* (cooked) developed. *Mevushal* wine (or *yayin mevushal*) was defined as wine that was heated to a point that is too hot to touch, to boiling. Because heating at such high temperatures affects the quality of the wine (boiling kills the "must" on the grapes and diminishes the tannins and flavors of wine), *mevushal* wine was considered to be "inferior" and would never be used in non-Jewish religious rites. The Rabbis allowed *mevushal* wine to be shared by everyone, only after it is declared *mevushal*. Today, this process of boiling the wine has advanced to "flash-pasteurization," in which the wine is heated very quickly to the point of boiling and then cools very rapidly, not affecting the flavor or quality.

Using the grapes that grew on their land, my father's family has a long tradition of making wine, both for their own family as well as for other Jewish families. This tradition continued post-Holocaust. I remember as a young child traveling to visit my father's aunt, Golda Moskovics, who lived in Chibat Zion, Israel. On Friday night, she would place a bottle of her homemade wine on the table for Kiddush. Her wine had a unique flavor, sweet with the sharp tart flavor of grapefruit, and a golden color. Because she did not grow grapes as her parents had grown in Hluboka, Czechoslovakia, before the Holocaust, my father's aunt, Golda, made her wine from raisins and grapefruit. I had never tasted any wine like this, but I loved it and looked forward to this tradition through the years, each time I visited her.

In my father's sister, Goldie Weinberger's home in Munkács in the Soviet Union (post-Holocaust), she and her husband Leib also made their own wine, firstly to ensure that they would have kosher wine, even while living under the communist regime, where kosher food was prohibited, and also because this was the family tradition. They had a large yard behind their home in Munkács, with an abundance of grapes. Each year, in preparation for Passover, they used these grapes to make simple red grape wine that lasted not only for Passover, but the entire year.

Through the centuries, the Jews have always made their own wine and distributed it or sold it to the Jewish community—simple wine used mostly for Jewish rituals, holidays and special occasions. However, over the past two centuries, significant changes in the kosher winemaking industry occurred. In the 1800s, the study and education of winemaking, indeed the wine industry, emerged in Israel.

Most notably, in the late 1800s Baron Edmond de Rothschild founded the Carmel Winery of Israel. This was in fact the beginning of the wine industry in Israel. Very careful to adhere to the laws of kosher wine, they produced and sold kosher wines around the globe. Then in 1983, the Golan Heights Winery in Israel was founded, competing with non-kosher wines in international wine competitions. In 1987, Yarden cabernet sauvignon from Golan Heights Winery won a Gold Medal at the International Wine & Spirit Competition.

The kosher palate has changed. The kosher perception has changed. Today, kosher wine has grown up; it has become more refined. Israel is producing some of the greatest wines in the world, *mevushal* as well as non-*mevushal*, kosher as well as non-kosher. Yarden's cabernet sauvignon 2004 (kosher) has won many prestigious awards. It was the only kosher and Israeli wine of Wine Spectator's Top 100 Wines of 2008, chosen from nearly 20,000 wines, kosher and non-kosher. However, Israel is not the only country where kosher wine is being produced today. Kosher wines come from all over the world. There are world-class kosher wines from, among other places, France, Italy, New Zealand, Argentina, Chile, Turkey, Hungary and California.

As you lift a glass of kosher wine to your lips during the Shabbos meal, the wedding ceremony and other religious events, remember that this tradition originated with our ancestors who made their own kosher wine. Wine not only gladdens the heart but it carries tradition from one generation to the next. And, even more, today's fine kosher wines are consumed all over the world in homes with different religions and cultures, thus gladdening many hearts. Truly, "*Yayin yesamach l'vav enosh*"!

The Holidays: Living and Celebrating
Through the Jewish Calendar
Lynn Kirsche Shapiro

"To everything there is a season."
— *3:1 Ecclesiastes*

Jewish life revolves around the Jewish Holidays. The week revolves around Shabbos and the year around the cycles of the Jewish holidays. This was especially true in the small towns of pre-Holocaust Europe: in Vásárosnamény, Hungary, my mother's hometown, and in Hluboka, Czechoslovakia, where my father's family lived. Both my parents were raised with a determined work ethic and a fervent religious dedication.

Shabbos

According to the Torah, God created the heavens and the earth in six days and rested on the seventh and final day. In recognition of this, we, the Jewish people, work six days, and on the seventh day, we stop. The quality of sanctity and a unique serenity together create the particular ambiance of Shabbos. The distinctive food, the particular wine for Kiddush, the dinner table set with a white cloth, formal dishes, two loaves of freshly baked, braided challah, the Shabbos candlesticks and the aromas of the meal, have all contributed to the sense of peacefulness and the extraordinary gift of Shabbos. My parents had many memories of Shabbos: my father walking to the shul (synagogue)

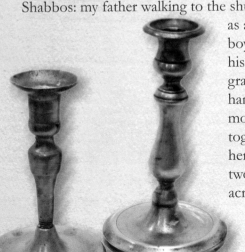

as a little boy grasping his towering grandfather's hand, my mother walking together with her girlfriends two kilometers across the Tisza

River to visit her grandparents in Gergely. And as Shabbos comes to an end, the *Havdalah* (literally "separation"), a ritual marking the end of Shabbos and the beginning of the new week, is said. In my mother's home, it was customary for the women to preface this ritual with a Chassidic prayer asking God for a week of blessing, *Got Fun Avraham*, which my mother still says each week.

Rosh Hashana

Rosh Hashana, (the New Year) the first day of the seventh month, Tishrei, is the day on which we pray for a "sweet New Year" filled with only

blessings. Many of the traditional foods for Rosh Hashana symbolize our wishes for the upcoming year. Challah, which is typically braided and twisted for Shabbos is made into round shapes, for the cycle of the year and of life. Challah (my parents' tradition) or apple is dipped in honey, while asking God "to renew for us a good, sweet year." My parents, as their parents before them, eat the challah dipped in honey through Hoshanna Rabba, the seventh day of Succos, because the Chassidic tradition believes that the gates of Heaven are open to our prayers through that day.

Sweet, candied carrots, and honey cake, *Lekech*, also represented the wish for a sweet year. Fish head was eaten, so "we should be like the head and not the tail." Rosh Hashana is still considered a somber holiday of judgment and prayer, as it was in my parents' childhood homes. My mother recalls walking with her family to the Krasna River (or going to the well in their yard) in the afternoon, bringing along challah crumbs to cast into the river, symbolically casting her sins of the previous year into the water, as she recited the accompanying prayer, *Tashlich*.

Yom Kippur

Yom Kippur (Day of Atonement) on the tenth of Tishrei, is a day of fasting, a day dedicated to beseeching God for forgiveness, repenting for one's sins, and praying for a *Gut Gebencht Yaar*, a good, blessed year. My father, believing in the power of a blessing, had the custom of benching (blessing) his children and grandchildren, just prior to the beginning of Yom Kippur, wishing them a blessed year. Reflecting the purity and holiness of these days, many men, including my mother's maternal grandfather, customarily wore a white *kittel* (ritual robe).

Erev Yom Kippur (the day preceding Yom Kippur) has many food-related customs, including the meal preceding the fast, which has always retained the traditional focus with my parents and their families. The meal is simple but appropriate for a holiday, beginning, of course, with challah dipped in honey, for a sweet year. My mother always served *falcse* fish for appetizer, followed by her famous chicken soup. For the entrée, she served chicken from the soup or simple broiled chicken, rice with mushrooms, sweet candied carrots, and for a light dessert, fresh fruit compote. This unusually simple meal, at least compared to our other holiday meals, was often enriched by our yearly conversation about whether it was better to eat more rice or more chicken, to prepare for the fast.

Succos

Succos (the Feast of Tabernacles), one of the *Shalosh Regalim*, the three pilgrimage-related Jewish festivals, is on the fifteenth of Tishrei and lasts for seven days. In five short days, we make an extremely sharp transition in our mood, from somber solemnity on Yom Kippur to lighthearted joy on Succos, which is referred to in the liturgy as "the time of our happiness." The temporary hut, *Succah*, that each family built, and which my mother so warmly recalls decorating with intricately handmade decorations, is reminiscent of the forty years that the Jewish people journeyed in the desert on the way to the land of Israel. The *Arba Minim*, which are traditionally used, symbolize the harvest season, the agricultural aspect of Succos. Traditional foods, such as dried food compote and stuffed cabbage, which my mother still prepares each year, abound on Succos.

Chanukah

Chanukah falls on the twenty-fifth day of the ninth month, Kislev, in the depth of winter. Commemorating the victory of the small Jewish army of Maccabim over King Antiochus and the Greeks in 165 BCE and the "miracles…strength and salvations that occurred in those days and in this era," the eight days of the holiday are spent in festive celebration.

In remembrance of the miracle of regaining control of the Beit Hamikdash (Temple in Jerusalem) and the small jug of oil used to light the Menorah (seven-branched candelabra) which lasted for eight days, until the priests had time to purify more oil, the culinary tradition of eating foods prepared with oil emerged. While it is traditional in the States to eat latkes, potato pancakes, my parents grew up eating pastries fried in oil (sufganiot), still popular in Israel today. As children, my brother and I were given "Chanukah gelt" (coins) each night after lighting the candles or oil on the Menorah, a custom my parents continued from their homes before the War. My mother recalls playing cards, specifically Blackjack or "21" as a child, using the gelt she received from her parents and the homemade cards that her brother, Morton, made. My mother still plays Blackjack each year, but now she plays with her grandchildren and even her great-grandchildren. Nearly forty years ago, when my father's family was finally allowed to leave the Soviet Union and came to Chicago, my mother began hosting an annual family Chanukah party. This Chanukah party, with all of our family customs (including singing all the verses of *Maoz Tsur*), which my mother began to simply bring us all together, has since blossomed into a treasured family tradition.

Purim

Purim, celebrated on the fourteenth day of Adar, is a uniquely joyful day, commemorating the defeat of Haman who, according to the Book of Esther, sought the destruction of the Jewish people. To celebrate this lively spirit, the children "dress up" as they did in generations past. The Book of Esther, Megillas Esther, is read in the evening and again in the morning of the holiday. At night, after the reading it was customary to have a Purim Shpiel, a satirical spoof or play. My mother recalls

the entire *Kehilla* (community) was invited to the Shpiel. To enhance the sense of peoplehood and community for Purim, families baked cakes and other goodies, such as Hamantaschen, as well as *Aranygaluska*, *Kindle* and Meringue Kisses, to send as *shalach manos* (Purim baskets) to neighborhood friends. Traditionally, the children in my parents' towns looked forward to delivering the food baskets and receiving a few pennies from each recipient. The Yeshiva Bochurim (students) would go from house to house dancing, singing, entertaining the families with small performances. And then, in the afternoon, each family enjoyed a Purim Seudah, a festive meal with delicacies. (We always waited eagerly for the roasted duck that my mother served each year). All these festivities were enhanced for my mother as she remembers that her mother's birthday was around Purim.

Pesach

Pesach (Passover), one of the *Shalosh Regalim* (festivals), along with Succos and Shavuos, falls one month after Purim, on the fifteenth day of Nissan, in the springtime. Historically, Pesach commemorates the freedom from bondage and exodus of the Jewish people from Egypt. Through the generations, one of the most widely celebrated and emotionally significant evenings of the Jewish calendar

is the night of Pesach, the Seder. The customs and the foods associated with the Seder reflect the retelling of the story of the exodus from slavery, the special *charoses*, which my mother has been making each year with her grandfather's recipe that is used for dipping the *maror* (bitter herbs); the *karpas* which we dip in salt water, either celery to remind us of springtime or the potato which my parents have both used since childhood, the wine, which was homemade in their homes before the Holocaust, and of course, the matza, which was home-baked, reminding us of the unleavened bread that the Jews made upon leaving Egypt in a frenzied hurry. Matza for the Jewish families of Hluboka was baked in the kitchen of the Kirschenbaum home. The house was cleaned of leavened food a few weeks before Pesach, long tables were set up for preparing the matza which was baked in a special oven.

My mother remembers the oven in the back of the shul, across the street from her family home in Vásárosnamény, in which their matza was baked. Many of the traditional foods are specific to the particular region, such as the *lukshin* (noodles), used for the soup, particularly since my parents did not eat *gebrockt* (matza broken in water); because they did not eat any foods that were *gebrockt*, our Pesach recipes are made mostly with potatoes and eggs. Each of my parents' shared their memories of Pesach, loving memories of special time shared with their parents and grandparents. Then the memories become blurred with the memory of their final Pesach at home, in 1944, when they were taken from their homes to the Ghetto and then to Auschwitz. And now, at our Seder, the story of the exodus of Egypt extends to include the story of the Jews of the Holocaust and the story of my parents' last Pesach with their family.

Shavuos

Shavuos, one of the *Shalosh Regalim* (festivals) is on the sixth day of Sivan, in late spring. As the holiday of the first fruits, we fill our homes with greens and flowers. Historically, because it commemorates the date when the Jewish people received the Torah at Mount Sinai and became a nation, the custom developed of (mostly) men staying up all night and learning Torah until the morning when they *davened* (prayed the morning service). Traditionally, the foods eaten on Shavuos are dairy; we have been enjoying cheese blintzes and cheese kreplach in our family for generations. Personally, Shavuos has taken on added meaning since the Holocaust. My mother's family entered Auschwitz, and most of them were taken immediately to the gas chambers, on the third of Sivan, just two days before the evening of Shavuos, 1944. My father's family entered Auschwitz on the evening of the sixth of Sivan, Shavuos, and his mother, grandmother, and many aunts, uncles and cousins were also taken to the gas chambers. However, even with only the few who survived the Holocaust, the Jewish people have flourished.

Shabbos and the Jewish holidays are special times, and many of the recipes in this book were prepared specifically for certain holidays, imbued with the tradition and the flavor of the holiday. As you read the recipes you will find more anecdotes describing holidays past and customs reflecting the Jewish life in my parents' childhood hometowns. The Survivors of the Holocaust carried these stories, along with the recipes, to the places they lived and the homes and families they built.

Jewish Calendar
Special Holidays

Tishrei:
September - October

Rosh Hashana, the Jewish New Year,
is on the first two days of Tishrei.
Yom Kippur is on the tenth and
Succos begins on the fifteenth of Tishrei.

Cheshvan:
October - November

Kislev:
November - December

Chanukah, begins on the night
of the 25th of Kislev.

Tevet:
December - January

Sh'vat
January - February

Tu B'Sh'vat, the fifteenth of Sh'vat,
celebrates the New Year of the trees

Adar:
February - March

Purim is on the fourteenth of Adar
and Shushan Purim is on the fifteenth.
Because the Jewish calendar is a lunar calendar,
periodically there is an extra month in the year,
Adar II, so the seasons do not change.

Nissan:
March - April

Pesach begins with the Seder in the evening,
on the fifteenth of Nissan (Erev Pesach is
on the fourteenth). Yom Hashoah VeHaGevuah,
remembering the victims of the Holocaust,
is on the 27th of Nissan

Iyar:
April - May

Yom Haatzmaut, Israel Independence Day,
is on the fifth of Iyar.

Sivan:
May - June

Shavuos is on the sixth of Sivan.

Tammuz:
June - July

Av
July - August

The first nine days of Av, ending on the "ninth of Av".
Tisha B'Av is the day when we commemorate the
destruction of the Temple in Jerusalem

Elul:
August - September

A time to reflect and prepare for Rosh Hashana.
Traditionally, the shofar (ram's horn) is blown daily.

Food, Family and Tradition

My First Shabbos
Nancy Ross Ryan

For an editor each new book promises new people and new experiences, in short, the "firsts" that make life exciting. Working on Lynn Shapiro's book *Food, Family and Tradition* has been full of "firsts."

I am the third generation of English-Irish-Scottish ancestors, all born in this country except for an Irish grandfather and a Scottish grandfather. I remember my grandparents well. Lynn was the first generation of Hungarian-Czechoslovakian Jewish ancestors, none born in this country. Lynn has no grandparents to remember, only stories about them. They were all killed in the Holocaust. I was raised a Christian but have been Buddhist since my twenties. Lynn was raised and remains an Orthodox Jew.

Despite our different religious and cultural backgrounds, as mothers we share an unconditional love for and close friendships with our adult children. As fellow members of the human race, we both try to lead the examined life, (Socrates said, "The unexamined life is not worth living.") As work on her book progressed, Lynn and I became not just author and editor, but friends.

The second "first" was devastating: hearing firsthand about the Holocaust through Lynn's family stories in this book. The family's life stories made me weep. When I retold just one of the stories to a friend, he said, "Do you keep a box of Kleenex nearby?" I replied, "I don't bother anymore. Too many tears."

Lynn is a great cook, and every week brought samples of her food and recipes, my "first" kosher food. The chicken soup was rich and golden, her pastries melted in my mouth, her challah (her mother's recipe) was light, crisp and delicious, so unlike bakery challah. There was the mysterious *Chrain*, a beet-horseradish relish that, once sampled, was eaten with every imaginable foodstuff until the last spoonful. Her quince preserves lasted a week in my fridge and the *lekvar*, or plum jam (her late father's favorite) was gone in less than a week.

The "first" I will never forget is my first Shabbos. I had met Lynn's mother, Mrs. Margit Kirsche, who had survived the Holocaust, but lost countless immediate family members including her mother and father, grandparents and her three younger brothers. She came to this country, worked hard, made a life, created a business, raised a family and, at the age of 75 was stricken suddenly and irreversibly blind. But Mrs. Kirsche continued to cook and still bakes and braids challah. And she invited me to her house for Shabbos.

We were seated around the big kitchen table: Mrs. Kirsche, her niece Alisa and Alisa's tow-headed toddler who was enraptured by my bright red lipstick, Lynn and her husband Irv. Lynn lit the Shabbos candles and recited the traditional blessing; everyone at the table washed their hands with water, and Mrs. Kirsche's challah loaves were broken and the challah passed. Irv had brought some excellent kosher wine. The courses kept on coming and I kept on eating: *Chrain* I already loved, Mrs. Kirsche's challah (with six braids), the famous *Falrse* Fish (chicken prepared in the manner of gefilte fish); rich, golden chicken soup, Mrs. Kirsche's tender stuffed cabbage rolls, her Stuffed Chicken Quarters, and more.

After dinner the traditional prayers were chanted, in rhythm and with melody. At my very first Shabbos, I was welcomed in so many ways: by the lovingly prepared food, the warmth of Lynn's family and the richness of their traditions. May my first Shabbos be one of many.

Part II
Recipes

More than Recipes

The recipes in this cookbook tell a story: the story of my parents' childhood homes with their Jewish-Hungarian-Czech traditions, and the survival of their traditions after the Holocaust. The story begins with the recipe titles, many of which have Hungarian or Yiddish names. They include family recipes from my parents' childhood, new recipes that my parents created for their store, Hungarian Kosher Foods, as well as a sprinkling of recipes from friends and family that help convey the Jewish life and culture in the regions where my parents grew up. Next, the recipe ingredients, seemingly basic, tell a story of their own, illustrating the natural food products available to my parents "at home." The cooking process itself tells of the fresh preparation of gourmet dishes in my parents' European homes, using simple but hands-on techniques and few appliances. Finally, the memories in the sidebars enrich the recipes with flavor, some sweet, some bittersweet and some bitter.

The process of compiling this cookbook for the modern cook entailed several adaptations. Some family recipes were handed down from my grandmothers: to my mother, from the Cheimovics-Weisz family, and to my aunt Goldie or my father, from the Moskovics-Kirschenbaum family. For these recipes, we translated from "handfuls" and "pinches" to precise measurements so that cooks could replicate the dishes in their own homes. For other recipes, such as the cheese blintz filling, we developed the recipes to taste (as the traditional homemade cheese had a slightly different consistency) according to the ingredients available today. Some of the recipes were actually hand-written recipes (in Hungarian) that my aunt, Goldie Weinberger, received from her mother, my paternal grandmother, before the Holocaust. But even theses written recipes had to be converted, from "a glazele" (glass) to a cup, from grams to teaspoons.

Bringing these century-old recipes to the modern kitchen cuts down the cooking time tremendously. While you may think that the meals were simple then, as a dinner could consist of homemade noodles with *lekvar* (plum jam), keep in mind two important distinctions. First, the dishes were cooked with the freshest ingredients producing optimum flavor. Trust me, one dish of homemade noodles with fresh jam trumps a three-course meal from the supermarket's freezer section. Second, remember that the noodles were made by hand, from scratch, and the *lekvar*, although it was preserved, was also originally cooked, stirring constantly, for up to twelve hours. Fortunately today, our gadgets, ingredients, and conveniences reduce both cooking time and labor. Examples include pre-ground chicken for the *False* Fish, canned sour cherries for the Sour Cherry Soup, the use of the food processor to purée the plums for the *lekvar*, and many more. Many of the baked goods are parve; however, you can substitute butter and milk as they did in Europe. When they wanted parve they traditionally used coconut oil or coconut shortening, which is enjoying renewed popularity today.

Many of the recipes have been long-time favorites at Hungarian Kosher Foods, such as Stuffed Chicken Quarters. Some of the recipes, such as *Kakáos* or Chicken *Paprikás* with *Nakidlach*, are family favorites and traditional Hungarian recipes.

In the ten chapters that follow, you will surely find recipes to fit your time, your taste and your own cooking style. The appetizers chapter alone offers a variety of textures and flavors, some simple, such as *Körözött* (Hungarian cheese spread) and some traditional such as Chopped Liver.

In Chapter 2 you will find soups for all seasons, some hearty, some light, some vegetarian, some for meat lovers, and, of course, my mother's famous chicken soup.

Chapter 3, Dairy and Egg Dishes, offers flavorful options for breakfast or brunch—blintzes and apple cheese pancakes—lunch and dinner—Cheese Kugel or Potato-Egg Casserole, and Farmer's Chop Suey.

Chapter 4, the Fish chapter, has, among a variety of other preparations, a selection of stovetop and oven-baked fish dishes that recommend themselves to today's busy cooks. They are easy to prepare, cook in a pot on the stovetop or bake in the oven, come out full of flavor and there is no fear of over- or undercooking the fish. One of my favorites is Whitefish with Carrots and Onions. Of course, my mother's Sweet and Sour Fish is hard to beat. And for something elegant but easy I recommend Poached Salmon.

Chapter 5, Poultry, has the famous *Falcse* Fish or Mock Fish, which is chicken prepared in the manner of Gefilte fish. There is my mother's famous roast chicken with rice and her equally famous stuffed-under-the skin chicken quarters. Chapter 5 has ultra traditional dishes such as Chicken *Paprikás* and completely contemporary recipes such as Chicken Schnitzel.

Chapter 6, Meats, offers old-fashioned recipes such as tongue, *Chulent*, goulash and Stuffed Cabbage. There are more contemporary dishes such as Chop Suey, Rib Roast and Meatloaf. You will also find guidelines for perfect roasts.

Chapter 7, Vegetables and Salads, holds the famous Tzimmes and also *Lecsó*, a Hungarian ratatouille-like vegetable stew, as well as Beet Salad, Israeli Salad, Pickled Vegetables and so much more.

Chapter 8, is a carbohydrate-lover's dream: Potato Kugel, Potato *Paprikás*, Latkes, My Mother's Homemade Noodles and other traditional hearty dishes from "at home."

Chapter 9, Breads, Pastries, Cakes and Cookies pretty much says it all. The chapter covers traditional baking from challah to Cheese Danish, from Sponge Cake to Honey Cake, and a variety of cookies including Mandel Bread.

Chapter 10, Fruit Soups, Sauces, Compotes and Preserves is one of my favorite chapters and a sweet ending for the book. You will discover recipes for fruit soups to serve hot or cold, plum preserves or *lekvár* (my father's favorite) along with a preparation method that cuts the traditional eight-to-twelve-hour preparation down to two to three hours. There is a recipe for exotic esrog preserves and candy, to put one of the "ingredients" for Succos to good use, and fresh and dried fruit compotes.

Each chapter begins with a complete list of the recipes. I hope you will find appealing dishes, start cooking, and embrace your friends, your family and your neighbors as you share the experience of "breaking bread."

Keeping Kosher
Lynn Kirsche Shapiro

Kosher food is an integral part of Jewish identity and Jewish faith. In many ways, kashrus is the most well known religious practice maintained by observant Jews. The laws of kashrus could fill hundreds of pages. Following is only a brief synopsis of these laws and their importance.

The laws of kashrus describe not only which foods are kosher, but also the process of preparing these foods. They tell us the following:

(1) Not all animals, fish and fowl are kosher. The Torah describes those that are and those that are not kosher. In order for meat to be kosher it must come from an animal that has split hooves and chews its cud. Kosher animals include the cow, deer, goat, and lamb. (The hindquarters of large animals, which contain the tenderest steaks, are not available as kosher because the sciatic nerve and blood vessels must be removed—a process few butchers can perform today—so these hindquarter cuts are sold to the general market.) Chicken, duck, geese, Cornish hen and turkey can also be considered kosher. Non-kosher animals include the camel, horse, pig and rabbit. And even among those that are kosher, care must be taken to prepare them in a way that is compatible with the laws of kashrus. For example, kosher animals must be slaughtered according to the strict laws of *shechita* (kosher slaughtering), and then they must be kashered, prepared according to laws that include salting of the meat.

(2) Most foods that are dairy are kosher, if they conform to the following principles: they come from kosher animals, they are free of meat derivatives, and they are prepared in a process compatible with the laws of kashrus.

(3) Foods that are neither meat nor dairy are called parve. In most instances, these types of foods— eggs, fruit, vegetables, and grains—are generally considered kosher. Fish also holds the status of parve: to be kosher, it must have fins and scales. (Although eggs are considered parve, chicken is considered meat.)

(4) Food products certified as kosher have been produced under the inspection of rabbis and Jewish religious organizations. Today there are many symbols representing various rabbinic organizations and supervisions found on food products that certify that these products are kosher. This makes it easy to shop at stores and markets. However, each person should consult with their rabbi when determining the acceptability of these symbols.

(5) Meat and dairy foods in any form, cannot be eaten together, nor can they be cooked together. Thus, a kosher kitchen contains at least two separate sets of pots and pans, as well as dishes and cutlery, and there are also separate sets used just for Passover. Additionally, since they cannot be eaten together, a meat meal for example, cannot offer a dessert made with a dairy product. Many of the baked goods in this cookbook are parve, allowing them to be served for dessert with either a meat or dairy meal.

(6) There are specific laws concerning the preparation of food on Shabbos as well as on Jewish holidays.

(7) On Passover, we are not allowed to eat any leavened food. We clean our homes from any leavened food; additionally there are laws regarding the pots and pans and dishes used during the year with leavened food. The Ashkenazic Jews (from Eastern European descent) have an additional custom that we do not eat *kitnios* or legumes, including rice. Some Jews, my parents among them, follow the custom of not eating *gebrockt* (literally "broken"), matza or matza meal broken in water. My parents shared this custom with many of the Jews from their region.

Recipe Guidelines

Unless otherwise specified:

*All fruits and vegetables have been washed, trimmed of unusable parts, stemmed, peeled, cored and seeded. To emphasize a frequent ingredient: All potatoes, unless otherwise described, have been peeled. Mushrooms are washed but not peeled. When fruits and vegetables are not peeled, the recipe will specify "peel on."

*All butter is unsalted

*All white flour is all-purpose unbleached, except as stated, such as bread flour

*All milk is whole milk

*All onions are yellow onions

*If prepared recipes are to be stored, refrigerated, they should be placed in non-reactive containers: glass, plastic, ceramic or stainless steel (no aluminum) and covered.

*All sugar is granulated cane sugar, unless specified as another variety.

*All cooked hot foods should be cooled down in an ice-water bath before refrigerating.

Seasoned Salt

We use seasoned salt in many recipes for added flavor. You can buy the well-known brand, or you can easily make your own. Seasoned salt is not as salty as table salt. Recipe instructions always say "to taste," so experiment, starting with a pinch and adding. You may want to decrease some of the regular salt listed in the recipe the more seasoned salt you add.

Makes about ⅓ cup

4 tablespoons salt
4 teaspoons sugar
1 tablespoon sweet Hungarian paprika
1 teaspoon turmeric
1 teaspoon garlic powder
1 teaspoon onion powder
½ teaspoon cornstarch or potato starch

Combine all ingredients in a small bowl and whisk to mix well. Transfer to a glass jar with a tight-fitting lid. Store in a cool, dark place.

To Kasher Livers:

Rinse the livers. Spread livers on a pan with slits or holes so the blood can drip through. Sprinkle kosher salt to cover the livers all over. Broil, or grill the livers over a fire, just until the blood drains, then turn the livers over and broil or grill on the other side. Remove the livers from the pan and rinse well under cold water.
(Some people rinse three times.)

Tip

If you are broiling the livers it is good to have a separate pan underneath to catch the blood.

The Ice-Water Bath

Bacteria multiply rapidly in food (in as little as 20 minutes) between 45°F and 140°F. An ice-water bath is essential to cool down cooked foods to cool room temperature before refrigerating them. Do not put hot foods directly in the refrigerator. They will raise the ambient temperature of the refrigerator; they will not cool down quickly enough; and they may release aromas that will be absorbed by other foods in the refrigerator.

To make an ice-water bath: Place a large shallow bowl or 12-inch sauté pan in the sink. Set the container of hot cooked food inside the bowl or pan. Add ice cubes and cold water around the hot food container halfway up (so it doesn't float). Stir the hot food until it is room temperature, then cover and refrigerate. It will cool down quickly in the refrigerator.

Chapter 1
Appetizers

Dill Dip
Cheese Spread, *Körözött*
Egg 'n Onion, *Eier mit Tzvibel*
Chopped Chicken Liver, *Májpástétom*
Sweet and Sour Gizzards, *Pupiks*
Chicken Fricasée
Gefilte Fish
Chopped Herring
Matjes Herring
Mini Stuffed Cabbage

See also:
Bean Dip (page 98)
Falcse Fish (page 139)
Mini Mushroom Blintzes (page 110)

Wine with Appetizers

Just as the appetizers introduce the meal, the wine you choose should work together with the appetizer to set the tone. To introduce a fun, festive meal, or for a light cocktail party, try Champagne or a light white sparkling wine, served cold. Our family's traditional drink for Matjes Herring, or any herring, is schnapps, and in particular, slivovitz plum brandy, which was my father's favorite, perhaps because of the plum trees that grew on his family's property. Slivovitz is also good with a bit of Chopped Liver or *Eier mit Tzvibel*. A modern take on slivovitz is to serve it right out of the freezer ice cold. And, of course, if you are enjoying *Eier mit Tzvibel* or Chopped Liver for Shabbos Kiddush, choose a traditional red Concord grape wine.

Food, Family and Tradition

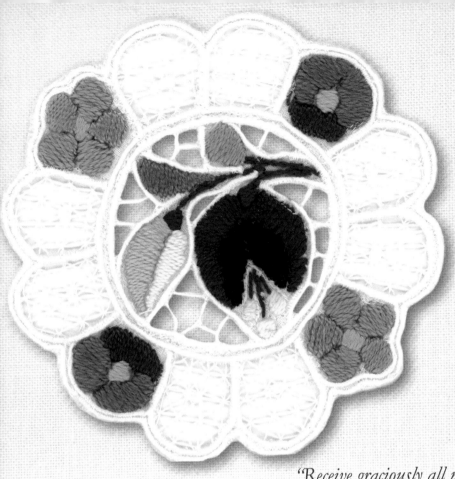

"Receive graciously all men with a friendly expression."

(Babylonian Talmud, Tractate Ethics of the Fathers)

Appetizers, or *forshpeiz* in Yiddish, are like first impressions. The word *forshpeiz* means not only the dish that is being served but also includes the response it evokes: keen anticipation, a whetting of the appetite.

As the recipes will show, food, family and personality were one when it came to the lives of my parents, Sandor and Margit Kirsche. In my parents' Eastern European homes, before the Holocaust—which they always referred to as "at home"—appetizers only set the stage on Shabbos, on other Jewish holidays, and at special occasions such as weddings. Because of the time-consuming nature of food preparation, daily meals consisted of few basic courses. Yet, on Shabbos and holidays, families put forth the extra effort to add several appetizers to their menus.

As you prepare your first recipe, I hope it will whet your appetite for more. Every recipe is seasoned with memories—and the personalities—of the original chefs of Hungarian Kosher Foods: Sandor and Margit Kirsche.

Dill Dip

P Makes about 4 cups, up to 20 servings

My mother Margit Kirsche created this recipe twenty years ago when one of the downtown Chicago hotels phoned Hungarian Kosher Foods to order nondairy dill dip. Rather than look for a recipe, she imagined how it should taste and simply made it. Thereafter, she produced it by the gallons for the hotels. Hungarian Kosher Foods then packed the surplus in small containers for customers at the store, and it sold out immediately.

We have been preparing this dip ever since. My mother liked the combination of salad dressing and mayonnaise; I simply use 2 cups of mayonnaise.

1 bunch fresh dill, about ½ pound
¾ cup parve sour cream
1 cup mayonnaise
1 cup salad dressing
2 cloves garlic
Salt and freshly ground pepper, to taste

Cut the roots, but not the stems, off the dill and discard. Soak the dill in a large bowl of cold water for 30 minutes, swishing often to remove sand and grit. Remove from water, place in colander and rinse well under cold water. Pat dry or spin in a salad spinner.

Place dill and remaining ingredients in the work bowl of a large-capacity food processor fitted with the metal blade. Pulse to process to a coarse purée.

Transfer to a medium bowl, add sour cream, mayonnaise and salad dressing and mix well. Season to taste with salt and pepper. Refrigerate, covered, for up to 4 days.

Serve as a dip with raw vegetables, crackers, chips.

Food, Family and Tradition

Cheese Spread, *Körözött*

(D) Makes 2 to 2½ cups, about 10 servings

Goldie Weinberger, my father's sister, made this with her own homemade farmer's cheese. Farmer's cheese is a fresh, unripened cow's milk cheese that is pressed, producing somewhat dry curds that can be mixed with various ingredients to enhance texture and produce a wide variety of flavors. The not-so-secret ingredient that provides the Hungarian flavor is the paprika.

1 pound farmer's cheese
4 tablespoons margarine or butter, softened
1 to 2 cloves garlic, minced
1 tablespoon sweet Hungarian paprika

In a medium bowl mix all ingredients together until smooth. Alternatively, pulse all ingredients to mix in a food processor using the metal blade. Refrigerate, covered, for up to four days.

Serve as a spread with crackers, cocktail rye, or as a dip for crudités.

The Taste of Home
Supermarkets today are full of rows and rows of cheese spreads. However, the original taste of this quick and easy spread can only be created at home. My cousin Ibi Gelb serves this—her mother's recipe—at brunch or a light dairy meal. The recipe was traditional in the Kirschenbaum home even before the Holocaust, when our parents and their communities made all of their own cheeses and dairy products. Restaurants in Hungary still offer this on their menus today.

Some traditional Hungarian recipes for this cheese spread include adding ½ to 1 teaspoon caraway seeds, or 1 to 2 teaspoons finely chopped chives.

Paprika
We use and recommend only genuine Hungarian paprika. Much Hungarian paprika comes from Szeged, both a city and a region in Hungary located between the Danube and Tisza rivers. It is well known for its red peppers, both sweet and mild as well as very spicy and hot. Ground into paprika, the paprika produced in Szeged is fragrant, flavorful and retains its rich, red color.

Egg 'n Onion, *Eier mit Tzvibel*

Ⓟ Makes about 4 servings

Certain foods transform shared times into strong family memories that can last for generations. Eier mit Tzvibel is one such recipe. This traditional Eastern European appetizer shows how the simplest ingredients can be combined for a flavor that is greater than the sum of its parts. Eier mit Tzvibel is the perfect Shabbos lunch accompaniment for crackers or challah.

3 hard-boiled eggs, shelled
¼ cup finely chopped onion
Salt and freshly ground pepper, to taste
2 tablespoons vegetable oil

Coarsely grate or hand-chop the eggs. In a medium bowl combine eggs and remaining ingredients and mix well. Refrigerate, covered, for up to 4 days.

Instead of serving as a spread with crackers or challah, place on a bed of lettuce with sliced tomatoes and cucumbers on the side.

When Margit Kirsche discovered avocados in the States, she began to add the flesh of 1 ripe avocado to this recipe. Preserve the avocado pit and place it in the center of the salad to preserve color, cover and refrigerate. This variation is best served shortly after being prepared.

A Shabbos Morning, by Margit Kirsche
"I grew up in Hungary in Vásárosnamény, a small town approximately thirty kilometers (about eighteen miles) from the Romanian and Czechoslovakian borders. My mother, Leah Weisz, had three brothers. The oldest, Aaron, lived in Hust, about sixty or seventy kilometers away. My mother's two younger brothers lived in Vásárosnamény. Chaim, lived near the railroad tracks, and Hersch Meilech, lived across the street from us and next to the shul (synagogue). Sometimes my mother went to shul on Shabbos morning, but on Friday evening she stayed home with me and my younger brothers; that was the custom for women with young children. There was no Kiddush in the shul on Shabbos morning; instead every family had Kiddush at home. After davening (reciting prayers), my uncle Hersh Meilech often crossed the street and joined us at our house for Kiddush.
My grandparents came often for Shabbos in the last few years before the War, because it had become too difficult for my aging grandmother to make Shabbos. Preparing for Shabbos in those days was not like today. There was no refrigeration, so everything had to be prepared at the last minute. Also, everything had to be prepared from scratch, even challah and noodles for the soup.
For Kiddush we had some cookies or cake that we had baked, along with wine or schnapps. And as for the Eier mit Tzvibel, we did not serve it for Kiddush. We served it after Kiddush, before lunch".

Chopped Chicken Liver, *Májpástétom*

Ⓜ Makes 6 to 8 servings

Chopped liver can also be made with beef or calf liver; however, chicken liver has the mildest flavor. As a delicacy "at home" both of my parents used this recipe with goose liver. The secret to good chopped liver is twofold: First, find a good source to buy kashered liver or else carefully kasher it at home. (For kashering, see Recipe Guidelines, page 66). Second, never cover the liver during or after cooking and never overcook it.

2 large onions, cut in half lengthwise, thinly sliced
Vegetable oil, as needed
1 pound chicken liver, kashered (page 67)
4 to 5 hard-boiled eggs, shelled
Seasoned Salt (page 66), to taste

Substitute calf or beef liver for chicken.

In a 12-inch stainless steel sauté pan over medium-low heat, heat oil. Add onions and sauté until onions are soft and translucent but not brown, stirring occasionally, about 20 minutes.

Add the liver and sauté uncovered just to heat through, a few minutes. Do not overcook. Do not cover.

Remove pan from heat. Scoop out onion-liver mixture, reserving oil. Grind onion, liver and eggs in a manual or electric grinder. Alternatively, hand-chop.

Transfer to a medium bowl, add the reserved cooking oil from the pan and mix well. Add Seasoned Salt, to taste. Add more oil, if necessary, for desired consistency.

Refrigerate, covered, for up to 3 days.

One Chicken Liver
"We did not buy a package of chicken livers," recalls Margit Kirsche. "We bought a live chicken at the open market which was in the town center on Sundays, Tuesdays, and Thursdays. We then took the chicken to the shoichet (ritual slaughterer). We used all of the parts of the chicken for cooking. The chicken feet were delicious for making soup. We added the chicken liver to the recipe for Eier mit Tzvibel and we had chopped liver."

Sweet and Sour Gizzards, *Pupiks*

Ⓜ Makes 6 to 10 servings

Chicken gizzards, often overlooked, are inexpensive delicacies. Margit Kirsche created this recipe in the States where gizzards were readily available, unlike in Hungary. "I wanted a new appetizer and thought this would be good—and it is!" she says.

2 pounds chicken gizzards
Water, as needed to cover the gizzards
1 medium onion, finely chopped
2 tablespoons vegetable oil
1 (15-ounce) can tomato sauce
1 cup water
¼ cup sugar
Juice from ½ lemon
4 to 5 mushrooms, sliced
⅓ cup dark raisins

Rinse gizzards well under cold running water because they are very salty from the kashering. Place in a 4-quart pot with water to cover and bring to a boil. Boil for 10 to 15 minutes. Drain and rinse again under cold, running water. Then trim away fat and gristle and discard trimmings. Transfer gizzards to a plate and reserve.

Rinse and dry the pot. Over medium heat, heat oil. Add onions and sauté, stirring, until the onions are soft and translucent but not brown. Add gizzards, tomato sauce, the 1 cup water, sugar and lemon juice. Add the mushrooms and raisins.

Bring to a boil. Cover and reduce heat to low. Simmer until the gizzards are tender, about 1 to 1½ hours.

Serve on a small plate with a little sauce for dipping challah.

> **How to buy kosher liver:**
> As today's home cooks are so accustomed to buying all pre-kashered meats, some kosher butchers sell pre-kashered livers, which have already been through the salting and grilling process. In contrast to other kosher raw meats, pre-kashered livers are already mostly cooked. If you choose to buy them this way, then be careful not to dry them out. However, un-kashered livers are the only un-kashered meats kosher butchers may sell today. So, if you buy un-kashered livers, see page 67 for how to kasher them at home.

Chicken Fricasée

Ⓜ Makes 12 servings

This recipe calls for under-utilized chicken parts—necks, gizzards and wings—but it has the fragrant aroma and tantalizing flavor of Chicken Paprikás (page 136). It can be served on appetizer plates with challah for dipping in the sauce. Or it can be served over mini mounds of white rice. My mother served our family "gourmet dinners" even during the difficult early years when they first arrived in the States. She worked all day and cooked a fresh dinner each evening. This dish costs very little, but has mouth-watering aromas, visual appeal and delicious flavor.

1 pound chicken gizzards
1 tablespoon vegetable oil
1 cup chopped onion
1 pound chicken necks, rinsed and patted dry, trimmed of excess fat
1 pound chicken wings, rinsed and patted dry, pinfeathers removed
1 to 2 teaspoons sweet Hungarian paprika
Seasoned Salt (page 66), to taste
2 tablespoons flour
Water, as needed

Rinse the gizzards well under cold running water because they are very salty. Then place in a 4-quart pot with water to cover and bring to a boil. Boil for 10 to 15 minutes. Drain and rinse again, trimming off and discarding any fat, gristle or tough parts. Reserve.

Rinse and dry the pot. Over medium heat, heat the oil. Add the onions and sauté until translucent, just a few minutes. Add the gizzards, necks, and wings. Season with paprika and Seasoned Salt to taste. Decrease heat to low. Cover and simmer until tender, stirring occasionally to prevent burning, about 1 hour.

Uncover and continue cooking on low heat, until the liquid has reduced considerably and color is deeper.

Sprinkle in the flour, stirring constantly until it is browned. Be careful not to burn. Add just enough water to cover the chicken, stirring constantly to mix in the browned flour, and cook covered for an additional 15 minutes.

Serve on a small plate with a little sauce for dipping challah.

A New Recipe

"We never made this dish 'at home' before the Holocaust because we did not buy the necks and gizzards separately," writes Margit Kirsche, "We took one of the live chickens we had bought in the market, to the shoichet (ritual slaughterer) to be slaughtered, then prepared the entire chicken. But during the years when my children were young and we lived in Chicago, even though we could barely afford our daily living expenses, we saved any money possible, to fly down to Florida in August to visit my brother, Morton, the only other member of my immediate family who survived. One summer we all went out to a Kosher Hungarian restaurant in Miami where I first tasted chicken fricassée. I liked it and so began to cook my own version, using gizzards, necks and wings, with the traditional Hungarian flavors that I learned 'at home.'"

Use only sweet Hungarian paprika for the best flavor.

Gefilte Fish

(P) Makes 10 to 12 servings

Literally "filled fish," gefilte fish is traditionally eaten on Shabbos and holidays. The name comes from the traditional method of preparation: first, debone the fish, removing the flesh from the bones, but leaving the skin, the head and tail intact. Then grind the flesh with the other ingredients, stuff it back into the fish skin, and you have "gefilte fish." The fish was cooked in a stock with carrots and onions, and most importantly, the bones and the head, which make the liquid jelled. It looks beautiful on a long platter, garnished with curly parsley. However, today, most gefilte fish is made into balls and patties, as in the recipe below. It is traditionally served with Chrain (page 195). The recipe suggests cooking the patties for 1½ hours, however, my mother always cooks her gefilte fish for 2 to 2½ hours.

For the gefilte fish:
2 pounds of ground skinless, boneless whitefish
1 medium onion, grated
1 carrot, grated
¼ teaspoon Seasoned Salt (page 66)
Pinch salt
4 eggs
½ cup dried breadcrumbs or matza meal

> Adding the fish head and bones makes for a rich, flavorful stock, which becomes jelled when chilled.

> Substitute 1⅓ pound whitefish and ⅔ pound pike for the 2 pounds of whitefish.

For the stock:
4 quarts water
2 whole, peeled carrots
1 large onion, sliced or chopped
2 teaspoons sugar
1 teaspoon sweet Hungarian paprika
1 teaspoon Seasoned Salt (page 66)
¼ teaspoon freshly ground pepper
Pinch salt
Whitefish bones and head, with "ears" (gill covers and gills) removed, optional

Ibi's Filled Fish

Ibi Gelb stills prepares gefilte fish in the traditional "filled fish" way. In today's world of customer service, Ibi says it is just as easy to prepare the gefilte fish in the skin. Have the fish store prepare the whole fish for you as follows: Ask them to debone the fish, grind the flesh, leaving you the skin with the head and tail intact. Save the bones for the stock. Then stuff the fish flesh mixture back into the skin, distributing evenly and smoothly, and cook the whole fish in the stock. After cooling in an ice-water bath, refrigerate the fish in the stock. When ready to serve, slice into steaks and serve.

In a medium bowl, mix the ground fish with the remaining gefilte fish ingredients. Reserve.

In an 8-quart pot over high heat, bring 4 quarts of water to a boil. Add the remaining stock ingredients. Place the fish head and bones, if using, in cheesecloth and tie securely. Add to the stock. Bring to a boil. If adding the fish head and fish bones, boil and cook for about ½ hour before adding the gefilte fish patties to make a stronger stock.

Form the reserved gefilte fish mixture into rounded oval patties. Use a standard ½-cup level ice cream scoop to measure each fish patty. Then form the scooped fish into rounded oval patties and drop into the boiling water. Raise heat until the water boils, and then decrease heat to lowest

possible, cover tightly and simmer until cooked through and tender, 1½ hours.

Remove the cheesecloth-wrapped head and bones. Discard bones and cheesecloth and, if desired, return the head to the stock.

Chill patties in their stock in an ice-water bath and refrigerate, covered. Before serving, slice carrots from the stock. Serve each piece cold, topped with sliced carrot and accompanied by *Chrain* (page 195).

Memories of Munkács

In Munkács, after the Holocaust, my cousin, Irving Weinberger, remembers going on Fridays to the market with his mother, Goldie. He remembers there were live fish swimming in a tank of water. The customers, mostly Jewish, would wait in line to choose a fish, as, during the post-War years, they waited in long lines, for staples such as bread and flour. They would then carry the fish home and kill it to be prepared for gefilte fish. My cousin vividly remembers his mother preparing the gefilte fish, stuffing the fish mixture into the fish skin with the head, and cooking it whole.

Chopped Herring

Ⓟ Makes 20 servings

In the early years of Hungarian Kosher Foods, a Chicago synagogue called with an order for "chopped herring" for Kiddush. So, on the spot, my mother just made this up. Thirty years later, it is still popular.

1 quart jar herring fillets with onions in wine sauce
2 red delicious apples, peeled, cored, seeded, quartered
1 cup dried breadcrumbs

Drain the herring and onions and discard the liquid. Either hand chop the herring and onions and apples finely, or place in the work bowl of a food processor fitted with the steel blade and pulse to chop finely.

Transfer the chopped herring-apple mixture to a medium bowl, add the breadcrumbs and stir to mix. Cover and refrigerate for at least 1 hour.

Serve in a bowl surrounded by crackers.

A Taste of Tradition

What a tradition—Kiddush on Shabbos morning—a sip of Schnapps and a bite of herring. I was raised with this tradition, which my mother and father brought from their childhood homes, and vividly remember watching my father Sandor Kirsche "have a Schnapps" and a bite of herring. My son, Sammy, loved to eat a piece of herring on Shabbos morning at Kiddush even when he was only 3 years old. Today, my husband, Irv Shapiro, known for his culinary talents and even more for his food presentation, makes his matjes herring for Kiddush for friends, for family, and in recent years for a Kiddush in Israel to honor the birth of our granddaughter Ma'ayan Libi. This one little taste of tradition has spanned four generations.

Herring's Humble Pedigree

Historically, in Eastern Europe, herring was the least expensive fish, a poor man's food. It was salted and transported in barrels from its countries of origin: England, Scotland, Holland and Norway. Jews were major importers and retailers of herring, transporting it by rail to Europe where it became a rich man's treat.

Matjes Herring

(P) Makes approximately 50 to 70 (¾- to 1½-inch wide) pieces

Matjes herring is mild salt herring made from young herrings and not as sharply brined. This recipe belongs to my husband, Irv Shapiro, who prepares it often for Kiddush on Shabbos morning. No matter how much he makes, there is never any left, but I am sure it would keep covered, refrigerated, for at least 4 days.

3 pounds jarred matjes herring fillets
3 heaping tablespoons of prepared lemon pepper
2 large onions, quartered and then sliced
1 cup vegetable oil

Rinse herring fillets well under cold running water. Slice into ¾- to 1½-inch thick slices. In the bottom of an 8 by 8-inch pan or glass or plastic container of similar size, place a single layer of herring.

Sprinkle evenly with ⅓ of the lemon pepper. Cover with ⅓ of the onions. Cover with ⅓ of the oil. Repeat with 2 more layers, finishing with oil.

Cover tightly and refrigerate for 36 to 72 hours before serving.

Serve with crackers or on a platter, with toothpicks in each fillet.

Mini Stuffed Cabbage

Ⓜ Makes about 90 pieces

My father's sister, Goldie Weinberger, prepared these delicacies while living in Munkács, in the Soviet Union, after the Holocaust. She served them as appetizers at weddings. When she came to the United States in 1973 and worked at Hungarian Kosher Foods, she and my mother prepared these for downtown Chicago hotels. Perhaps the most famous person to enjoy these little delicacies was Prime Minister Menachem Begin (1913–1992). The former Prime Minister of Israel visited Chicago in May, 1978, and dined in a hotel in downtown Chicago on mini stuffed cabbages (and other dishes) that had been prepared at Hungarian Kosher Foods. During Prime Minister Begin's stay, my mother and Aunt Goldie remember that the store was bristling with the secret service agents who came to oversee the preparation and transportation of all the food prepared for the Prime Minister, including the stuffed cabbage.

For the cabbage:
2 heads of cabbage, enough for
45 whole cabbage leaves, plus
additional for shredding
16 ounces refrigerated sauerkraut,
well drained

For the filling:
2 tablespoons vegetable oil
1½ cups diced onion
½ cup finely chopped mushrooms,
optional
1 pound ground beef/turkey/chicken
¾ cup uncooked long grain white rice
¼ teaspoon salt
Dash pepper

For the sauce:
1 (16-ounce) can tomato sauce
1 teaspoon salt
½ cup sugar
Pinch Seasoned Salt (page 66)
Dash pepper

You can freeze half of the cabbage rolls by placing flat, not touching, on a parchment paper-lined sheet pan that will fit the freezer. Let freeze until solid then store rolls in self-sealing plastic bags for later use. Cook as directed in recipe, reducing the amount of sauerkraut but not reducing the sauce.

Cut the recipe in half, but do not reduce the amount of sauce. Mix ground turkey and chicken, half and half.

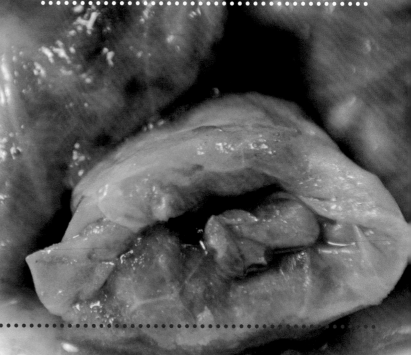

Prepare the cabbage leaves. You can do this in 2 different ways, my mother's way or the hard way.

My mother's way:
Core the cabbage and discard the core. Freeze the cabbage overnight. Defrost in warm water until the leaves can easily be pulled off. Trim the center heavy rib off the leaves and reserve for chopped cabbage (the cabbage leaf will be easier to roll when filled).

The hard way:
Core the fresh cabbage and immerse the cabbage in a large pot of boiling water just until the leaves become pliable and easily separated, about 5 minutes. Don't leave the cabbage in the water until it becomes too soft or the leaves will tear when you try to fill and roll them. Drain the cabbage and, when cool enough to handle, pull off the leaves, trim and reserve the center rib on each.

Choose large cabbages with loose outer leaves, rather than small cabbages with tight leaves. Use the large outer leaves for stuffed cabbage and reserve the inner tight cabbage for other uses such as shredding (for this recipe), cabbage soup or coleslaw.

Cut each leaf in half. Shred remaining heads of cabbage using a four-sided grater as for coleslaw. Finely chop reserved center ribs of cabbage. Reserve.

Make the filling:
In a 12-inch stainless steel skillet or sauté pan, over medium heat, heat the oil. Add the onions, and the mushrooms if using, and sauté until soft and translucent, but not brown. Add the meat, and brown for a few minutes mixing with a fork so it does not form large clumps, but stays crumbled. Then add the seasonings and the uncooked rice and stir to mix.

Trim the cabbage leaves so they are as uniform in size as possible and roughly square in shape. Reserve the trimmings.

Put 1 rounded teaspoonful of filling in the center of each halved cabbage leaf. Roll the cabbage up from the thickest end in the shape of a cone. Tuck in the top, wider part. Alternatively, fold the bottom up over the filling, fold in the two opposite edges, and fold over the remaining top, making a rectangular package. Or, roll the leaf over the filling into a cylinder, tucking in the outer edges.

Cover the bottom of a 6-quart saucepot with some of the reserved cabbage trimmings and shredded cabbage and half the sauerkraut. Place the stuffed cabbage rolls, seam side down, neatly on top. Cover with remaining cabbage trimmings, shredded cabbage and sauerkraut.

Combine all sauce ingredients, mix well. Pour over the cabbage to cover. Add more water, if necessary, so top cabbage layer is covered.

Over high heat, bring to a boil. Decrease heat to lowest possible setting and cover. Simmer for about 2 hours. Check to see that the rice is fully cooked. Alternatively, bake at 350°F for about 2½ hours.

Chapter 2
Soups

Russian Vegetable Borscht
Sweet and Sour Cabbage Soup with Meat
Roux, *Reistle*
Potato Soup, *Krumpli Leves*
Creamy Green Bean Soup, *Intergeshlugina Bundlach*
Sweet and Sour Green Bean Soup
Famous Chicken Soup
Quick and Easy Cabbage Soup
Mushroom Barley Soup
Bean Soup and Bean Dip
Meatball Soup, *Frikadelki*

See also:

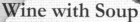

Wine with Soup
Your choices of wine for soup should be as diverse as the soups in this chapter. For a light, vegetable soup, no wine is necessary, but if you would like a glass of wine, try a dry riesling. If you are enjoying a heartier soup, serve it with fresh bread and a nice glass of red wine, bistro style. A moscato wine, with bright acidity, or a chenin blanc, served cold, is a perfect complement to a fruity dessert soup, such as Sour Cherry Soup (page 254).

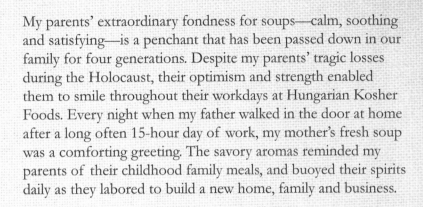

"Worries go down better with soup,"
according to an old Yiddish proverb.

My parents' extraordinary fondness for soups—calm, soothing and satisfying—is a penchant that has been passed down in our family for four generations. Despite my parents' tragic losses during the Holocaust, their optimism and strength enabled them to smile throughout their workdays at Hungarian Kosher Foods. Every night when my father walked in the door at home after a long often 15-hour day of work, my mother's fresh soup was a comforting greeting. The savory aromas reminded my parents of their childhood family meals, and buoyed their spirits daily as they labored to build a new home, family and business.

As a child, I loved watching my father's ritual of soup. I would sit next to him at the table, watching closely, as he lifted the soupspoon slowly to his lips and then returned it to the bowl, untried. He mixed the soup to cool it a bit, and then again lifted the spoon, repeatedly until finally he took his first sip of now perfect-temperature soup.

Most of my mother's soup "recipes" originated at her childhood family lunch table in Vásárosnamény, Hungary. Lunch, the main meal of the day, consisted of soup and bread together with noodles or chicken. The children came home from school and the entire family ate together, including my mother's father, who took a lunch break from his store in the town's main square.

My father's sisters also continued serving soup during the main meal in the Soviet Union. My cousin, Ibi Gelb, recalls that as a child in the Soviet Union after the Holocaust they ate soup every day—both because of its comfort and its economy. They used the cheapest and most readily available ingredients, such as potatoes or cabbage. They mostly prepared dairy or vegetable soups, but on Friday night they had the traditional chicken soup.

Enjoy the savory aromas that emanate from your home kitchen when you cook a fresh soup, and feel free to adapt the recipes to the vegetables most abundant and available.

Russian Vegetable Borscht

Ⓓ Ⓟ Makes 8 to 10 (8-ounce) servings

This is Goldie Weinberger's recipe. "We made this soup every week 'at home' in the Soviet Union," says her daughter Ibi. The soup can be served hot, room temperature, or cold. If you are looking for a sweet and sour cabbage-based soup, which is not typical, this is perfect. It is spicy, refreshing and healthy. For a complete meal Goldie often served this with cheese blintzes.

1 small to medium head cabbage, cored and shredded

1 carrot shredded

1 carrot sliced into thin rounds

12 cups water

½ tablespoon sweet Hungarian paprika

1 teaspoon salt, or to taste

¼ teaspoon freshly ground pepper

2 bay leaves

2 tablespoons vegetable oil

2 cloves garlic, minced

1 onion, chopped

2 small beets, peeled and shredded

1 (15-ounce) can crushed tomatoes

1 (15-ounce) can dark red kidney beans, drained

1 (7-ounce) can tomato sauce

Scant ⅛ teaspoon hot Hungarian paprika, optional

Fresh chopped dill, as needed, optional garnish

Yogurt or sour cream, as needed, optional garnish

1 hard-boiled egg, thinly sliced, optional garnish

In an 8-quart pot, add cabbage and carrots and 12 cups of water. Add paprika, salt, pepper and bay leaves to the cabbage soup. Bring to a boil, decrease heat to low and simmer, covered, for 1 hour.

Meanwhile, in a separate sauté pan, heat oil over medium heat. Add garlic and sauté until soft and translucent, but not browned. Add onion and beets and sauté until beets are soft and onion is golden but not browned, about 5 minutes. Remove from heat and reserve.

Add tomato sauce, tomatoes, and beans to the soup. Taste for seasoning and adjust. Bring to a boil, and cook for an additional 10 minutes.

Add the reserved onion-beet mixture to the soup, heating through. Taste for seasoning again. If desired, add the hot paprika for an extra kick, and the chopped dill. Remove bay leaves and discard.

Serve soup ladled into bowls and garnish each with the chopped dill (if you haven't added it to the soup), and a dollop of sour cream and/or a slice of hard-boiled egg.

> The beets are best bought fresh with the leaves still on.

> For a thicker soup, start with 10 cups of water.

The Traditional Pesach Borscht

Preparing for Pesach "at home" was a major event, nothing like today. If you wanted potato starch, you started with potatoes and water. If you wanted matza, you baked your own. If you wanted wine, you started with the grapes. And if you wanted borscht, you made this traditional Pesach borscht that my aunt Goldie Weinberger learned to make from her mother, my grandmother, Chaya Zisel Kirschenbaum. According to my cousin Irving Weinberger, this is how his mother made borscht. "Fill a 1-gallon jar halfway with peeled and quartered beets. Meanwhile prepare a mixture of water, salt and sour salt so the water is salty to the taste, but not too salty. Add the water to the jar with the beets up to 1 to 2 inches from the rim. Cover with a clean towel or a mesh screen because white foam will form on the top which must be removed and discarded every few days. Do not seal the jar tightly. Let beet-water mixture ferment for 2 weeks. Taste, making sure it is sour. Strain the borscht liquid into a clean jar, cover and refrigerate. Discard the beets. To serve, transfer the borscht to a pot. Heat over medium heat, but do not boil. Meanwhile in a small separate bowl beat 4 eggs. Slowly stir some of the hot borscht mixture, little by little, into the eggs, whisking constantly. Then pour the egg-borscht mixture slowly into the hot (not boiling) borscht and whisk to thicken. Remove from the heat, refrigerate and drink cold with a meat dish, or serve it cold with a dollop of sour cream."

Sweet and Sour Cabbage Soup with Meat

Ⓜ Makes 8 to 10 (8-ounce) servings

Traditional Hungarians cook cabbage in a variety of ways. Here is a rich and tasty sweet and sour cabbage soup, with the deep flavor of meat. I like to cook it for a few hours to develop the flavor. For a sweeter taste, add raisins. I always do.

1 to 2 tablespoons vegetable oil
1½ to 2 pounds short ribs,
cut into large chunks
1 medium onion, diced
1 medium head cabbage, cored,
cut into small squares or shredded
1 (28-ounce) can whole tomatoes
quartered
or
1 (28-ounce) can diced tomatoes
1 cup tomato sauce
½ tablespoon lemon juice
⅓ cup sugar
¼ teaspoon freshly ground black
pepper
1 teaspoon salt
⅓ cup dark or golden raisins, optional

In an 8-quart pot over medium-high heat, heat oil. Brown short ribs with onions, turning so ribs brown on all sides. Decrease heat to low, cover tightly and steam until meat is tender, about 30 minutes to 1 hour.

Add the cabbage, the tomatoes together with their juice, and the remainder of ingredients to the meat, including raisins if using.
Add 6 cups of water.

Bring to a boil, decrease heat to low and simmer, covered, until the cabbage and the meat are both tender, about 1 hour. Taste and adjust seasonings. For a richer flavor, cook an additional 30 minutes to 1 hour.

Serve ladled into heated bowls.

Fresh Ingredients
My mother, Margit Kirsche, recalls that "at home" they made their own tomato juice, which they used for this soup. She says, "We purchased tomatoes at the open market in the center square of Vásárosnamény during the tomato season, which was late summer and early fall. Then we washed the tomatoes, cooked them, sifted out the skin and the seeds, and we bottled them, storing them in our root cellar to have during the winter months."

For a parve, meatless soup, omit short ribs, sauté onions according to recipe instructions and add 3 teaspoons parve powdered chicken-flavor soup base or parve meat-flavor soup base along with the water.

Roux, *Reistle*

D **P** Makes enough roux to thicken 2 quarts of liquid

You can thicken any soup with what is known in French cooking as a roux, a mixture of fat and flour. My mother calls it a reistle, in Yiddish. In Hungary, my mother prepared a reistle with schmaltz. Since schmaltz is meat fat, all of her roux-based soups were originally fleishig, or meat based. Today, she sometimes uses margarine, butter or oil, for a non-meat based alternative. To thin the roux into a soup broth, add water to the finished roux. For a creamy soup, add milk, or to make it parve, add either nondairy creamer or soymilk.

2 tablespoons vegetable oil
or margarine or butter
2 tablespoons flour

In a 1-quart saucepan over medium heat, heat the oil, margarine or butter. Slowly add the flour, mixing with a whisk or spoon until smooth. Continue stirring and cooking until the roux is golden. Be careful not to burn. Remove from heat.

To add the roux to the soup, begin by slowly adding some water or liquid from the soup into the roux, 1 tablespoon at a time, stirring until the roux is smooth and free of lumps. Then add the roux to the pot of hot soup, stirring and cooking until the soup thickens.

Have Reistle, Will Travel

Margit Kirsche remembers: "I went to Budapest a few months before the War to visit my brother, Morton. He had recently moved there after being released from an insane asylum. He could not live at home, because after being transferred from a slave labor camp to an insane asylum on staged grounds of mental illness, he feared that our hometown neighbors would inform the Nazis that he was, indeed, sane. He hoped to live undetected in the large city of Budapest. I wanted to cook for my brother in Budapest, to give him a taste of home, but without too much fuss. So I took a jar of reistle with me from home. When I arrived in Budapest, I bought green beans, added water to the reistle and cooked the green beans into a sweet and sour soup for Morton and myself. It was delicious." Shortly after she returned home to Vásárosnamény, my mother was taken to the ghetto and from there to Auschwitz. Her brother Morton remained in Budapest until early summer 1944, when he was captured by the Nazis, sent to Auschwitz and then to Buchenwald.

When making a soup using sautéed vegetables, you can simply sauté the vegetables, add the flour directly to the sautéed vegetables, and mix as directed above. Then, slowly add the water or broth for the soup, while stirring to be sure the soup stays smooth. You can, as did my mother, make a large batch of roux and refrigerate it, covered, for use as necessary. The ratio is 1 to 1: flour to fat. For a thinner or thicker soup, try varying the proportions of flour to fat.

Potato Soup, *Krumpli Leves*

(P) Makes 3 quarts, 12 (8-ounce) servings, or 8 (12-ounce) servings

On our family journey back to my parents' childhood homes in the summer of 2000, we spent a few days in Budapest, where we dined at each of the kosher restaurants. We ate an especially tasty potato soup at a kosher hotel that reminded my mother of the potato soup her mother made for the family meal when her father returned home for lunch every day. Notice the garlic and paprika, both of which appear in many Hungarian recipes.

1 to 2 tablespoons vegetable oil

2 large onions, diced

4 ounces fresh mushrooms, diced

1 clove garlic, minced

½ teaspoon sweet Hungarian paprika

1 to 2 tablespoons flour, optional

1 carrot, thinly sliced

1 to 2 stalks celery, thinly sliced

1 parsley root, thinly sliced, optional

8 cups water

1 teaspoon parve powdered chicken-flavor soup base, or to taste

1 teaspoon salt

Dash fresh coarsely ground black pepper, to taste

¼ teaspoon Seasoned Salt (page 66), optional

2 pounds russet potatoes, diced

½ cup finely chopped fresh parsley for garnish

In an 8-quart pot over medium heat, heat oil. Add onions, mushrooms and garlic and season with paprika. Sauté, stirring, until onions are translucent and the mushrooms are soft.

If using flour, add it now, stirring to avoid lumps. Then add some of the water slowly, mixing to keep the roux smooth. The roux will add body to the soup.

Add carrots, celery, and parsley root. Add the remaining water to cover, the soup base, and season to taste with salt, black pepper and Seasoned Salt. Bring to a boil.

Decrease heat to low, and simmer, covered for about 30 minutes. Add the potatoes. Taste for seasoning after a few minutes, adding more salt, paprika, pepper, or Seasoned Salt as desired. Cook for about 20 minutes or until the potatoes are soft. Do not overcook the potatoes.

Serve ladled into heated bowls, and garnish with the parsley.

The Store in Vásárosnamény

My mother, Margit Kirsche, describes her family's store on the main square in the center of the town of Vásárosnamény. There were yards goods for sale as well as a small selection of eyeglasses and wedding rings. Her father, a trained watchmaker, used part of the storefront to fix watches. On Sunday, according to law, the store was only allowed to be open from 8 to 10 a.m. It was also closed on Shabbos as were all of the Jewish-owned stores, which constituted most of the stores in town. My mother attributes the high ratio of Jewish-owned stores to the laws prohibiting Jews from obtaining a higher education and from owning more land than that of their home. Consequently, many Jews chose career paths in the business world.

Creamy Green Bean Soup, *Intergeshlugina Bundlach*

Ⓓ Makes 2 quarts, 8 (8-ounce) servings

A traditional Hungarian cream soup uses sour cream, which lends distinctive taste and texture. The full recipe contains green beans, mushrooms and potatoes, but you can make it with either. The egg yolk is optional but makes a thicker, fuller soup.

1 pound green beans, cut into
1-inch pieces
6 mushrooms, thinly sliced, optional
Water, as needed
2 teaspoons salt
1 pound red potatoes, diced
2 cups sour cream
1 egg yolk, optional
Dash pepper, to taste

> Use half green beans and half yellow wax beans, which have a different flavor and also make the soup more colorful.
> Use frozen cut green beans to cut down the cooking time; cook the beans for 15 minutes.

Nourishing Four Generations

"We cooked Intergeshlugina Bundlach once a week 'at home'," remembers Margit Kirsche. "We made it with either green beans or potatoes, easy to get in our area. My mother never combined the two vegetables in the same soup, but today I like to mix them. On Pesach, we do not use green beans, as there is a tradition among Ashkenazic Jews not to eat Kitniyos (rice, millet or legumes); so we use just potatoes and mushrooms. For the past 15 years, I have been cooking this soup for two of my grandsons, Sammy and Aaron, who loved to eat it on Friday afternoon, when they came home early from high school in preparation for Shabbos. Now that they are grown and living in different cities, whenever they come to visit, this soup is waiting."

In a 6-quart saucepan combine green beans and mushrooms, if using, with 6 cups water. The water should cover the beans and mushrooms. Add 1½ teaspoons of the salt and bring to a boil over high heat. Decrease heat to low and simmer, covered, until beans are very tender, about 1 hour.

Add the potatoes with the remaining ½ teaspoon of salt, raise heat to high and bring to a boil again. Decrease heat to low and simmer, covered, for about 10 to 15 minutes, until the potatoes are soft.

Meanwhile, place the sour cream in a small bowl and mix well. Slowly add 1 cup of water to the sour cream in ¼ cup increments, mixing well after each addition. Mix in the egg yolk, if using.

Ladle about 1 to 1½ cups of hot liquid from the bean soup into the sour cream mixture in small increments, 1 tablespoon at a time for about 8 tablespoons and then ¼ cup very slowly, mixing constantly after each addition. Be careful that the sour cream does not curdle.

Stir the sour cream mixture very slowly into the soup, stirring constantly, so that it does not curdle, keeping the consistency smooth and creamy, until it is heated through.

Serve ladled into heated bowls. To serve cold, chill to room temperature in an ice-water bath, then refrigerate covered. Ladle into chilled bowls.

91

Sweet and Sour Green Bean Soup

(P) Makes 8 to 10 (8-ounce) servings

This hot or cold soup recipe belonged to my aunt, Goldie Weinberger. Her daughter Ibi remembers, "We cooked this almost every Shabbos for lunch during the summer months in Munkács, as it is a perfect soup to be served cold." Under Communism, after World War II, Jews were prohibited from having a synagogue, attending services, studying the Torah or displaying religious articles. In Munkács, however, the government looked the other way, and there were at least six small shteiblach (prayer house in a private home) for daily services, all with Torah scrolls which had survived the Holocaust. After services Shabbos morning, there was Kiddush. Kichel and pastries baked by the women of the community and homemade Schnapps were served. After Kiddush, people went home to eat and my father's sister Goldie often served this soup, cold, in summer.

1 recipe roux (recipe, page 89)
2 quarts water
1 to 1½ pounds green beans or yellow wax beans, cut into 1-inch pieces
2 tablespoons sugar
½ teaspoon salt, or to taste
¼ teaspoon sour salt
or
2 tablespoons white vinegar
1 teaspoon sweet Hungarian paprika, optional

In an 8-quart saucepan over medium heat, make the roux according to recipe directions. Add 2 quarts of water, slowly, stirring to mix after each addition, so the consistency stays smooth. Cook until water thickens. Add the green beans and seasonings. Bring to a boil. Decrease heat and simmer, covered, until the green beans are soft, approximately 1 hour.

Serve hot, or chill in an ice-water bath, refrigerate covered and serve cold.

Widely available, sour salt, also called citric salt or citric acid, is a substance derived from acidic citrus fruit, such as lemon and limes, dried and processed into a powder or crystal.

My great aunt Golda Moskovics made a version of this soup which she only served cold: Increase sugar to ½ cup. Omit sour salt, vinegar and paprika. Add 1 tablespoon of lemon juice and 1 teaspoon cinnamon. Prepare recipe according to directions, chill in an ice-water bath and refrigerate, covered.

Becoming Free

My great aunt Golda Moskovics was the youngest child in her family and the only sister to survive the Holocaust. She grew up in her parents' home (my father's grandparents), across the street from the Kirschenbaum house in Hluboka. Although she was his aunt they were so close in age that she and my father felt more like brother and sister. Golda was a young woman before the Holocaust.

At 16 years old she worked in Ungvár (Uzhgorod), not far from Hluboka, as a hat designer. During the Holocaust, she hid out in the trees of the forests with her sister, Rachel, and Rachel's husband, Tzvi. They ate food that they foraged. One day Tzvi went looking for food, leaving Golda and Rachel hiding in the trees. When Tzvi returned they were gone. They had been found and captured by Nazis. They were taken to Dachau where Rachel was killed. At the end of the war, while on the Death March from Dachau, Golda had no strength left and collapsed in a field on a bed of thorns. A priest found her, took her home and fed her. He wished to convert her to Catholicism, but she declined, saying, "I survived to be a Jew."

After the Holocaust, she was living briefly in Opava, Czechoslovakia, where she married. She declared to her husband, Eliezer Moskovics, that she only wanted to live in Israel. So in January 1949 she and her husband, together with their small son Moshe, and her brother Yitzchak and his new family, made the then-long and dangerous journey to Israel, where she lived for the rest of her life.

Soup and Schnapps

In the summer of 1968, I traveled to the Soviet Union with my father. For the past 20 years, he had been trying to free his sisters and bring them to Chicago. They had been unable to leave the Soviet Union ever since they returned home at the end of the Holocaust and the borders were sealed. My father was unable to obtain papers for their release, and he was very lonely for them. He wanted to see them face-to-face, first, because he longed to see his family, and second, because he wanted to speak privately and openly to them. In those days, he had to be careful about the content of his letters, as the KGB might decide to read any mail. In fact, he could not even be certain that they would receive the letters. So, my father and I set out on a journey that started with two-days' delay: First, we were delayed in Chicago, then we missed our connection in London and had to fly from London to Prague and from Prague we took a train to Uzhgorod. Obtaining kosher food was very difficult, especially because of the communist control at that time, so we ate almost nothing on the way. When we arrived, we were a day late. My aunts, who had used their travel permit to come the day before to the hotel in Uzhgorod, could not come again the next day. But my father's sister, my aunt Goldie, sent her sister-in-law, who lived in Uzhgorod, to see if we had in fact arrived. Knowing that we could not get kosher food unless it was home-cooked, she brought Goldie's homemade sour cream green bean soup along with some schnapps for my father. The family all agreed, "A Schnapps would be good for him, even on an empty stomach."

Famous Chicken Soup

(M) Makes 12 to 16 (8-ounce) servings

This recipe from my mother's family (the Weisz family) has been prepared for four generations. We serve it every Friday night for Shabbos in our own homes. In addition, we prepare this soup fresh daily at Hungarian Kosher Foods; it seems that the soup flies out of the store. At home, we serve it with the traditional egg noodles, and a bowl of fresh radishes on the side. As you eat the soup you take a bite of salted radish. On Rosh Hashana, we serve it as my mother's family did, with kreplach. The secret to our flavorful chicken soup is the ingredients my mother added over the years. One ingredient from "home" which she used until they became unavailable was chicken feet.

1 (3-pound) skinless chicken, quartered
2 carrots, coarsely chopped
2 celery stalks, coarsely chopped
1 onion, coarsely chopped
1 leek, light green and white parts, thoroughly cleaned and coarsely chopped
1 turnip, coarsely chopped
1 clove garlic, whole
1 turkey neck, optional, tied in cheesecloth
12 cups water
2 teaspoons salt, or to taste
¼ teaspoon freshly ground pepper
Seasoned Salt (page 66), to taste
1 bunch fresh dill, optional
8 ounces dry egg noodles, cooked

In an 8-quart pot add chicken and vegetables. Add optional turkey neck, if desired, for a richer soup.

Add water and seasonings. Bring to a boil over high heat, decrease heat to low and simmer until chicken is tender and soup stock is rich, 1½ to 2 hours. (For richer soup, my mother cooks hers for 3 hours.)
Taste and adjust seasoning, if needed.
Remove turkey neck and discard.

Ladle broth into preheated bowls.
Add chicken meat and vegetables as desired, along with cooked noodles.

The Magic of Shabbos Candles

Margit Kirsche always lights one more than the number of candles for everyone in her immediate family. Here is why: "One Friday night, after the War, I was living in Freising, Germany, with my brother Morton. I was not yet married and so I didn't light Shabbos candles. 'At home' a woman only lit Shabbos candles after she was married. That night I dreamed about my middle younger brother Yitzchak Isaac. He was 12 years old when we entered Auschwitz, and he was sent directly to the gas chambers. In my dream I asked him if he was alive, and he said no. I asked him if he liked it better to be alive or not and he said he liked it better to be alive. In my dream there were two candles on the wall. I said to my brother Morton, 'Keeck, Meilach, Isaac is alive. Du (Look, Morton, Isaac is here). He'll light the candles.' Isaac made the candles light three times. The first two times he lit the candles, they went out, until the third time. Then they stayed lit. When I woke up I said to myself that he came to tell me where there is a Jewish home, candles should be lit on Shabbos. From then on I started lighting candles on Shabbos. When I got married I added a candle so I lit three candles instead of the customary two. With each of my children I lit an extra candle, as my mother had done before me. To this day I light five candles (instead of four), and each week I think of my brother Yitzchak Isaac."

Quick and Easy Cabbage Soup

(P) Makes 2 quarts, 8 (8-ounce) servings

My mother says, "I made up the recipe for this soup while in Desert Hot Springs, California, with my husband. He loved soup and we were looking for a quick soup to cook for lunch. I have since shared this recipe with many people and everyone loves it. It is easy to prepare and quite delicious. You can chop or shred the cabbage, but I prefer to chop."

1 small head cabbage (about 2 pounds), chopped or shredded
or
2 (14- to 16-ounce) bags of shredded cabbage
2 small onions, diced
2 (8-ounce) cans of tomato sauce
4 tablespoons sugar
2 teaspoons parve powdered chicken-flavor soup base
Dash of freshly ground pepper
1 teaspoon salt
4 cups water
½ pound red potatoes, diced, optional

In an 8-quart pot, add the cabbage, onion, tomato sauce, sugar, soup base, salt, pepper and water. Over medium-high heat, bring to a boil. Stir, decrease heat to low and simmer, covered, until cabbage is cooked, about 30 minutes. Taste and adjust the seasonings.

If you are adding potatoes, add now. Bring the soup to a boil again. Decrease heat, cover and cook until potatoes are just cooked, about 15 to 20 minutes. Taste for seasoning. If the soup is too thick, add 1 cup of water. Adjust salt to taste.

> For more depth of flavor, heat 1 tablespoon vegetable oil in the pan and sauté the cabbage and onions until tender, then proceed with the recipe steps.

Desert Hot Springs

Desert Hot Springs, California, is just 15 minutes from the center of Palm Springs and its airport. Surrounded by magnificent mountains, it is dotted with motels and spas offering studio motel rooms with a full kitchen and dining area. Many survivors of the Holocaust, my parents and their landsmen (countrymen) were drawn here for the natural healing hot mineral water spas, Jacuzzis and swimming pools, as well as for the warm dry weather.

For more than 25 winters my parents kept company with the group of Holocaust survivors who vacationed here. Cooking and living independently, group members rented an extra motel room to use as a shul with daily minyan (group prayer) and shiurim (Torah/Talmud lectures). This was a wonderfully therapeutic and refreshing time for my parents and they formed friendships that were stronger than ordinary; they were all Survivors. Sitting outside in the sunshine the group discussed everything from cooking to Jewish history, politics and the future. Many conversations relived memories of "home," and in fact, they often discovered landsmen that had survived or shared family members.

My parents loved to host dinners as well as Kiddush on Shabbos. My mother always prepared a special Kiddush in celebration of my father's birthday at the end of January. Being who they were, my parents used their vacation time to create new recipes, for example, this Quick and Easy Cabbage Soup.

Mushroom Barley Soup

P   Makes 8 to 10 (8-ounce) servings

This recipe could not have originated in my mother's hometown in Hungary where her mother never cooked with mushrooms. In this country, my mother cooked this soup often during the week, especially in the winter. It is a favorite of my niece, Alisa. It is thick, filling, and filled with chopped vegetables and makes a complete meal when served with fresh bread. It also makes a nice starter soup, served in small bowls or cups.

1 to 2 tablespoons vegetable oil
1 medium onion, finely chopped
1 pound mushrooms, chopped
1 tablespoon flour
8 cups water
½ cup pearl barley
1 carrot, thinly sliced or shredded
1 stalk celery, thinly sliced
2 bay leaves
1 tablespoon parve powdered
chicken-flavor soup base
1 teaspoon salt
⅛ teaspoon pepper
Seasoned Salt (page 66), to taste,
optional
Freshly chopped parsley, for garnish

> Omit the soup base and
> increase the salt to 2 teaspoons.

> Substitute 1 tablespoon chopped
> fresh dill instead of the bay leaves.

In an 8-quart pot over medium heat, heat oil. Add onion and mushrooms and sauté until vegetables are soft but not browned, about 5 to 10 minutes. Add flour and continue to cook on a low heat, stirring, until flour is medium brown. Be careful not to burn.

Add 8 cups of water, the barley, carrot, celery, bay leaves and seasonings. Bring to a boil over high heat. Decrease heat to low, cover, and simmer, stirring occasionally. Taste after 30 minutes and adjust seasonings. Depending on how thick you like the soup, you may want to add up to 2 more cups of boiling water. Cover and continue cooking until the barley is tender and vegetables are soft, about 30 to 45 additional minutes. The soup gets very thick the longer it cooks, so be sure to stir from the bottom frequently so it does not burn. Remove bay leaves and discard.

Serve ladled into heated bowls and garnish, if desired, with parsley.

Bean Soup and Bean Dip

P Makes 8 to 10 (8-ounce servings) of soup, and 6 to 8 servings of dip

All of my cousins who grew up in the Soviet Union, including Ibi who gave me this recipe, say that this was a popular dish. Beans are a great source of protein, and as such, prized in the Soviet Union where meat was scarce. The recipe is a great time saver, actually two recipes in one: a soup and a dip. The bean dip reminds me of the hummus which my Israeli grandchildren love today.

For the soup:
1 pound dried white beans
(Great Northern, cannellini)
8 to 10 cups or water, or as needed
2½ teaspoons salt, divided
1 teaspoon sweet Hungarian paprika,
divided
⅛ teaspoon freshly ground pepper
3 tablespoons vegetable oil
1 extra large onion (or 2 large onions),
diced
¼ cup dry small soup pasta
(farfel, orzo, alphabets)
¼ cup chopped parsley

For the dip:
1 clove garlic, pressed or minced
¼ teaspoon salt, or to taste
Pinch freshly ground black pepper
Sweet Hungarian Paprika,
as needed for garnish

Soak the beans in water to cover, overnight. Drain the beans, remove any stones or debris, rinse and drain.

Into an 8-quart pot, add the beans together with enough water to cover, 8 to 10 cups. Add 2 teaspoons salt and ½ teaspoon of the paprika and the pepper. Over high heat, bring to a boil. Decrease heat to low, cover loosely (with lid slightly ajar) and simmer until beans are soft, about 2 hours.

Meanwhile, in a separate small sauté pan over medium heat, add oil and heat. Add onion and sauté, adding ½ teaspoon salt and the remaining paprika, until the onions are soft and golden. Reserve. Divide onions in half; half will be used for the soup and half for the dip.

When the beans have cooked, remove half of the beans from the pot using a slotted spoon to drain as much liquid as possible, and transfer to a large bowl. Reserve.

Make the soup:

In the pot, which has half of the beans, add the dry soup pasta and half the reserved onions. Bring to a boil, decrease heat to a simmer and cook, covered, until the noodles are soft. Serve ladled into bowls. Garnish with parsley.

Make the dip:

Mash the reserved beans with a fork or potato masher for a chunky consistency, or for a smoother consistency, purée in a food processor.

Add garlic, ¼ teaspoon salt and pepper and stir to mix. To serve, spread on a flat plate. Make a dimple in the middle. Put the remaining reserved onions in the dimple and sprinkle with paprika. Serve as an appetizer or a side dish.

Meatball Soup, *Frikadelki*

(M) Makes 12 to 14 (8-ounce) servings

Frikadelki translates as "meatballs," and many cultures have a version: The Jewish matza ball soup, the Italian Wedding Soup and the Eastern European Frikadelki Soup. Veronica Sporia of Hungarian Kosher Foods, tells me that her family in Romania, also made a version of this meatball soup on New Year's, using rice in the meatball instead of breadcrumbs. My cousin Ibi tells me that the following recipe was prepared often by her mother, Goldie, during the cold winter in Munkács. Ibi's mother made the meatballs from ground chicken, easier for her to find in Communist Russia than kosher beef.

For the soup:

1 to 2 tablespoons vegetable oil
2 carrots, shredded
1 onion, diced
12 cups water
2 stalks celery, thinly sliced
1 tablespoon powdered chicken soup base
¼ teaspoon pepper
2 bay leaves
2 teaspoons salt
Dash Seasoned Salt (page 66), optional
⅓ cup orzo (or another small soup pasta)
1½ to 2 cups cauliflower florets
or shredded cabbage
Chopped parsley for garnish, as needed
Thickly sliced fresh bread, as needed

For the meatballs:

1 pound ground chicken or beef
1 small to medium onion, shredded
1 egg
2 tablespoons dry breadcrumbs
½ teaspoon salt, or more to taste
¼ to ½ teaspoon fresh ground pepper, to taste
1 clove garlic, minced

Veronica Sporia prepares her meatballs with rice instead of breadcrumbs. Some of the rice escapes into the soup adding an interesting texture. At the same time that she adds the meatballs to the soup, she also adds 1 tomato chopped and ½ of a red pepper, diced. Here is her meatball recipe: 1 pound ground beef, ½ cup uncooked white long grain rice, 1 tablespoon paprika, 1½ tablespoon chicken soup base, ½ teaspoon pepper, and 1 teaspoon seasoned salt.

Winter in Munkács

My cousin Ibi remembers the winters in Munkács were a procession of dark, cold, windy, rainy, damp days, varied only by, at times, snow falling from the grey skies. The streets were not paved and so on the rainy days, they were rivers of mud. People could not shake the chilling cold that crept into their bones. The only heating in the homes was from a tall, wood-burning clay oven in the living room. In the kitchen they had a coal or wood-burning stove on top of which they could cook three to four pots. There was an oven alongside heated with the same coals or wood. (This was the exact same heating method that both my parents had in their homes prior to the Holocaust.) In such weather, this soup filled them with a warm, cozy feeling and offered relief from the bitter cold.

In a small sauté pan over medium heat, heat oil. Sauté the carrots and onion together until soft. Reserve.

Meanwhile, in an 8-quart pot over high heat, bring the 12 cups of water to a boil. Add the reserved carrots and onions, the celery, soup base, pepper, bay leaves, salt and Seasoned Salt to the boiling water. Bring to a boil. Decrease heat to low, cover loosely (with lid slightly ajar) and simmer.

While the soup is cooking, prepare the meatballs. Mix the chicken or beef, onion, egg, breadcrumbs, salt, pepper and garlic together in a medium bowl. Shape mixture into meatballs between ½ to 1 inch in diameter.

Add the meatballs to the soup. Raise heat and bring to a boil. Decrease heat to low and simmer until the vegetables are soft and the meatballs are cooked through, about 30 to 45 minutes.

Add orzo and cauliflower. Adjust seasonings to taste. Continue cooking until the pasta and vegetables are cooked through, about 20 minutes. Remove bay leaves and discard.

Serve ladled into a deep soup bowl, garnished with chopped fresh parsley and accompanied by a thick slice of fresh bread.

For a deeper flavor, add 3 to 4 beef bones to the boiling water and cook for 1 to 1½ hours before adding the meatballs. When soup is fully cooked, remove and discard bones.

Chapter 3
Dairy and Egg Dishes

Wine with Dairy

When selecting a wine for your light, dairy meal, choose a crisp, light white wine that will balance the sweetness and creaminess of the entrée. Select a chenin blanc and serve it nice and cold. The acidity in the wine helps to cut the richness of the dairy. If you prefer a sweet taste, serve a light bubbling, moscato wine for an extra flair to the flavor.

"A land flowing with milk and honey"
(Exodus 3:8)

This Biblical description of the land of Israel captures an image of abundant fresh milk combined with the sweet taste of honey, just like the dairy foods that my mother, Margit Kirsche, and my aunt, Goldie Weinberger, prepared. Their dairy dishes were made from the freshest milk products—sweet and rich, and yet light and refreshing.

My father always began his day with a strong cup of freshly brewed coffee. He drank his coffee with a lot of sugar and American half-and-half, similar to the thick cream he had "at home." His breakfast, which he often enjoyed sitting in his office at Hungarian Kosher Foods, was either a plain fresh roll, to dip in his coffee, or toast spread with fresh butter, or sliced cheese on a freshly baked roll. My father remembered churning butter as a child. He sat outside his home in Hluboka, Czechoslovakia, churning the butter by plunging the wooden paddle up and down in the cream-filled wooden churn until butter formed and separated from the buttermilk. When his mother had kneaded and pressed the butter, he then spread the fresh butter on homemade bread.

My mother, Margit Kirsche, has always been discriminating in the cheese that she uses for cooking and baking, because she ate only the freshest milk and used only homemade cheese as a child in Hungary. The milk was used not only for their drinking milk, but also for making homemade butter, yogurt, sour cream and farmer's cheese. Because farmer's cheese is the only cheese that my mother had "at home," fresh farmer's cheese appears in many of the following recipes.

Two special recipes that epitomize my family's Eastern European dairy dishes are blintzes and kreplach. The preparation is time consuming but well worth the effort.

Homemade Hot Cocoa

D Makes 1 cup

Today, the only hot cocoa many people drink comes from a mix. As a young child, I believed my mother made the very best hot chocolate. Her secrets: she uses only the highest quality Dutch cocoa, fresh whole milk and cream, and a to-taste ratio of cocoa to sugar. My children and grandchildren love to top it with a mound of whipped cream.

1 cup whole milk
1 (level) tablespoon cocoa, preferably Dutch process
1 to 1½ tablespoons sugar, or to taste
Whipped cream, optional garnish

My son Aaron puts a pinch of ground cinnamon in with the cocoa before adding milk. In his words, "it adds a little spice."

In a small saucepan, over low heat, heat the milk to just below boiling, stirring from the bottom.

Meanwhile, in a mug, mix the cocoa and sugar, keeping the ratio 1:1½ or to taste.. When the milk is hot, pour a small amount, about 1 tablespoon into the cocoa-sugar mixture. Mix until it is a smooth paste. Slowly add ¼ cup of milk to this paste, mixing to keep the smooth consistency. Slowly add the rest of the milk, mixing so that the cocoa is smooth and creamy. You can top with whipped cream.

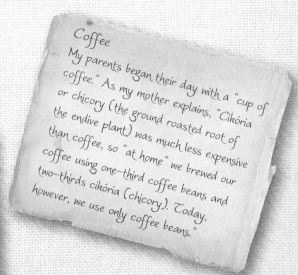

Fresh Milk "at Home"

My mother, Margit, remembers that every morning "at home" her mother would send her on a five-minute walk to the farmer in Vásárosnamény. My mother took along her family's personal bucket as well as kosher soap. The farmer, who was not Jewish, would have his wife wash her hands with the kosher soap, and then, while my mother was watching, milk the cow into my mother's family's bucket. Thus, they ensured that the milk was indeed kosher, and contained no non-kosher products, such as pig's milk or other animal products that were sometimes added in those days. "I wanted to get out of there in a hurry," my mom says, "so the farmer's wife taught me how to milk. When I was twelve years old I used to milk one of the cows so I could go home faster." When my mother returned home, her mother would boil the milk, and then it was ready for use.

Coffee

My parents began their day with a "cup of coffee." As my mother explains, "Cikória or chicory (the ground roasted root of the endive plant) was much less expensive than coffee, so "at home" we brewed our coffee using one-third coffee beans and two-thirds cikória (chicory). Today, however, we use only coffee beans."

My Mother's Blintzes

(D) Makes about 16 (8½-inch) blintzes, or 20 (6-inch) blintzes

I have been eating my mother's wonderful blintzes all my life, and today, her great-grandchildren look forward to this specialty. Traditionally, blintzes are served on Shavuos (in spring, one of three major holidays) when it is customary to eat dairy foods, but we like to make them anytime for a brunch, lunch, or light dinner. To make smaller blintzes use a smaller, 7-inch pan. If the batter thickens toward the end of cooking, add a little milk to thin it. Crepe pans vary in size as do sauté pans and skillets. In general a 10-inch diameter measured from the top, makes a 7-inch blintz or crepe. An 8-inch pan measured from the top, makes a 6-inch blintz or crepe.

For the batter:
3 extra large eggs
2 tablespoons vegetable oil
3 tablespoons sugar
½ teaspoon salt
1 cup flour
2 cups milk
Butter, as needed, for frying,
about ½ tablespoon per blintz

For the filling:
1 pound farmer's cheese
2 ounces cream cheese
½ teaspoon salt
½ teaspoon cinnamon
⅓ cup sugar, or to taste
1 egg

Mix the batter: In a large bowl, whisk eggs, oil, sugar, and salt until sugar is dissolved. Then slowly mix in flour until completely smooth. The batter will be thick and dough-like. Lastly add the milk, very slowly, in three parts, mixing well after each addition until the batter is the consistency of thick cream.

Make the blintzes: In a crepe pan over medium heat, melt ½ tablespoon of butter or enough to film the bottom of the pan. When butter sizzles, pour or ladle in a scant ¼ cup of batter, and swirl the pan to distribute batter evenly. Fry until golden on one side, until cooked through, about 2 to 3 minutes, then turn over and fry briefly on the second side. Do not wait until the blintz browns, the lighter it is, the prettier. Turn blintzes out on a wax paper- or parchment paper-lined plate browned side up. Cover with waxed paper so blintzes do not dry out. Repeat until all the batter is used, lifting the wax paper cover and replacing it with every new blintz that is added to the stack.

Make the filling: In a large bowl, using a sturdy spoon, knead the cheeses together until well mixed. Add salt, cinnamon, sugar to taste, mixing well. Add egg and mix well. Cover and refrigerate for about 10 minutes, so the filling holds together.

Fill the blintzes: Place 2 tablespoons of the filling in the center of one blintz, fold over each side, then fold up each end to form a rectangle or square. Repeat until all blintzes are used. You can freeze blintzes at this point by placing on flat sheets in the freezer until frozen solid then transferring them to self-sealing plastic bags for later cooking. If you cook frozen blintzes, it is not necessary to defrost, just allow extra time for frying or baking.

If you wish to defrost, place frozen blintzes in the refrigerator until defrosted.

Cook the blintzes: In a 12-inch sauté pan over medium heat, heat enough butter to film the bottom of the pan. Fry blintzes seam side down in batches (do not crowd the pan) in butter as needed, until filling is cooked through and blintz is golden but not brown, turning once. Or, alternatively, place seam side down in a single layer on a buttered baking sheet, brush tops with melted butter, and bake in a preheated 350°F oven in a single layer until filling is cooked through, about 20 minutes.

Serve 1 to 2 blintzes per person topped with sliced fresh strawberries, jam or fruit compote.

107

Goldie Weinberger's Blintzes

(D) Makes about 15 (8-inch) blintzes

Ibi says, "This is a translation of the original recipe, written in Hungarian, which my mother, Goldie Weinberger, received from her mother, Chaya Zisel Kirschenbaum, before the Holocaust. In our home in Munkács, after the War, we had blintzes at least twice a week, maybe with a different filling, sometimes with mushrooms. It was good for a main meal, because kosher meat was very difficult to obtain in the Soviet Union. Additionally, cheese blintzes also had protein." Ibi does not use egg in her filling and does not refry or bake the filled blintzes as in my mother's recipe (page 106). Try these with Ibi's special raspberry sauce and sour cream for a garnish that looks as good as it tastes.

For the batter:
⅔ cup flour
½ teaspoon salt
4 tablespoons margarine or butter, melted
3 large eggs
1½ cups milk

For the filling:
1 pound farmer's cheese
½ teaspoon vanilla
¼ cup sugar
Dash cinnamon, optional
or
½ teaspoon freshly finely grated orange zest, optional

For the Raspberry Sauce:
1 pint fresh raspberries
1½ tablespoons sugar

Sour cream, as needed, for garnish

> For a softer filling, add 4 ounces cream cheese.

Mix the batter: In a medium bowl, add the flour and salt, stirring well to mix. Add melted margarine or butter and stir to mix. Add the eggs, one at a time, mixing well after each addition, to a smooth consistency, like a thick dough. Lastly add the milk, very slowly, in three parts, mixing well after each addition until the batter is the consistency of thick cream.

Fry the blintzes: It is best to use an electric crepe maker, following the manufacturer's directions. Otherwise use a nonstick 8-inch crepe pan as follows:
Brush the pan with melted butter or spray with nonstick cooking spray. Heat pan over medium-high heat. The pan must be hot. Ladle scant ¼ cup of batter into the pan, tilting the pan to spread the batter evenly. Fry until light brown on one side, then turn. Cook about 10 seconds on the other side then remove blintz to a plate, browned side up. Cover with waxed or parchment paper, repeating until all the batter is used. Lift and replace the paper cover for each blintz. The lighter and softer the blintz is, the easier it is to fill and fold. You do not want hard edges.

Make the filling: In a medium bowl mix the farmer cheese with the vanilla, sugar and choice of optional ingredients, using a sturdy spoon. Mix until smooth.

To make the raspberry sauce: In a small bowl, mash the raspberries with a fork or spoon until the raspberries are creamy. Add the sugar. Continue mixing until almost liquid consistency. Refrigerate, covered, until using.

Fill the blintz: In the center of each blintz place about 2 tablespoons of the filling. Fold sides of blintz over filling, leaving ends open. Serve topped with a dollop of sour cream and Raspberry Sauce on the side.

To freeze blintzes after filling, freeze them, wrapped individually and when you are ready to use them, simply take out of freezer and defrost in refrigerator. Coat the bottom of a 10-inch frying pan with butter or spray. Fry the blintzes on medium for a few minutes on each side. Alternatively you can coat the bottom of a shallow casserole pan with butter. Bake at 350°F for 8 to 10 minutes.

109

Mini Mushroom Blintzes

Ⓓ Ⓟ   Makes about 50 appetizer mini-blintzes

Margit Kirsche first made this recipe thirty years ago using nondairy ingredients in the blintz recipe to satisfy the kosher catering needs for hotels in downtown Chicago. The original filling recipe was for 100 blintzes, but I have reduced it by half for the home kitchen. Because of the labor intensity, I recommend making extra blintzes and freezing half for another day.

8 to 9 blintzes (page 106), for parve,
see Variation
Vegetable oil, as needed
1 large onion, finely diced
6 ounces mushrooms, minced
Pinch each of salt, freshly ground
pepper, sweet Hungarian paprika
Farina, as needed, optional

For parve blintzes, substitute parve creamer or soy milk for milk in the blintz recipe. Dilute thick parve creamer with water in equal amounts.

Wild Mushrooms
Margit Kirsche remembers: "My mother never used mushrooms "at home" because there were no cultivated mushrooms—they grew wild. And she was never sure which were poisonous and which were safe to eat. All of the mushrooms in my recipes have been added since I came to the States."

Prepare blintzes according to recipe.
Cut each blintz in half.
Cut each half into 2 or 3 triangles.
Reserve, covered.

In a 12-inch stainless steel sauté pan over medium heat, add oil as needed and heat. Add onions and mushrooms and sauté, stirring, until onions are translucent but not browned and mushrooms are tender. Season with salt, pepper and paprika. You can thicken the filling with 1 to 2 tablespoons of farina as needed, if desired.

Remove pan from heat and let cool to lukewarm.

Preheat oven to 350°F. Spoon about 1 rounded teaspoon of mushroom filling in the center of each blintz triangle. Fold in each of the bottom opposite corners of the triangle to the center over the filling and roll to the top point. Seal the blintz by brushing a bit of raw blintz dough or water on the inside of the blintz at the tip. Place, seam side down, on a lightly oiled baking pan in a single layer.

Bake just before serving until filling is heated through and blintz is golden, about 10 to 15 minutes.

Apple Cheese Pancakes

(D) Makes 8 to 12 pancakes

My cousin Ibi learned to make these pancakes from her mother, Goldie. The cheese used is farmer's cheese; her mother's was homemade. Combining farmer's cheese and tart green apples creates a wonderfully refreshing flavor. Serve with fresh jam or sour cream, or fresh fruit, for breakfast or brunch. The cinnamon is optional, but I like the added kick. Sautéeing in butter is delicious but take care because butter quickly burns. The safe option is to sauté in a little vegetable oil in a nonstick skillet.

Vegetable oil, or butter as needed
1 pound farmer's cheese
2 eggs
1 teaspoon vanilla
Pinch salt
4 tablespoons sugar (all white or 2 white and 2 brown, packed)
4 tablespoons all-purpose flour, plus additional for coating pancakes
½ teaspoons cinnamon, or to taste, optional
1 cup finely diced Granny Smith apple

In a medium bowl combine cheese, egg, vanilla, salt, sugar, flour and cinnamon if using. Using a large sturdy spoon mix until well blended. Gently fold in apples. Cover and refrigerate for at least 30 minutes. (Refrigeration helps the pancakes hold together when cooking.)

Remove apple-cheese mixture from the refrigerator, scoop out ¼ to ⅓ cupfuls and form with your hands into round patties 2 to 3 inches in diameter and about ½ inch thick. Dip the patties, turning once, into a plate of flour.

Heat a 12-inch nonstick skillet lightly sprayed with nonstick cooking spray over medium heat until hot. Sauté patties in batches, without crowding pan, on one side until browned. Turn once and sauté until golden on the other side.

> Top with fresh jam or sour cream; serve with fresh fruit or berries on the side.

> Omit apples. Substitute farina for flour in the pancake batter. Substitute graham cracker crumbs for the flour in coating.

Cheese Kreplach

Ⓓ Makes about 40 to 50

My mother has made Cheese Kreplach every single year on Shavuos. It can be served as a main dish or a side dish, but our family has always served it as a main dish in a huge bowl smothered in melted butter. We love the taste of the light, fresh cheese combined with the warm, melt-in-your-mouth kreplach dough. It is time-consuming to make, but well worth the effort. Serve it for brunch with fresh fruit on the side. Ibi likes to coat hers in a mixture of ground walnuts with sugar (see Variation). My father liked kreplach filled with lekvar (plum preserves) (page 259) and dipped in buttered breadcrumbs.

For the Dough:
4 cups flour
1 cup eggs, about 4 large eggs
½ cup oil
½ cup water

For the filling:
1 pound farmer's cheese
1 egg
½ teaspoon salt
2 tablespoons sugar, or to taste

Water, as needed, for cooking
1 teaspoon salt, for water
1 teaspoon oil, for water

8 tablespoons of butter, or as needed, for coating kreplach.

Memories of Shavuos
Margit Kirsche remembers: "At home, for Shavuos, we brought green leaves and flowers from the garden and decorated the whole house with them. We didn't have too much time, because we cooked dairy, which takes a long time to prepare, and everything was made from scratch: noodles, cheese blintzes, cheese kreplach, the butter and even the cheese. But we were so excited! We had greens coming out of drawers, stuck in windows, covering dressers—wherever we could put them."

Ibi suggests that you dip the kreplach in finely ground walnuts mixed with sugar immediately after tossing it with melted butter. The flavor is dramatically different.

My father savored the kreplach filled with *lekvar* (page 259), and dipped in buttered breadcrumbs made from dried challah (page 224).

Make the dough: In a large bowl, place the flour. Make a well in the middle. In a separate small bowl, mix the eggs, oil, and water together. Pour the egg mixture into the well. Knead the eggs and flour together for about 10 minutes until a thick dough forms, which does not stick to your hands. If necessary, after kneading for 10 minutes, add flour, little by little, "as much as it takes up" according to my mother, for the proper dough texture.

On a lightly floured surface, roll the dough with a rolling pin into either a square or rectangular shape, about ⅛-inch thick.

Cut into 2- to 3-inch squares. Fill each square in the center. If you have a 2-inch square, use ½ to 1 teaspoon of the cheese filling; if you have a 3-inch square use ½ tablespoon of the filling. Then fold one corner up to the opposite corner, forming a triangle, pressing down the edges to seal the kreplach, so they do not open while cooking. If they are dry and do not seal, you can use a bit of raw egg white on the inside edge to seal the edges.

Cook the kreplach: Fill an 8-quart pot half way with water. Add 1 teaspoon salt. Bring to a full boil. Add 1 teaspoon of oil to the water to prevent the kreplach from sticking together during cooking. Carefully drop the kreplach into the boiling water in batches of about 20. Do not crowd; allow the kreplach space to cook. Be sure the water is continually boiling. Cook uncovered on medium-high heat for about 15 to 20 minutes, until the kreplach float to the top. Using a metal mesh spider or flat slotted spoon carefully remove kreplach and transfer to a serving bowl.

While they are still hot, toss gently with the butter. The butter will melt and the kreplach will melt in your mouth.

Potato-Egg Casserole, *Rakott Krumpli*

(D) Makes 1 (8- by 8-inch casserole), 8 main dish servings

This potato casserole is traditionally Hungarian, and the non-kosher version is made with both sour cream and sausage. The sautéed onions add a rich, moist flavor. Rakott Krumpli was traditionally served as a main course at the main meal of the day, "at home." Today you can serve it for a breakfast, brunch or a light meal. Add a salad and you have a complete meal. Use russet potatoes, not red or waxy potatoes.

Water as needed with 2 teaspoons salt
1½ pounds peel-on russet potatoes
2 tablespoons vegetable oil
2 medium onions, thinly sliced
2 cups sour cream
½ cup cream or half-and-half
6 hard-boiled eggs, peeled and
sliced ¼ inch thick
4 tablespoons butter, melted
⅛ teaspoon freshly ground pepper,
or to taste
Salt, as needed
1 teaspoon sweet Hungarian paprika,
plus as needed for garnish
Chopped fresh parsley, as needed,
for garnish

Ibi likes to substitute mayonnaise for the half-and-half. She suggests mixing 2 cups of sour cream with 1½ cups of mayonnaise.

"The Nine Days"

The first nine days of the month of Av (which always falls in summer), commemorate the nine days leading up to the destruction of the Temple in Jerusalem. It is a time of mourning. In addition to the laws of mourning, we refrain from eating meat. On the ninth day (Tisha B'Av) we fast for 25 hours, from just before sundown until after the stars come out the next night. My mother remembers the evening of Tisha B'Av. All the men, including her grandfather and father, went to the Synagogue to hear the chanting of the Eicha. My mother along with a dozen women gathered in her grandmother's home; they sat on the floor as a sign of mourning. Her grandmother read to them Eicha in Yiddish from Tzena Urena (the Yiddish translation of the Torah, Megillot and Haftarot for women).

Fill a 6-quart pot halfway with water and 2 teaspoons of salt. Add whole potatoes. Add water as necessary to cover completely. Bring to a boil. Decrease heat to medium and cook, with lid ajar, until the potatoes are just cooked, but not overcooked about 20 to 30 minutes. Test with a fork for doneness. Gently remove the potatoes and rinse in cold water until cool enough to handle. Peel the potatoes; the skins slip off easily. Slice the potatoes into ¼-inch-thick rounds.

Meanwhile, in a large sauté pan over medium heat, heat oil. Add onions and sauté until golden, stirring, about 15 minutes. Reserve.

In a medium bowl, mix together the sour cream and the half-and-half until smooth and creamy. Reserve.

Preheat oven to 350°F.

Coat the bottom and sides of an 8- by 8-inch or 2-quart casserole with butter. Place half the potatoes on the bottom. Layer half the onions. Next layer half the eggs, and half the melted butter. Sprinkle with half the pepper, salt and paprika. Pour half the sour cream mixture on top.

Repeat the layers, ending with the sour cream mixture. Sprinkle the top lightly with additional paprika. Bake, covered with aluminum foil sprayed with nonstick cooking spray, until casserole is golden and bubbling, about 45 minutes. Uncover and bake an additional 15 minutes.

Garnish with fresh parsley before serving. Cut 2 by 4 for 8 servings.

Before baking and topping with last half of the paprika you can mix ¼ cup dry breadcrumbs with 1 tablespoon melted butter, sprinkle on top, add paprika and bake. Do not garnish with parsley.

A modern variation is to top the casserole with 2 to 4 ounces shredded cheddar cheese. Then sprinkle top with paprika and bake.

Noodles with Farmer's Cheese

Ⓓ Makes 4 to 6 servings

Noodles with Farmer's Cheese is a traditional Hungarian recipe—very simple, very light and very satisfying. This was a special favorite of my mother's when she was young. Although she made her own fresh noodles, I make it with good-quality dry egg noodles and fresh cheese, and it is still delicious.

Water as needed with 2 teaspoons salt
2 tablespoons butter
1 pound dry wide egg noodles
8 ounces farmer's cheese
Sugar to taste, optional

Prepare this recipe using Homemade Noodles (page 216).

In a 6-quart pot over high heat, bring 4 quarts of water with 2 teaspoons of salt to a boil. Add noodles and cook, stirring occasionally until noodles are cooked through, 8 to 10 minutes. Drain noodles.

Meanwhile, in a 5-quart sauté pan over medium heat, melt the butter. Remove from heat. Add noodles, and toss with butter to coat.

Transfer the noodles into a large serving bowl. Break the farmer's cheese into pieces and toss with the noodles and butter to soften. Add the sugar, to taste, and toss. Or drizzle the sugar on top of either the serving bowl, or each individual bowl.

The "Kirschenbaum Cousins' Club"

After the Holocaust, my father was living in Freising, Germany, where he met an American soldier who helped him locate his father's brother, Ben Kirschenbaum. Uncle Ben had emigrated from Europe to the States with his half sisters and half brothers in the 1920s and was living in Chicago. Upon learning that my father had survived, Uncle Ben, who had no children of his own, sponsored my parents to come to the States. Unfortunately Uncle Ben died two months prior to their arrival. When my parents arrived in Chicago they were welcomed by Uncle Ben's wife, Aunt Mary, and a large group of cousins, all related through the Kirschenbaum family. These cousins, mostly a generation older than my parents, met every month at each other's homes to eat and play cards. They served coffee and cake. They loved coming to our house, because my mother always served a complete dinner. It was for these meetings that she first made the Cheese Kugel (page 117).

Food, Family and Tradition

Cheese Kugel

D Makes 8 servings

My mother says she never made cheese kugel "at home," in Hungary, but she made it often in the States, and served it frequently when "the Kirschenbaum Cousins' Club" met at our house in Chicago. She created this as a take-off of the noodles with farmer's cheese dish from her childhood. For a more robust flavor, add the raisins and top with cinnamon and sugar. It can be served as a main course, a side dish or even a dessert.

Water as needed for cooking,
with 2 teaspoons salt
½ pound dry medium egg noodles
3 eggs
½ cup cream
½ cup sugar
Pinch salt
1 teaspoon vanilla
½ to 1 teaspoon cinnamon
4 tablespoons melted butter, plus
additional for casserole
½ pound farmer's cheese
2 tablespoons cream cheese
½ cup raisins, optional
Cinnamon–sugar, for topping, optional
Corn flake crumbs, for topping, optional

Preheat oven to 350°F.

In a 6-quart pot over high heat, bring 4 quarts of water with 2 teaspoons of salt to a boil. Add noodles and cook until al dente, about 8 to 10 minutes. Drain and reserve.

In a medium bowl, mix the eggs with the cream, until light and fluffy. Add the sugar, salt and vanilla and cinnamon.
Add the melted butter and the cheeses and mix until smooth. Add the raisins, if using. Place noodles in a large bowl. Pour egg mixture over the noodles and mix together.

Butter an 8 by 8-inch casserole generously. Pour the noodle mixture into the casserole. Top with cinnamon–sugar and, if desired, sprinkle with corn flake crumbs.

Bake, uncovered, in the oven until bubbling and golden, 45 to 60 minutes. Cut 2 by 4 for 8 servings, or serve scooped with a large spoon.

Deviled Eggs

(P) Makes 12 servings

My mother has been making deviled eggs forever. While I was growing up and her house was full of company on Shabbos (as it still is today), she prepared and served them fresh for seudat shlishit (the third and informal meal served at the end of Shabbos). The original recipe did not use mustard, but I have added it for a kick. This dish is easy to make, serves beautifully and goes wonderfully with a salad.

6 hard boiled eggs, shelled
¼ cup mayonnaise
1 teaspoon mustard
¼ teaspoon salt
Dash pepper, optional
Sweet Hungarian paprika, as needed, for garnish

Cut the eggs in half lengthwise. Gently, remove the yolks and put all the yolks in a small bowl. Mash the yolks with a fork. Add the mayonnaise, mustard, salt and pepper and mix well. Adjust seasonings to taste.

With a pastry tube pipe the yolk mixture back into the white halves of the eggs. Or spoon it back in with a small spoon, carefully, so as not to break the whites. Arrange on a platter on a bed of lettuce, and sprinkle with paprika.

For easy peeling, drain the eggs after cooking and fill the pan with cold running water until the eggs are cool. Let the eggs sit in the cold water for 30 minutes, then crack the shells.

Got Fun Avraham (Yiddish prayer recited at the end of Shabbos)
As Shabbos ends, the women, for centuries, have prayed that the coming week would be a week of blessings, as my mother still does today. At the end of Shabbos as the men would go to shul, the women of my mother's family would recite this version of Got Fun Avraham.

Got fun Avraham, fun Yitzchak, un fun Yaacov
Heit dayn leib heiliger faulk Yisrael Fun alle bisz tzu dannen loib.
Vie de liber heiliger Shabbos gait ahin Zal himen de libe vaach
Tzu gezint tzu parnassa Tzu oisher Tzu havod
Tzu besoros tovos Tzu gezeros tovos
V'yitnu refuah shlema U'noimar Amen

God of Abraham, Isaac and Jacob, protect the Jewish people;
As Shabbos departs, let the new week bring health, prosperity, happiness, and good news.

Farmer's Chop Suey

D Makes 4 servings

I am not sure where my mother heard the name Farmer's Chop Suey, but that is how she has referred to this dish through the years. My mother developed this salad from the original recipe that her mother prepared in Vásárosnamény, which used just radishes, salt and sour cream. In both the original recipe, as well as the newer version, the salad retains the crisp flavor of the vegetables, along with the refreshing flavor of the cottage cheese or sour cream. My grandchildren love it with the cottage cheese. This is best prepared just prior to serving.

2 tomatoes, chopped
1½ cups chopped seedless cucumbers, peeled or peel on
2 radishes thinly sliced
Salt to taste
1 cup farmer's cheese
or
2 cups cottage cheese
or
1 cup sour cream

In a medium bowl toss together tomatoes, cucumbers and radishes with the salt. Top with farmer's cheese, cottage cheese or sour cream and toss gently. Serve immediately.

Chapter 4
Fish

Wine with Fish

The flavor of fish often demands a light, crisp clean white wine, especially refreshing since white wine is best served cold. For the Poached Salmon, you may want to try a white wine with more body and substance, for example a buttery chardonnay. Try a sauvignon blanc with the whitefish recipes, for a flavor that is lighter and more "citrusy." A heartier fish entrée, for example Baked Rainbow Trout, will hold up to a red wine such as a pinot noir, sangiovese, gamay or cabernet franc.

*"…God provides for all
who show devotion:
clothes to wear,
plentiful bread, meat, fish
and all sort of delicacies…"*
Excerpts from a Shabbos song

Fresh fish is a true delicacy in any time and any place. Before the War, my parents cooked only perfectly fresh fish, because lack of dependable refrigeration made preserving fish for any length of time impossible. While gefilte fish loaves today are conveniently located in the freezer section of supermarkets, my mother recalls the gefilte fish of her childhood, "We were able to obtain fish for gefilte fish when the farmers in the area went fishing in the Tisza River and then came to sell it. In addition, beginning in approximately 1940, someone in Vásárosnamény had a business selling carp. We bought one carp each week. The carp was farm-raised in clear water."

In post-War Germany, in the first years after my parents survived the Holocaust, kosher fish was easier to come by than kosher meat, so fish often substituted for meat on Shabbos or special occasions. The laws of kosher fish are simpler. They only concern the presence of fins and scales, not the slaughtering process as with meat, so by eating fish they were able to preserve their parents' traditions, and observe the laws of keeping kosher.

However, obtaining fresh fish was still far from easy, and the quest sometimes led them down strange paths (see "A Long Journey Back," page 122).

Many of these fish recipes begin with the same basic ingredients: onions, carrots and paprika. But each recipe's unique flavor emerges during the wide range of cooking methods: baking, broiling, boiling, or poaching the fish.

Whitefish with Carrots and Onions

(P) Makes about 6 servings

This is Ibi's recipe from her mother Goldie. Ibi recalls, "We prepared this on Friday and served it for lunch on Shabbos, usually in the summer. Because we did not heat food on Shabbos, my mother served it cold or room temperature. It was a summer dish because the fisherman would bring the fish they had caught and sell it door to door in Munkács. It was too cold to go fishing in the winter."

1 whole whitefish, 2½ to 3 pounds
1 to 2 tablespoons oil, or as needed, for sautéing
6 to 8 carrots, shredded
3 medium onions, diced
Kosher salt, to taste
Freshly ground black pepper, to taste
1 teaspoon sugar, optional
1 (15-ounce) can tomato sauce
1 lemon, thinly sliced
Fresh chopped parsley, for garnish

Clean and wash the fish in cold, running water, leaving whole, head and skin on.
In a 12-inch stainless steel or nonstick sauté pan over medium-high heat, heat the oil. Add carrots and onions, season to taste with salt and pepper, and sugar, if using, and sauté, stirring, until vegetables are soft but not browned. Add the tomato sauce and mix, until heated through. Remove from heat. Reserve.

Preheat oven to 375°F. In a lightly oiled ovenproof baking dish or casserole, large enough to fit the fish, place fish on its side. Season fish lightly with salt and pepper, inside and out. Place 2 slices of lemon in the fish. Cover the fish with the reserved carrots and onions in tomato sauce.

Bake until fish is cooked through and browned, about 45 minutes. Then remove from oven, cover and let steam for 10 minutes.

Serve fish on a platter. Surround the entire fish with the carrots and onions. Sprinkle the vegetables with chopped fresh parsley and garnish with remaining fresh lemon slices on top. Cover again and let stand for 10 minutes.

A Long Journey Back

Margit Kirsche remembers, "After The War, when I was living in Freising, Germany with my brother, Morton, there was no kosher food available for the first year. I had just recently decided to eat only kosher food once more. Let me explain. I had been raised in a large close-knit family of four brothers, parents, grandparents, aunts, uncles and cousins. Immediately upon entering Auschwitz, my mother, grandparents and three younger brothers were sent to the gas chambers. At the end of The War, when I was liberated, I had no idea if anyone else in my family had survived. I decided that if no one else had survived, I did not want to know from Yiddishkeit and would not care what I ate or what I did. I was a young woman in my early 20s left alone. A few months after liberation, I found out that my older brother, Morton, had in fact survived. Having found my brother, I decided that I would once again eat only kosher food. During this time, my brother bought me a fish not easy to obtain at that time. We did not have refrigeration, so it was swimming in the bathtub for a few days until my brother killed it (in the bathtub) for Shabbos. And, if you are wondering if I used the same bathtub in which the fish was swimming, I did not—because there was no hot water. There was a bathhouse in Freising, and I used to go there to bathe."

Boiled Fish

Ⓟ Makes 6 servings

This simple dish keeps its flavor served cold. My mother still cooks fish this way and we still appreciate the fresh, pure taste. "This is the fish I cooked for my wedding. It is a recipe that I have from my mother and is always delicious. The trick is to have clear-water fish, which is very fresh," says my mother. "At home, we never baked or broiled fish, or prepared it in an oven." A few years ago, I vacationed with my husband Irv in Door County, Wisconsin. The town prides itself on its legendary "Fish Boils." I, however, felt that I had grown up with fish boils. My mother cooks her fish for 2 to 2½ hours; however, I often cook it for 1 hour.

6 whitefish or carp fish steaks,
1½ to 2 inches thick
or
1 whole whitefish or carp,
2 to 3 pounds
Kosher salt, as needed
Water, as needed
1 large onion, diced
1 carrot, sliced into rounds
2 teaspoons sugar
½ teaspoon sweet Hungarian paprika
2 pinches freshly ground black pepper
2 to 3 small red potatoes,
sliced into ¼-inch thick rounds

If you have purchased a whole fish, cut into 6 steaks. Discard the tail; reserve the head to cook with the steaks. It enhances the flavor of the fish. (Always remove and discard the "ears" or gill covers from the fish head before cooking.)

Spread the fish steaks in a single layer on parchment paper. Sprinkle the fish all over with kosher salt on both sides, as you would do when kashering meat. Let the fish rest for about 1 hour. Then rinse under cold running water.

Meanwhile, in a 6-quart pot over medium-high heat, bring enough water to cover the fish to a boil. Add the onion, the carrot, the fish and seasonings. Bring to a boil, then decrease heat to low and simmer covered for about 2 to 2½ hours. Add the potatoes for the last half hour. Bring to a boil again. Cover and cook on low for an additional ½ to 1 hour.

This is usually served cold, or room temperature. But it is also delicious served warm. Serve on individual plates with some of the vegetables and just enough liquid for dipping challah.

Food, Family and Tradition

My mother and father were married in Freising, Germany twice. First in a civil ceremony on June 1, 1947, which allowed her to apply for emigration papers on my father's application as his wife. The second ceremony, on October 21, 1947, was according to Jewish law and tradition. At that time in Freising my mother was the only one among her group of survivors who kept a kosher kitchen. There was no rabbi in Freising, no kosher meat, no kosher restaurant. Both the chupah ceremony (performed by a rabbi who came from Munich) and the wedding reception took place in the banquet hall of the Coliseum restaurant. Guests included her brother Morton, who arranged the wedding, my mother's cousin and her husband, friends and fellow survivors. Despite the loss of family and the ordeal of the Holocaust, it was festive. My mother wore a wedding gown (designed by her cousin, Piri Apfeldorf) and my father a suit. A violinist played traditional music. The restaurant catered the food. My mother wanted to make sure that at least the head table had kosher food. So for her table of seven, she baked the challah and cooked seven pieces of Boiled Fish (page 124).

Poached Salmon

Ⓓ Makes 10 to 12 small servings

Ibi's simple recipe for poached salmon can be made 1 or 2 days in advance. The finished dish looks as good as it tastes. A fish poacher is the best pan for cooking the large salmon fillet, but lacking that, a long roasting pan or even a disposable foil roasting pan covered with foil will work. There is a parve variation below.

For the fish:
1 boneless, skinless side of salmon,
about 2½ to 3 pounds
Scant 2 tablespoons kosher salt,
or to taste
10 whole peppercorns
2 to 3 bay leaves

For the garnish:
4 tablespoons unflavored yogurt
1 tablespoon sour cream
1 garlic clove
1 bunch dill, chopped, divided
1 seedless cucumber, very thinly sliced

> The Whole Fish
>
> In Munkács after the War, Ibi's mother Goldie Weinberger used to buy a whole salmon from the fisherman. It was a huge fish for one family, so she used it for many meals. With half she would make the Poached Salmon and with the remaining salmon she would either make a fish-and-vegetable soup or salmon baked in her homemade flaky puff pastry dough—an old-fashioned version of today's elegant coulibiac of salmon.

For a parve garnish, substitute ⅓ cup mayonnaise in place of yogurt and sour cream.
Cut the fillet into serving-size pieces and poach in a 12-inch sauté pan for 7 to 15 minutes, depending on the thickness of the fillet. Decorate according to recipe directions.

Ibi's mother did not have a fish poacher so she wrapped the fish fillet in cheesecloth before poaching, making it easy to lift the cooked fish from the poaching liquid.

Sprinkle salt evenly all over salmon. Let fish rest for 10 to 15 minutes. Rinse under cold running water.

Place fish gently in a fish poacher or in the bottom of a long roasting pan or disposable foil roasting pan. Add enough water to come up halfway the depth of the fish. The top surface of the salmon should not be under water.

Bring to a boil over medium high heat. Add peppercorns and bay leaves. Decrease heat to low, cover poacher with lid or foil pan with aluminum foil. Simmer until salmon is cooked completely through, about 30 to 40 minutes. When tested with a fork the flesh should be lightly pink, not red.

Remove pan from heat. Remove salmon gently from water. Slide onto a large fish platter (Fish poacher has a rack that is easily lifted.) To lift salmon from roaster, slip 2 broad spatulas underneath fish and lift gently from water. Slide onto platter and let it cool until the fish is room temperature. Remove any accumulated liquid on plate using a folded paper towel.

In a small bowl combine yogurt and sour cream, stirring to mix well. Press garlic through a garlic press and add to yogurt-sour cream mixture, stirring to mix well. Spread mixture over the top and sides of the fish. Sprinkle half the dill evenly over the sauce on top of the fish. Place the cucumber slices like fish scale over top and sides of the fish. Sprinkle the remaining dill on top of the cucumbers. Serve at room temperature or wrap with plastic wrap and refrigerate for up to 2 days. Serve cold.

127

Sweet and Sour Fish

P   Makes 6 to 8 servings

The flavor of the fish in this recipe is enhanced by the contrast of the sweet and the sour elements. My mother prepares this for Shabbos and it is still one of everyone's favorites. It is a perfect appetizer or main dish for Shabbos lunch because it can be served cold or at room temperature. My mom dips challah in the sauce and serves Chrain (page 195) on the side. She also cooks the fish for 2 to 2½ hours. I reduce the cooking time to 1 to 1½ hours.

1 whitefish, skin on, about 3 pounds,
sliced into 1½-inch thick steaks, head
reserved
Kosher salt, as needed
2 large onions, thickly sliced
¾ cup sugar
3 cups water
1 to 2 pinches of sour salt

Remove and discard the "ears" or gill covers located just under the fins on the fish head. Reserve the head.

Spread the fish and head in a single layer on parchment paper. Sprinkle both sides with kosher salt. Let the fish rest for about 1 hour. After an hour, rinse in cold running water. Pat dry.

Meanwhile, put the sugar and onions in the bottom of a 6- to 8-quart pot. Do not add water or oil. You want the onions to caramelize, a crucial step.

Brown the onions in the sugar on low heat, stirring constantly, until the onions are dark brown. Watch this very carefully so that the onions and sugar do not burn. When onions are well browned, remove the pot from heat.

Add approximately 3 cups of water and the sour salt. (The sour salt gives the fish the "sour" flavor.) Return the pot to medium-high heat. Add the reserved fish and head.

Bring to a boil. Decrease heat to low, cover and simmer for 2 to 2½ hours, or until fish is cooked through and infused with flavor.

Cool the cooking pot with fish in an ice-water bath. Then cover and refrigerate. This fish is best served cold or room temperature. If prepared properly and cooked with the head, the water becomes jelled when cooled.

Serve each steak on individual plates with some of the jelled cooking liquid on the side. Accompany with sliced challah and *Chrain* (page 195). It is customary to eat the fish head on Rosh Hashana, and many enjoy the fish head on Shabbos as well.

All Carp Are not Created Equal

"In Hungary, before the Holocaust, we did not have a lot of fish," recalls Margit Kirsche. "We had one carp every week, which we used for boiled fish. The carp was farm-raised in clear water and brought from Budapest. When I first came to the States, I saw carp in a supermarket for 19 cents per pound! I bought one and cleaned it and cooked it, and then I threw the whole thing in the garbage. For me that was pretty extreme, as I never throw out food, especially after surviving the Holocaust. Apparently, the carp I bought here in the States was a scavenger fish and it smelled like the dirty water. I did not eat carp again until we began selling it at Hungarian Kosher Foods—only carp raised in clear water."

Simple Broiled or Baked Fish

Ⓟ Ⓓ Makes 1 to 8 servings

This is a quick-and-easy recipe for your favorite fillet of fish. We have used whitefish, salmon, tilapia, sea bass and golden trout. Olive oil gives the fish a fragrant flavor, but butter is more delicate. Fresh herbs complement the flavor of the fish. Remember, the only secret is to use very fresh fish.

1 to 8 fish fillets of choice,
skin-on or skinless
Olive oil or melted butter, as needed
Freshly squeezed lemon juice, to taste
Salt and freshly ground pepper, to taste
1 to 8 teaspoons finely chopped herbs:
dill, parsley, rosemary, thyme, any
combination

Preheat the broiler or preheat oven to 400°F. Lightly oil or butter a shallow baking or broiling pan. Lay fish fillets in pan in a single layer. Brush tops of fish with oil or butter.

Season fillets lightly with lemon juice, salt, pepper and sprinkle with teaspoon fresh herbs.

Broil until fish flakes easily, about 10 minutes, or bake for 10 to 15 minutes.

Serve with crisp, tender vegetables, a baked potato and a green salad for the perfectly balanced low-calorie, low-fat meal.

A "Mir Schit Arain" Recipe
My mother had many recipes she referred to as "Schit" recipes, much to my daughter Rocky's shock the first time she heard that. "Mir Schit Arain" means "we pour in" and this simple, creative recipe allows the cook to throw in any herb or combination of herbs available and still come up with a light, flaky, fresh full-of-flavor main dish.

Tuna Salad

Ⓟ Makes 4 servings

This tuna salad is one of my mother's most popular recipes, and we have been told that nobody's tuna salad is as tasty. It is simple but it has its secrets. One is the grated egg; another is the oil-packed tuna. You can substitute water-packed tuna if you want a lighter salad, but the depth of flavor will not be quite the same.

1 (12-ounce) can or 2 (5-ounce) cans oil-packed tuna, well drained
3 hard-boiled eggs, shelled
¼ cup minced onion
1 stalk celery, very finely chopped
⅓ to ½ cup mayonnaise

Place tuna in a medium bowl and mash with a fork. Grate the egg and add to the tuna, stirring to mix. Add the onion and celery, and mix well with the mayonnaise.
Cover and refrigerate for up to 3 days.

131

Baked Rainbow Trout

(P) Makes 2 servings

Each year in Desert Hot Springs, where my parents spent some time each winter, my mother looked to the supermarkets for a supply of fresh fish. The fish sold there was always very fresh. When my mother found rainbow trout, this is how she prepared it. The vegetables are moist and flavorful, and it is a complete meal.

2 whole fresh rainbow trout, scales and fins removed
Kosher salt, as needed
2 tablespoons butter
1 medium onion, thinly sliced
4 to 6 small red potatoes, thickly sliced
1 zucchini, cut into chunks,
8 baby carrots
or
2 carrots, cut into chunks
¾ cup frozen or fresh peas
2 tablespoons olive oil
Freshly ground pepper, to taste
Sweet Hungarian paprika, to taste

Use skin-on trout fillets. Bake vegetables for 45 minutes until they are tender, then add fillets and bake until fish flakes with a fork, 7 to 15 minutes.

Rinse trout under cold running water. Pat dry. Sprinkle kosher salt on both sides and let rest on parchment paper for 1 hour. Rinse under cold water and pat dry.

In a separate skillet over medium heat, heat butter. Sauté the onions in the butter, until they are golden. Reserve.

Preheat the oven to 375°F. Place the fish in a shallow baking pan. Place the vegetables around the fish. Drizzle the fish and the vegetables with the oil. Season the vegetables with salt, a dash of ground pepper and paprika. Toss to coat. Then season the fish with a dash of the pepper and paprika. Top with the reserved sautéed onions. Bake uncovered for 1 to 1½ hours.

Food, Family and Tradition

Mom's Salmon Patties

P   Makes 6 to 8 patties

When I was a child this was one of my favorite recipes that my mother made. The sautéed vegetables add moistness to the fish patty. It is a perfect use for leftover salmon, good served hot as a main entrée or cold as a fish sandwich.

2 tablespoons oil, plus more as needed for frying patties
½ cup diced onions
⅓ cup diced red or green pepper
1 pound of cooked salmon (baked, boiled, broiled, sautéed)
or
1 (14- to 15-ounce) can red salmon, drained, some liquid reserved
2 eggs, beaten
¼ cup dry breadcrumbs
⅛ teaspoon freshly ground pepper, or to taste
¼ teaspoon salt
¼ teaspoon Seasoned Salt (page 66)
Cornflake crumbs, optional

In a small skillet heat oil over medium heat and sauté the onions and peppers for 5 to 7 minutes until golden and soft. Reserve.

Remove and discard any salmon bones. Mash the salmon well with a fork and add the sautéed onions and peppers. If using canned salmon, add some reserved liquid for moistness. Add the beaten eggs, the breadcrumbs, and the seasonings. Mix well. Form into 2½-inch round patties ½ inch thick. If desired, dip into cornflake crumbs.

In a 12-inch sauté pan over medium heat, heat oil. Fry patties until crispy, turning once, about 3 to 5 minutes on each side.

Tuesday Dinners

Alisa Kirsche Oler writes: "I was the eldest of the six grandchildren and for a few years I had the undivided attention of my grandparents, Margit and Sandor Kirsche. It was great: they took me shopping for toys and clothes, entertained me on Saturday nights. They always made me feel special.

"When I finished graduate school with a degree in nutrition, I decided my grandfather needed help with his nutrition. He was always thin (he had stomach surgery in 1958) and worked long hard hours. I felt it was my duty as the oldest grandchild and a dietitian to be sure my grandfather ate a relaxing dinner at least once a week. Tuesdays seemed to be the best nights, so after a few months of having dinner at our family's former dairy restaurant, Tuesday night dinners evolved to dinner at my grandparents' home. My grandmother, despite being blind, would cook dinner. When I was able to come early I was lucky to have a personal cooking lesson and learned the tricks of such dishes as nakidlach. But I usually came after work, arriving in time to watch Wheel of Fortune with my grandmother while we waited for Grandpa Sanyi to come home and have dinner with us. It was just like old times: I had my grandparents' undivided attention. But this time around I was able to appreciate them on a different level and enjoy conversations ranging from life in Europe to personal and political opinions, to how to make a firm, but light matza ball. After my grandfather passed away, my grandmother and I continued our Tuesday night dinners until I finally moved into the apartment above hers with my husband and our small son. Now we see each other every day and my son watches Wheel of Fortune with Bubbie."

Chapter 5
Poultry

Chicken *Paprikás* with Dumplings, *Nakidlach*
Stuffed Chicken or Goose Neck, *Helzel*
Mock Fish, *Falcse* Fish
Schmaltz
Whole Roasted Chicken with Rice for Shabbos
Chicken *Chulent*
Chicken Schnitzel
Stuffed Chicken
Chicken Stuffed in Chicken
Stuffed Chicken Breast
Chicken Patties
Duck Simply Roasted
Duck Roasted with Fruit

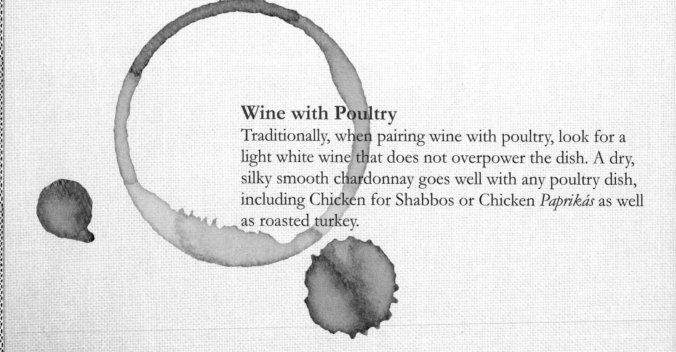

Wine with Poultry
Traditionally, when pairing wine with poultry, look for a light white wine that does not overpower the dish. A dry, silky smooth chardonnay goes well with any poultry dish, including Chicken for Shabbos or Chicken *Paprikás* as well as roasted turkey.

Food, Family and Tradition

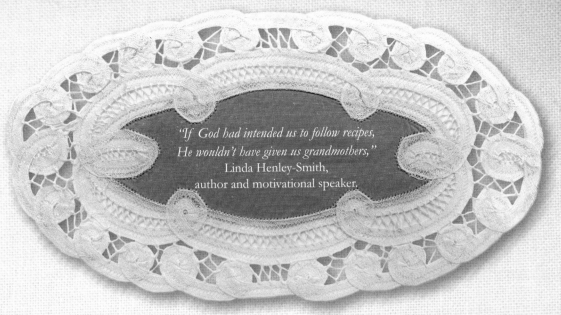

*"If God had intended us to follow recipes,
He wouldn't have given us grandmothers,"*
Linda Henley-Smith,
author and motivational speaker.

When I think of my mother's poultry dishes, I realize that, in so many ways, they remind me of the grandmothers I never knew, and of traditional Jewish life in Eastern Europe before the Holocaust. Chicken was the central dish that my grandmothers prepared for Shabbos, and the recipes conjure up all of the stories of purchasing at the market, *schecting* (ritual slaughtering), preparing and finally eating the chicken at my parents' childhood family Shabbos meals.

I never knew how it felt to grow up with grandparents. The Nazis killed all of mine and my memories of my grandmothers come only from the images that my mother and father painted for me. I did not watch my grandmothers cook in the natural settings that my parents describe, nor did I walk into their house and smell the aromas of their Shabbos chicken delicacies.

Of all the foods my mother cooks, chicken seems to me to be the most therapeutic. I don't remember my mother using any

recipe for chicken while growing up, and yet her chicken dishes were my favorite. Many of the recipes here are very family-friendly, simple to prepare and use basic ingredients that kids tend to like. (You will notice that my grandmothers' recipes use every part of the chicken, wasting nothing.)

There is no recipe for roast turkey, but my parents always celebrated Thanksgiving (a national, not a religious holiday) in the States, their new home. In fact, my parents had never seen nor tasted turkey prior to coming to the States. There is much rabbinic literature discussing the kashrus of turkey, as it is not mentioned at all in the Torah, presumably because there were no turkeys during the Biblical Era. However, it is mentioned in later Talmudic literature and is referred to as *"ofe hodu"* (Hebrew for turkey). There are recipes for duck, goose, and even *Helzel*, stuffed chicken or goose neck. One of my special favorites and one of my mother's signature dishes is *Falce* Fish, or Mock Fish. It is chicken made in the manner of gefilte fish, a true delicacy.

Chicken *Paprikás* with Dumplings, *Nakidlach*

(M) Makes 8 servings

This is an authentic, traditional Hungarian recipe. My mother's Chicken Paprikás is renowned. Her grandchildren love the nakidlach. There may be a few bites of chicken left but there are never enough nakidlach.

For the Chicken *Paprikás*:
2 tablespoons vegetable oil
2 medium onions, chopped
1 (3½-pound) skin-on chicken,
cut into eighths
or
8 leg-thigh quarters
2 teaspoons sweet Hungarian paprika
1½ teaspoons Seasoned Salt (page 66)
½ teaspoon salt
⅛ teaspoon freshly ground pepper
2 tablespoons flour
Water, as needed

For the dumplings, *nakidlach*:
1 cup eggs, about 4 large eggs
¼ cup vegetable oil
½ cup water
2 ~~tablespoons~~ flour   *2 cups*
2 teaspoons salt
or
¼ teaspoon salt with 1 teaspoon
powdered chicken soup base

The Best Dumplings

Margit Kirsche writes: "I was in Budapest in December of 1945 a few months after the War had ended. There were two girls, both my friends, in this household, one was my age, both survivors. Before the War, their family was living in a five-room apartment at Dob Utca (street) 5, and rented out bedrooms for people who did business in Budapest. My brother Morton and I had both rented rooms here at different times before the War. After the War, I had gone home to Vásárosnamény and found no one alive there. When I heard that my brother Morton had survived, I left with just the clothes on my body and went to Budapest to see if I could find him. I arrived at my friend's apartment at Dob Utca (street) 5, and the girl who was my age was married and living in the apartment. Her husband really liked nakidlach and she wanted to cook it but did not know how to make it. I offered to make it but then she said she had no eggs, which were hard to come by. So I made it without eggs. You can only cook with what you have. What you don't have, you don't have. As I was cooking the dish, my friend was sewing and there was a knock on the door. 'I'll get it,' I said. And when I opened the door, there stood my brother Morton. He had been on his way back to Vásárosnamény to find me. The nakidlach were delicious, even without the eggs."

Omit dumplings and make the recipe with the rice: When the chicken is almost cooked and most of the liquid has reduced, add 1 cup of rice and 2 cups of water to the chicken. Bring to a boil, decrease heat to low, cover and cook for 20 minutes until the rice is cooked.

Omit dumplings and make the recipe with potatoes: When the chicken is almost cooked and most of the liquid has reduced, add 4 peeled russet potatoes, cut into chunks. Add enough water to almost cover the potatoes. Bring to a boil, decrease heat to low, cover and cook until the potatoes are cooked through, about 20 minutes.

Food, Family and Tradition

Make the chicken:

In an 8-quart pot over medium heat, heat oil. Add the onions and chicken. Cover the pot, decrease heat to low and simmer for 15 minutes.

Remove cover, and season with the salt, Seasoned Salt, and paprika.

Cover and cook on low heat for about 1 to 1½ hours, stirring occasionally, to make sure the chicken or onions do not burn. Uncover and continue cooking, until the liquid has reduced to ½ cup, about ½ hour.

Add 2 tablespoons flour and stir until it browns, similar to making a roux. Then slowly add enough water to just cover the chicken, stirring to mix. Cook just until it thickens. This makes the gravy for the nakidlach. Reserve, keep warm.

Make the dumplings, *nakidlach*:

While the chicken is cooking, in a 3-quart bowl, mix the oil and water. Beat the eggs and add to the oil-water mixture. Stir to mix. No salt is necessary since you will cook the *nakidlach* in salted water. Very slowly, in ¼ cup increments, add the flour to the egg mixture, stirring until completely smooth.

In a 6-quart pot, add water to the halfway mark. Bring water with the salt or the salt and chicken soup base to a boil. Drop the dumpling mixture by ½ teaspoonfuls into the boiling water. Scoop the noodle dough in one teaspoon, then use the second teaspoon to scrape it into the boiling water. Periodically, mix the cooking dumplings gently with a large spoon, so the dumplings do not stick together. Cook until the *nakidlach* rise to the top, about 10 minutes. Drain the *nakidlach* gently in a strainer.

Transfer the drained *nakidlach* onto a large platter and place the chicken with its gravy over. Alternatively add the drained *nakidlach* to the chicken in the pot and cook together for a few minutes. This infuses the rich flavor of the chicken to the *nakidlach*.

Stuffed Chicken or Goose Neck, *Helzel*

Ⓜ Makes 5 to 6 slices as a side dish with the meal

My mother removed the skin from the chicken neck, rinsed and cleaned it of all pinfeathers. (The neck meat and bones were used for soup.) She stuffed it according to the size, sewed up both ends with needle and thread, and cooked it in the pot with the chicken soup or stew. She often roasted the neck afterwards to brown it. Then she sliced it and served it with the meal. The directions below still work, although today a helzel needs to be ordered from your butcher because chickens come with their necks skinned and the skin discarded. And you are far more likely to get chicken than goose, even though a goose neck is larger and serves more.

1 chicken neck skin or *helzel*
1 cup Bread Stuffing (page 232) or
mix for Chicken Patties (page 149)
as needed
2 hard-boiled eggs, shelled, optional

Rinse and clean the helzel, pat dry with paper toweling. Stuff to capacity with the stuffing. If using eggs, start with the stuffing, then add one egg lengthwise, and repeat, ending with the stuffing. Sew the ends closed using a needle and thread. Add the stuffed *helzel* to a pot of soup and cook with the soup or add to the roasting pan with the chicken and roast together with chicken.

Remove *helzel* from the soup pot or roasting pan, remove thread and discard, slice *helzel* in 5 to 6 slices.

Mock Fish, *Falcse* Fish

Ⓜ Makes approximately 20 to 24 *falcse* balls, or 6 to 8 servings

Literally "false," falcse fish was and still is a flavorful stand in for gefilte fish, although it is made of chicken. "I learned to make this dish 'at home' from my mother, who was a very good cook" Margit writes. "It was another method of using the chicken breast. We often served falcse fish on Shabbos as an appetizer for lunch. We would prepare it on Friday, and keep it fresh in our cellar." Falcse fish, mock fish, is cooked exactly like gefilte fish and, in fact, it tastes so much like gefilte fish, most people do not believe that it is chicken. It can be a light dinner served with challah, or a light and refreshing appetizer. It is best served cold or at room temperature., with Chrain (page 195) on the side.

For the *falcse* balls:
1 pound ground chicken breast
½ medium onion, grated
½ carrot, grated
1 dry challah roll or thick challah slice, soaked in water, squeezed dry
2 eggs
½ teaspoon salt
Pinch freshly ground pepper
Pinch Seasoned Salt (page 66)

For the stock:
2 quarts water
1 medium onion, sliced
1 to 2 carrots, peeled, sliced
1 teaspoon sugar
¼ teaspoon Seasoned Salt
Pinch salt
Pinch freshly ground pepper
½ teaspoon sweet Hungarian paprika

In a medium bowl, mix together the ingredients for the *falcse* balls. Reserve.

In a 4-quart pot over high heat, bring 2 quarts of water to a boil. Add the remaining stock ingredients and decrease heat to medium.

Form reserved chicken mixture into small balls, about 1 inch in diameter, and drop them gently into the water. When the water again reaches a boil, decrease heat to low, cover and simmer until the *falcse* fish balls are cooked through and tender, about 30 to 45 minutes.

Remove from heat, cool to room temperature in an ice-water bath. Refrigerate the *falcse* fish balls in their liquid, covered. Serve with a little of the poaching liquid spooned over and a slice of carrot.

Schmaltz

Ⓜ Makes about ½ cup schmaltz, depending on chicken

Margit Kirsche writes: "In Europe, we made schmaltz from a goose. This lasted us a long time, almost a whole year, until we could get another goose. If we did not have a goose we made it from the chickens we had and collected it as we made it. We stored this for almost a whole year. We did not use oil. We did not have parve oil, only coconut oil. But we liked the schmaltz better and used this for everything: frying, potatoes, etc. We even stored some of this away, to be used on Pesach." This was also done after the Holocaust in Munkács, ensuring that the Jews were able to have kosher oil or fat for cooking, especially for Pesach. There was no store where one could buy "kosher for Passover" products. The schmaltz was stored in the root cellar. The following recipe is as much anecdote as formula; however, the adventurous cook can still make schmaltz. A word of warning: at Hungarian Kosher Foods it takes 20 chickens to make 1½ pounds of schmaltz. On the other hand, you will never use that much today. Please see the tip for instant schmaltz at the recipe's end. Speaking for myself, nothing tastes better than homemade mashed potatoes with schmaltz.

You will need the skin and fat of 1 to 2 chickens. Remove the skin that has fat attached to it, along with the fat that is under the dark meat.

> Add 1 onion, diced, in the beginning, and cook all the way through. The onions will become crispy also and will add flavor.

> When you make chicken stock or soup and refrigerate, the chicken fat will rise to the top of the container. Before reheating the soup, remove the fat with a spoon and place in a covered jar and refrigerate: instant schmaltz! Then use by the tablespoon to sauté instead of oil, or in place of margarine in mashed potatoes or rice.

Cut the skin into pieces about 1-inch square. Pour ½ cup water or less into a heavy pot. Cook uncovered over medium heat, adding the skin plus the fat. Continue cooking over medium heat, until the water cooks down and evaporates and the skin becomes crispy. Drain the fat and reserve fat and skin separately. Cool schmaltz to room temperature. Refrigerate cooled schmaltz, covered.

To make *griebenes*, return the skin to the pot and continue to cook on low until the skin is brown and crispy. Nibble on *gribenes*, sprinkle on bread, or add to dishes such as mashed potatoes for flavor.

My father's sister, Goldie, did not add water. She melted the fat along with the skin in a heavy cast iron pot (we also used this pot) until the fat was melted and the skin was crispy. So, to follow her directions, follow all the steps above, without the water! She stored the *griebenes* in some of the fat.

Whole Roasted Chicken with Rice for Shabbos

(M) Makes 4 to 6 servings

My mother made this every Shabbos for years. The aroma defined Shabbos for us. It was her signature Shabbos dish. There have been variations, but to this day it is still the favorite dish of my grandchildren who live in Israel, just as my mother made it. Their mother, my daughter Rocky, thinks this is the perfect family dish: you carve it at the table and everyone gets to pick their favorite part.

For the chicken:
1 whole chicken, about 3½ pounds
1 ounce wine of choice, optional
1 teaspoon Seasoned Salt (page 66)
1 teaspoon sweet Hungarian paprika
2 to 3 cloves minced garlic
or
¼ teaspoon garlic powder, or to taste
½ teaspoon freshly ground pepper, or to taste
1 onion, chopped
3 cups cooked white rice

Preheat oven to 350°F. Place chicken in roasting pan. Pour wine, if using, over chicken. Rub the chicken with seasonings and garlic. Sprinkle onions alongside.

Roast the chicken, covered, until cooked through and juices run clear, when thickest part is pierced with a fork, about 1 to 1½ hours. Uncover, baste with pan juices, and bake uncovered for an additional ½ hour.

Serve chicken on platter garnished with parsley. Bring to the table to carve. Serve rice in a separate bowl.

Buying the Right Chicken
In my mother's home in Vásárosnamény, she went with her mother to the market to buy a chicken, but, unlike today, they bought what was available because the chickens were all live. The farmers brought the corn-fed chickens to the market and each week there were different sizes. Today we would call them fryers, spring chickens and broilers (2½ to 3½ pounds), or capons or roasters (4 to 7 pounds), and hard to find today, old hens or soup chickens. When hens lived past their egg-laying years, they were big and tough and appropriate only for the long cooking of the soup pot. My mother says that they bought the chicken according to the family's needs, "A big chicken served more people." From the market my mother took the chicken to the shoichet (kosher slaughterer). Then she would go home and together with her mother, remove the feathers and internal organs, clean and kasher the chicken by salting. Finally she would rinse the chicken and begin preparation. My grandmother cooked chickens by frying or sautéing, roasting, and boiling. The fat was rendered for schmaltz, and the skin was used to make gribenes (cracklings), stuffed helzel (chicken neck) or left on the chicken for extra flavor. And even the feet were used; they are delicious in soup.

My mother always adds some of the roasted chicken juices to her white rice as it cooks, making her rice more flavorful.

When my father roasted chicken, he would rub oil on the chicken before roasting, making the skin extra crisp.

Chicken *Chulent*

(M) Makes 8 servings

This is perfect for Shabbos lunch. You should leave the skin on the chicken, in which case you will need very little oil for the pan. Traditional chulent is made with beans, but my mother created this dish in the States for Pesach when we do not eat beans. The chicken is so tender, it just melts in your mouth. It also makes a nice, easy hot cold-weather lunch.

1 tablespoon vegetable oil, as needed
4 medium onions, cut into large pieces
6 russet potatoes, cut into large pieces
2 chickens, skin on, 3 pounds each, cut in fourths or eighths
1 teaspoon salt or
Seasoned Salt (page 66)
½ teaspoon freshly ground pepper
4 garlic cloves minced
1 tablespoon sweet Hungarian paprika

Preheat oven to 350°F. You need to start preparing this 2 hours before Shabbos begins on Friday, even though you are not going to serve it until noon on Saturday.

Pour oil on bottom of a heavy roasting pan with cover (I use an enameled cast iron Dutch oven). Layer the pan beginning with potatoes and onions on the bottom and then the chicken and sprinkle on half the seasonings. Repeat until all ingredients are used.

Cover pan, sealing tightly, so the *chulent* will not dry out. If your pan does not have a tight-fitting lid, line the pan with 2 layers of foil, then cover tightly and crimp to seal. Bake for about 1 hour.

> Substitute sweet potatoes for some of the russet potatoes.

> Prepare in the slow cooker on high for 1 hour, then turn to low for the remainder of the cooking time.

Decrease heat to 225°F and leave in the oven overnight. Remove from oven at lunch. If your Dutch oven is presentable, bring it to the table with a large spoon.

Serve with a salad. Dip your fresh challah in the sauce as my father did.

Chicken Schnitzel

Ⓜ Makes 8 servings

Schnitzel is authentically European, whether veal or chicken. My mother's chicken schnitzel is special. She debones her own white meat from the chicken, then slices it thin and pounds it to about ¼ inch uniform thickness. Also she uses fresh breadcrumbs for the breading. Pounding the chicken breasts uniformly thin allows them to cook faster and more evenly. For added flavor I often mix breadcrumbs with cornflake crumbs, half and half.

6 to 8 boneless skinless chicken breast halves, about 2 pounds
1 cup flour
1 teaspoon Seasoned Salt (page 66)
½ teaspoon sweet Hungarian paprika
¼ teaspoon garlic powder
¼ teaspoon freshly ground pepper
2 eggs, beaten, mixed with 1 tablespoon water
1 cup fresh bread crumbs
or
½ cup fresh breadcrumbs and
½ cup cornflake crumbs
Vegetable oil for frying, as needed

Slice each chicken breast in half horizontally. Cover each piece with plastic wrap. Using a meat mallet or rolling pin, pound chicken breasts, to an even thickness of ¼ inch. Some tears are okay; even thickness is the most important step.

Place flour and seasonings in 1 shallow bowl; stir to mix. Place egg, and crumbs in 2 additional separate shallow bowls.

Dip each chicken piece first in flour, then egg and then the crumb mixture. Transfer to a tray or plate and repeat until all chicken is breaded.

In a 12-inch skillet over medium-high heat, heat oil as needed. Fry schnitzel on each side, in batches, turning once, until golden brown and cooked through, about 5 minutes for each side.

Serve immediately or transfer to a parchment-lined baking pan and keep warm in a 250°F oven.

Serve on individual plates with vegetables and potatoes or rice of choice.

> When I prepare schnitzel, I place the crumbs and the flour on a 12-inch length of foil. That way the two pieces of foil can be folded up and discarded.

> Chicken schnitzel is a popular dish in Israel where the breasts are sold already pounded paper thin. If you buy pre-pounded breasts, fry the schnitzel for only 2 or 3 minutes on each side.

Stuffed Chicken

Ⓜ Makes 4 to 6 servings

"At home" in Vásárosnamény my mother's family always stuffed the chicken with bread stuffing because nothing was wasted and this was the perfect use for leftover challah. When the stuffing is baked inside the bird the flavors are intense. This was a traditional Shabbos meal with many variations. Today I serve it both for family and company dinners. When baking this on Erev Shabbos (the eve of Shabbos) the aromas fill the house and welcome the Shabbos in through all your senses. For a one-dish meal, carrots, onions and mushrooms are added to the baking pan.

1 whole skin-on chicken,
about 3½ pounds
1 recipe Bread Stuffing (page 232),
prepared
1 ounce wine of choice, optional
1 teaspoon Seasoned Salt (page 66)
1 teaspoon sweet Hungarian paprika
2 to 3 cloves minced garlic or
¼ teaspoon garlic powder, or to taste
¼ to ½ teaspoon freshly ground
pepper, to taste
3 carrots, cut into chunks
8 to 12 mushrooms
2 onions, cut into chunks

Preheat the oven to 350°F. Stuff the chicken with the prepared stuffing. Close the chicken either by sewing or with wooden skewers.

Season the chicken first with wine, if using, then sprinkle on remaining seasonings and garlic. Put chicken in roasting pan. Place vegetables in pan close to the chicken. If you have leftover stuffing, place it around the chicken.

Bake uncovered for about 2 hours, basting every 20 minutes. Serve the chicken on a platter and carve at the table; place vegetables and stuffing in a serving dish.

Stuffed Chicken Quarters:
You have the chicken and its side dish all in one and it looks very appetizing on the plate. Stuff 8 skin-on bone-in chicken quarters under the skin with Bread Stuffing. Lay the quarters in a shallow baking pan, seasoning tops as desired with salt, Seasoned Salt and paprika. Baked until cooked through, basting every 20 minutes with pan juices, about 1½ to 2 hours. Serve 1 chicken quarter per person.

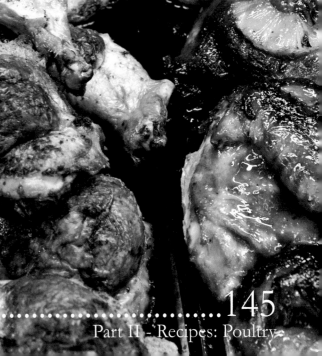

Turning the Clock Back Fifty Years

In the summer of 1992, my niece and nephew, my two daughters and I traveled with my mother and father back to their homes in Hungary and what was once Czechoslovakia. On the way to my father's home in Hluboka, which is in the Ukraine today, we stopped in Uzhgorod (or Ungvar as it was known before the War), which is a larger city nearby. Strolling through the city we arrived at a large square surrounded by shops. On the right side is a large, beautiful building, a concert hall at that time. The building was locked, but the caretaker was outside the building and my father asked if we could go inside and look around. After some persuasion, he let us in. It was quite emotional for us, because it was apparent from the traditional Jewish symbols that this concert hall had been a magnificent Jewish Synagogue before the Holocaust.

Many of the stores in the square had been owned by Jews and on any typical Thursday or Friday, it had been brimming with Jewish life. As we continued walking, we arrived at the main square near the Ung River. My father painted the picture for us of what it looked like before the Holocaust: bustling with Jewish merchants and customers shopping for Shabbos. At this point my nephew Daniel turned to me and said, "I wish I could just stand here and turn the clock back fifty years."

Chicken Stuffed in Chicken

(M) Makes 8 to 10 servings

Here is a gourmet dish with frugal beginnings: to "stretch" the chicken. If you debone and grind your own chicken as my aunt Goldie did, then the dish is economical but labor-intensive. She used the bones and some of the chicken meat for soup for Shabbos and some of the chicken meat for schnitzel. However today, it is much simpler to prepare. You can ask the butcher to bone out the chicken and then grind the breasts for you. The finished dish looks beautiful on a platter, slices easily, and serves many people. It's an elegant dish for the holidays and it perfectly reflects the cooking philosophy of our grandparents.

1 whole chicken, about 3½ pounds, skin on but deboned except for wing bones and thigh bones, breast meat ground (see note)
3 tablespoons vegetable oil, divided
2 cups diced onion
2 cups cooked rice, room temperature
3 to 4 small mushrooms, diced
2 cloves garlic, minced
3 tablespoons chopped fresh parsley
1 tablespoon chopped dill or cilantro, or to taste, optional
1 teaspoon sweet Hungarian paprika, divided
½ teaspoon salt
¼ teaspoon freshly ground pepper
2 eggs

Preheat the oven to 350°F. You will be stuffing the skin and using the ground breast meat to prepare the stuffing.

In a 12-inch skillet over medium heat, heat 2 tablespoons of the oil. Sauté the diced onions and mushrooms for about 10 minutes, or until golden. Add the minced garlic along with the parsley, and, if using, dill or cilantro. Remove from heat.

Add the rice, ground chicken, eggs, salt and pepper and ½ teaspoon of the paprika to the onion-mushroom mixture. Now you are ready to stuff the chicken skin. Gently, push the stuffing inside the skin. As you do, you will notice that it takes on the form of a chicken. Using a needle and thread, sew the chicken together at the neck and tail openings. You also sew together any spot that has pulled apart.

Spray the bottom of a roasting pan with nonstick cooking spray. Place the stuffed chicken in the pan. Mix together the remaining one tablespoon of oil and ½ teaspoon paprika. Rub the chicken with the oil-paprika mixture. Bake uncovered for about 2 hours.

Serve on a platter with greens, and slice the chicken into 1-inch thick slices.

Ask the butcher to remove all bones except wing and leg bones and all meat except wing and leg meat leaving the chicken skin intact. Then ask him to grind once only the chicken breast meat. Reserve the thigh meat and all the bones for soup.

Stuffed Chicken Breast

Ⓜ Makes 6 to 8 servings

This is similar to Chicken Stuffed Chicken (page 146), but uses only the chicken breast. And, like its similar recipe, looks beautiful on the plate and serves a great many people. The stuffing is made with challah instead of rice. Once again, you can ask the butcher to debone a whole breast, leaving the wings attached, then grind the breast meat once, saving the bones for soup. Or, (see Tip) you can do this yourself.

1 whole deboned skin-on chicken breast, wings attached, from a 3½-pound chicken, breast meat ground and reserved
2 tablespoons vegetable oil, divided
1 medium onion, diced
1 clove garlic, minced
3 to 4 slices of dry challah (scant ¼ pound), soaked in water then squeezed dry
⅛ teaspoon freshly ground pepper
⅛ teaspoon salt
¾ teaspoon sweet Hungarian paprika, divided
2 eggs

> To dry fresh challah, bake slices in a 350°F oven for 15 minutes. To debone your own chicken breast, slip your fingers carefully underneath the skin and break the wing bones where they join the breast. Now separate the skin, removing the chicken breast meat and bone, trying to leave the skin in one piece. Reserve the skin with the wings attached. Remove the breast meat from the bones (reserving bones for soup) and grind the meat coarsely. Proceed with the recipe.

Preheat the oven to 350°F. In a 12-inch sauté pan over medium heat, heat 1 tablespoon of the oil. Add onion and garlic and cook, stirring, until soft and golden but not brown. Remove from heat.

Add the challah, pepper, salt and ¼ teaspoon of the paprika and stir to mix. Add the reserved chicken meat and eggs and mix well.

Stuff the skin with this chicken mixture. Fold skin under and sew to close.

Mix remaining 1 tablespoon of oil with remaining ½ teaspoon of paprika and rub chicken breast all over.

Spray bottom of a small roasting pan with vegetable oil spray, and place chicken in pan. Bake, uncovered, until chicken is golden brown and cooked through, about 1½ to 2 hours.

Serve sliced ½- to 1-inch thick. Accompany with cooked carrots or a green vegetable.

> You can also make the stuffing with fresh challah.

Chicken Patties

Ⓜ Makes 8 to 10 patties

Chicken Patties are a good use for chicken breast because it extends the number of people that one whole breast can serve. The whole breast from one 3- to 3½-pound chicken will yield about 1 pound of ground chicken. Ask the butcher to grind it only once, which makes for better texture. You can also prepare the recipe using pre-ground chicken sold in packages. The patties take on a rich flavor from being fried with the onions. It is equally good served cold the next day, as my mother's mother did, for Shabbos lunch.

1 to 1¼ pounds coarsely ground
chicken breast meat
2 eggs
3 to 4 slices pre-sliced dried challah
(scant ¼ pound) soaked
and squeezed dry
1 clove garlic, minced
⅛ teaspoon pepper
⅛ teaspoon salt
⅛ teaspoon Seasoned Salt (page 66)
3 tablespoons vegetable oil,
or as needed
1½ cups diced onion, divided

In a medium bowl, combine the ground chicken with the eggs, bread, garlic and seasonings. Stir to mix well. Form into 2½- to 3-inch round patties about ¾-inch thick.

In a 12-inch skillet over medium high heat, heat oil. Add half the onions, sauté for 2 minutes. Add half the patties and cook until cooked through, 7 minutes on each side, turning once and stirring the onions as the patties cook. Repeat with second batch of onions and patties.

Serve patties on individual plates with mashed potatoes and a small green salad, or serve on a bun with condiments. Or, serve cold or at room temperature accompanied with potato salad.

The Golden Goose

Today, goose is regarded as a delicacy. "At home" in Hungary before the Holocaust, and after, goose was a poultry which provided food for a whole season, everything from schmaltz to smoked goose. It was stored in the cellar and preserved. A few of the possible recipes and uses follows:

Smoked Goose

My mother's family in Vásárosnamény smoked goose in the chimney of their house. In the fall and winter when a wood fire was built in the house, they climbed up to the roof using a ladder and tied the breast and thighs with strings, hanging them from the bars inside the chimney. After a few days the goose was nicely smoked and they stored it in the cold cellar where it kept all winter. When my mother's cousins would visit on their way to Budapest, my maternal grandmother often sent smoked goose with them. It was not only a delicacy but kept well.

Goose Liver

Chopped Goose Liver. Both sets of grandparents used goose liver in the recipe for chopped liver (page 72). Goose liver, as mentioned earlier, was so large and such a delicacy, that the family could sell it for enough money to buy another goose. Then they would have all the goose meat as well as the skin and the fat, instead of just one goose liver.

Goose Liver Cut in Pieces Roasted with Garlic and Onions. My grandparents used goose liver in the recipe for fried liver and onions (page 156).

Goose Fat and Skin. My grandparents used goose fat and skin in the recipe for schmaltz (page 140). The goose provided quite a lot of schmaltz and *griebenes* that could be stored and used for an entire season.

Tza'ar Ba'alei Chaim
My mother's maternal grandparents in Hungary never ate geshtopte geese (force-fed geese). My maternal great grandfather, Yaakov Yehuda Cheimovics, was the rabbinic advisor for the town of Gergely, Hungary. He felt that the common practice of force-feeding geese presented problems regarding their kashrus in terms of cruelty to animals as well as other legal issues. When they visited my mother's family for Shabbos, my maternal grandmother never cooked with force-fed goose or its schmaltz knowing her father's religious concerns.

Duck Simply Roasted

M Makes 4 to 6 servings

My mother roasted duck for many years for the festive meal that our family ate on Purim. I love duck, but it takes hours to clean a kosher duck of its pinfeathers. Once my mother finally finished cleaning the duck, the rest was easy. Kosher duck is already quite salty, so it needs no salt. My mother seasoned it only with some garlic and pepper, and of course, a bit of wine.

1 cleaned, dressed kosher duck,
about 4 to 6 pounds
2 garlic cloves, minced
Freshly ground pepper, to taste

Preheat the oven to 350°F. Season the duck inside and out with the garlic and pepper. Place the seasoned duck in a roasting pan and roast covered for 2 hours. Then uncover, roast an additional ½ hour, basting with the pan juices. If the duck is larger than 4 pounds, roast until tender, an additional ½ to 1 hour.

Serve on a platter garnished with orange slices and carve at the table. Accompany with rice and Candied Carrots (page 184).

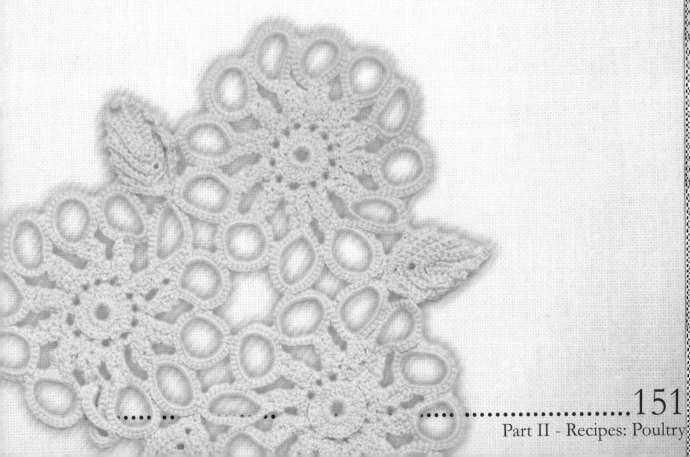

Duck Roasted with Fruit

(M) Makes 4 to 6 servings

This is Ibi's recipe for duck. The fruit is not only stuffed inside the duck's cavity, where it infuses the duck with delicious flavor during roasting, but it is cooked as a compote of stewed apricots, prunes and onions to serve alongside. This duck is traditionally served on Rosh Hashana or Succos.

For the duck:

1 duck, about 4 to 6 pounds
1 to 2 Granny Smith apples, cored and chopped
10 pitted prunes
1 whole clove garlic
1 clove garlic, minced
Freshly ground black pepper, to taste

For the sauce:

½ cup freshly squeezed orange juice
1 teaspoon honey
¾ cup apricot jam or orange marmalade

For the compote:

1 tablespoon vegetable oil
1 large onion, halved, thinly sliced
12 ounces pitted prunes
4 ounces dried apricots

Roast the duck: First clean the duck. Cut off the neck and any hanging fat and discard. Preheat the oven to 350°F. Stuff the apples, the 10 prunes and 1 clove of garlic inside the duck. Season the top with minced garlic and pepper.

Place the duck in a roasting pan. Add about ¼ cup of water. Roast, covered, 2 hours. If the duck is large, roast until soft and tender, an additional ½ to 1 hour.

Meanwhile, make the sauce: in a small bowl mix apricot jam or orange marmalade with the orange juice and honey.

Uncover and roast the duck for an additional ½ hour and baste often with the sauce.

Make the compote: In a 12-inch skillet over medium heat, heat oil. Sauté the onion until translucent but not browned, about 10 minutes. Add the dried fruit and continue sautéing, stirring, for about 3 to 5 minutes. Add 1 to 2 tablespoons of water, cover, decrease heat to low and let steam to plump fruit, about 5 minutes. Remove from heat and keep covered.

Serve the duck on large platter. Surround with compote.

Duck at Rosh Hashana

As I was photographing this duck dish for the cookbook, one of the staff at Hungarian Kosher Foods broke into tears. He and his family had lived under Communist rule in the Soviet Union (outside of Munkács), and were prohibited from observing any Jewish laws. The anti-semitism was so harsh that one had to be careful to be able to keep a job and not be arrested as a political prisoner. The few traditions they kept were behind closed doors. But his mother managed always to serve this duck on Rosh Hashana, and he says that always reminded him of his Jewish heritage.

Chapter 6
Meat

Fried Liver with Onions and Potatoes
Chop Suey
Lamb Stew
Hungarian Goulash, *Gulyás*
Stuffed Cabbage, *Gefilte Kraut*
Stuffed Peppers
Chulent
Meatloaf with Beef or Veal
Brisket
Rib Eye Roast
Boiled Tongue
Sweet and Sour Tongue
Veal Breast
Veal *Paprikás*
Veal Schnitzel

Wine with Meat

In this chapter, there are recipes for beef, as well as veal, and lamb. Veal, which is lighter than beef, goes well with a white viognier wine. Viognier is a dry, aromatic, medium-bodied white wine, which will offer complex herbal flavors, as well as a mouth-feel that complements the texture of veal. Lamb and beef both demand the richness of red wine to accompany the full flavor. Cabernet sauvignon is the most full-bodied and robust of the red wines, and is perfect for Rib Roast or for Goulash. For Brisket try a red wine that is not quite as heavy, perhaps a merlot or syrah, which has a hint of a fruity flavor. For lamb try a pinot noir, a lighter red wine generally from Italy or a malbec, a medium red wine with ripe fruit flavors generally from South America.

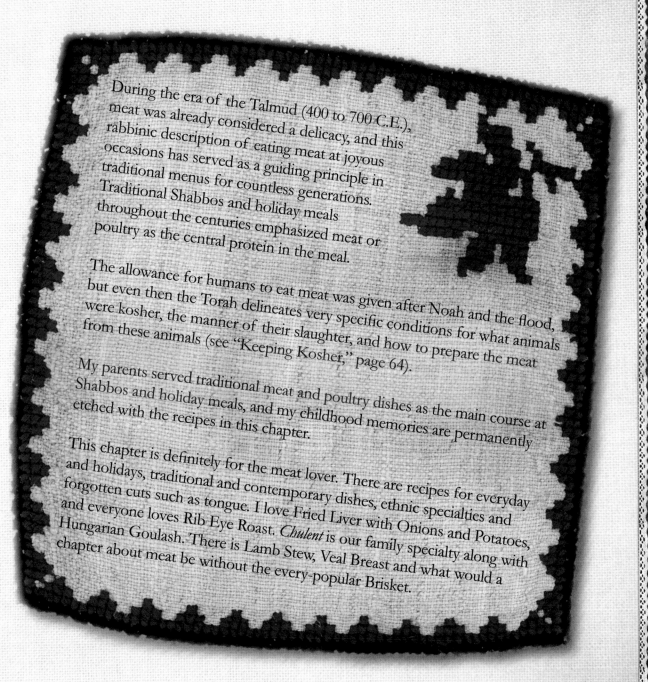

"There is no joy except with meat and wine."
(Talmud Pesachim 109a)

During the era of the Talmud (400 to 700 C.E.), meat was already considered a delicacy, and this rabbinic description of eating meat at joyous occasions has served as a guiding principle in traditional menus for countless generations. Traditional Shabbos and holiday meals throughout the centuries emphasized meat or poultry as the central protein in the meal.

The allowance for humans to eat meat was given after Noah and the flood, but even then the Torah delineates very specific conditions for what animals were kosher, the manner of their slaughter, and how to prepare the meat from these animals (see "Keeping Kosher," page 64).

My parents served traditional meat and poultry dishes as the main course at Shabbos and holiday meals, and my childhood memories are permanently etched with the recipes in this chapter.

This chapter is definitely for the meat lover. There are recipes for everyday and holidays, traditional and contemporary dishes, ethnic specialties and forgotten cuts such as tongue. I love Fried Liver with Onions and Potatoes, and everyone loves Rib Eye Roast. *Chulent* is our family specialty along with Hungarian Goulash. There is Lamb Stew, Veal Breast and what would a chapter about meat be without the every-popular Brisket.

Fried Liver with Onions and Potatoes

(M) Makes 4 servings

In the time it takes the potatoes to cook, you can complete this entire dish. It is like step one of making chopped liver. It is also a great Passover dish, no chametz (leavened food). Just mound the potatoes on a large platter, top with liver and onions and garnish with parsley. In Europe beef liver was used because it was most readily available. In Israel I tasted a lighter option served over a green salad rather than potatoes. Serve the salad version immediately, or cool the liver first so as not to wilt the lettuce.

4 medium russet potatoes,
cut into large chunks
2 tablespoons vegetable oil
5 medium onions, sliced in half,
then thinly sliced
1 pound beef or veal liver, sliced and
kashered (page 67)
Seasoned Salt to taste (page 66)

....
Substitute 1 pound of kashered
chicken livers for beef or veal liver.
....

Fill a 4-quart pot halfway with salted water and bring to a boil over high heat. Cook the potatoes until they are soft when pierced with a fork, but do not fall apart, about 20 minutes.

Be careful not to overcook. Drain and reserve. In a 12-inch sauté pan over low-medium heat, heat oil. Sauté the onions, stirring, until they are soft and golden, about 20 minutes. Drain and reserve.

Add the liver to the onions and cook for just a few minutes. It is not necessary to cook the liver longer, as it has already been cooked in the kashering process. Do not cover the livers even after they have been fried, or they will become rubbery and bitter.

Serve the liver and onions over the boiled potatoes or mash the potatoes on a platter.

Food, Family and Tradition

In the 1990s when the grandchildren were young, Hungarian Kosher Foods was so busy before Pesach, too busy for the as-yet small hired staff. So the grandchildren worked through many pre-Seder nights alongside the parents and grandparents. Although the children attended Jewish day schools, they were not on vacation until just before Pesach. Completely exhausted from the lack of sleep, they nevertheless looked forward with great anticipation going to work late at night during this season. They stocked the shelves with Passover items or worked in the kitchen filling and assembling Seder dinner orders, making charoses (traditional Pesach fruit-and-nut paste) with my mother, or just peeling eggs or potatoes. Somehow every year, my father, also working in the kitchen, would kasher the chicken livers and then sauté them with onions, in the middle of the night. This was a favorite midnight snack for the grandchildren. Although it was a stressful time of work, these nights were a deep bonding experience for the siblings, cousins, and grandparents. The hours flew by full of stories about my parents' childhood and their preparations for Pesach "at home." These stories told in those late night hours filled us all with memories that will last a lifetime.

Chop Suey

Ⓜ Makes 8 servings

My mother had never heard of chop suey much less cooked or tasted it "at home" until she came to the States. My parents' first apartment was in Humboldt Park, Chicago, and that is where she first saw chop suey being cooked by Jewish neighbors. It became a family favorite, like an Asian variation on Hungarian goulash. My mother always used canned bean sprouts, but today fresh sprouts are readily available. We allow for ¾ cup rice per person.

2 tablespoons vegetable oil
2 pounds bonelsss beef stew meat, cut into 1½-inch chunks
2 medium onions, chopped
½ teaspoon Seasoned Salt (page 66)
¼ teaspoon garlic powder
¼ teaspoon freshly ground pepper
3 stalks celery, sliced
10 small white mushrooms, sliced
2 (15-ounce) cans bean sprouts, drained
or
1 pound fresh bean sprouts
2 (8-ounce) cans bamboo shoots, drained
1 (8-ounce) can water chestnuts, drained and sliced
3 tablespoons cornstarch
1 tablespoon powdered chicken soup base
1½ cups water
2 tablespoons mild, unsulphured molasses
4 tablespoons soy sauce
6 cups cooked white rice

In an 8-quart pot over medium heat, heat oil. Add stew meat and onions and dry seasonings. Decrease heat to low, cover and simmer until meat is tender, about 1 hour. There will be considerable liquid. Add all the vegetables, and stir.

In a small bowl add cornstarch and soup base and whisk to mix. Add ¼ cup water, mixing until smooth. Add remaining water in batches, slowly, stirring constantly. Stir in the soy sauce and the molasses. Slowly add the cornstarch liquid mixture to the meat and vegetables in the pot, stirring until thickened.

Bring to a boil. Cover, decrease heat to low and simmer until meat is tender, 30 minutes to 1 hour.

Serve ladled over cooked rice.

Lamb Stew

(M) Makes 6 servings

Margit Kirsche says, "We never had lamb 'at home.' The farmers didn't raise much lamb in Hungary, but after the War we had lamb in Germany. When we moved to Chicago, I started making this version of goulash. I always made goulash, and this is the same idea. Bone-in lamb is more flavorful."

3 tablespoons vegetable oil
1 cup chopped onion
2½ pounds bone-in lamb stew meat
½ pound mushrooms, sliced, optional
3 medium carrots, cut into chunks
1 teaspoon sweet Hungarian paprika
½ teaspoon salt
½ teaspoon Seasoned Salt (page 66)
2 cloves chopped garlic
3 russet potatoes, cut into large chunks

In a 6-quart pot over medium heat, heat the oil. Sauté the onions together with the lamb in oil until the lamb has browned, approximately 10 minutes. Stir constantly.

Add the mushrooms, if using, and carrots and brown for a few minutes. Cover, decrease heat to low and simmer until the lamb is tender and the liquid has reduced for 1½ to 2 hours, stirring frequently.

Uncover pot and add enough water to cover the lamb. Then add the seasonings and garlic and potatoes. Bring to a boil. Decrease heat, cover and simmer, until the potatoes are cooked, about 30 minutes. Taste while cooking and adjust seasoning as necessary.

New Lives, New Neighborhood
Humboldt Park in Chicago in the late 1940s and 1950s included a vibrant Jewish community. The magnificently landscaped park, designed by 20th-century famed landscape architect Jens Jensen, sat between two distinct neighborhoods. The east side, and the west side of the park (west of Kedzie avenue), where our family lived. When my parents first arrived in Chicago, in February 1948, they went to live with "Aunt Mary," the wife of my father's Uncle Ben, on the South Side of Chicago. Recently widowed, she was selling her home and moving to the North Side of Chicago, so after one month my parents looked for another place to live. They found a bedroom with kitchen privileges for rent in the home of an elderly Jewish widow, Mrs. Bernstein, who had a kosher kitchen and lived on Beach Avenue, just west of Humboldt Park. Although they were renting one bedroom with kitchen privileges, they welcomed my mother's cousins Suri (Muschel) and Brindy (Cziment) for a Jewish holiday. A large group of Holocaust survivors found their way to this Chicago neighborhood, which offered low-cost housing and a beautiful park, as well as an active shul, Ateres Zion, located on Spaulding Avenue just south of Division Street. Once there, my parents signed up at Crain School to learn English. Their lives were hectic but productive: They worked during the day and went to school at night. They always looked to the future, a future with children. While learning English, the survivors still spoke to each other in Yiddish and their native Eastern European languages. My parents learned English quickly, and were reading the newspaper as well as novels, within two years.

Hungarian Goulash, *Gulyás*

Ⓜ Makes 6 servings

We sell Hungarian Goulash in Hungarian Kosher Foods; it is authentic goulash, made with only meat, potatoes, and onions. For this recipe I have added optional mushrooms and carrots. The secret to making a good goulash is, first, sautéing the meat without any liquid, and second, adding authentic Hungarian paprika. Liquid is only added later with the potatoes. Non-kosher Hungarian goulash also calls for sour cream; however, we do not mix meat and dairy.

2 tablespoons vegetable oil
1½ pounds boneless beef stew meat, cut into 1½-inch chunks
1½ cups chopped onions
2 cloves garlic, minced
1 teaspoon sweet Hungarian paprika
⅛ teaspoon fresh ground black pepper
1½ tablespoons flour
Water, as needed
4 russet potatoes, cut in large chunks
½ teaspoon salt, or to taste
8 ounces sliced white mushrooms, optional
1 carrot, thinly sliced, optional

Film the bottom of an 8-quart pot with oil. Add the beef, onions, garlic, paprika and pepper. Sauté, on low, stirring frequently, until the meat is browned, then cover, and cook on low, stirring often, until the liquid from the beef and onions has mostly evaporated, about 1 hour. If the liquid has not sufficiently evaporated at the end of cooking, uncover and cook until ½ inch of liquid remains.

After the liquid has evaporated, add flour and stir. Cook to brown, stirring, about 10 minutes, being careful not to burn. Add enough water to cover the meat, stirring until smooth. Add the potatoes and salt. Add carrots and mushrooms if using. Bring to a boil.

Cover, decrease heat to low, and simmer until potatoes are cooked and meat is tender, about 30 to 45 minutes.

Serve ladled into large bowls, and accompany with fresh bread.

Gulyás in Freising

Although my mother learned to cook Gulyás as a young girl in Hungary, her family was not able to cook or eat the dish or, in fact, any beef, from 1942 until after the Holocaust. During the last years before my parents were taken to the Ghetto and to Auschwitz, the Nazis declared it illegal to "shecht" (ritual kosher slaughter) beef because they, ironically, considered ritual slaughter of animals cruel. However, my mother remembers cooking this recipe in Freising, Germany, where she lived after the Holocaust.

While living in Freising, my father had befriended an American Jewish soldier who was helping survivors connect with relatives in the States to assist them in obtaining papers to emigrate. The soldier posted ads in the Jewish Forward, a widely read Stateside Jewish newspaper. After he submitted an ad that my father had survived, one of my father's cousins, Laura, who was living in Chicago, read the ad and sent it to my father's Uncle Ben, his father's brother, who had been living in Chicago since 1920. Uncle Ben, who had no children, was thrilled to hear that my father had survived and immediately offered to sponsor my father and mother.

When my parents went to the American embassy in Freising to apply for emigration papers, they met an American army officer who struck up a conversation with my mother about Hungarian cuisine, especially goulash. So my mother, who throughout her life has cooked for everyone, everywhere, prepared some goulash and brought it to him. My mother remembers, "He liked what I cooked and asked for the recipe, but I don't cook from recipes."

Stuffed Cabbage, *Gefilte Kraut*

Ⓜ Makes 20 rolls

This is very similar to the recipe for Mini Stuffed Cabbage (page 82), but you get more bang for your buck. The rolls are larger and you may serve one as an appetizer or two as an entrée. The number of servings depends on the size of the head of cabbage, but I get 20 large leaves from a large cabbage head with plenty left for shredding. Choose large cabbages with loose outer leaves rather than small cabbages with tight leaves. If you like your cabbage very sweet, use ½ cup of sugar. Not so sweet? Use ¼ cup.

For the rolls:
1 large head of cabbage
8 ounces refrigerated sauerkraut,
well drained

For the Filling:
1 pound ground beef, turkey, chicken
or a mixture
¾ cup uncooked long grain white rice
1 medium onion, finely diced
2 tablespoons vegetable oil
¼ teaspoon salt
Pinch pepper

For the Sauce:
1 (15-ounce) can tomato sauce
or
2 cups tomato juice
1 teaspoon salt
¼ teaspoon Seasoned Salt (page 66)
¼ to ½ cup sugar, to taste

No Rice for Stuffed Cabbage
During my mother's childhood in Hungary, rice (prized in stuffed cabbage) was expensive because it was imported from China and considered a delicacy. In the early 1940s, the first years of World War II, my mother remembers, "We couldn't import rice anymore. So my mother made stuffed cabbage using dried chopped corn kernels from the open market in place of rice. My three younger brothers and I didn't want to eat it because without the rice it wasn't true stuffed cabbage. Behind our house lived a poor Jewish widow with three children who often could not even afford to buy wood for cooking. So my mother gave her the stuffed cabbage. This woman said that her children loved it so much they 'licked their fingers.'"

Prepare cabbage leaves in two different ways: my mother's way or the hard way.

My mother's way:
Core the cabbage and discard the core. Freeze the cabbage overnight. Defrost in warm water until the leaves can easily be pulled off. Trim the heavy center rib off each leaf as if you were shaving it and reserve the shavings. Do not cut the leaf in half.

The hard way:
Core the cabbage and discard the core. Immerse the cabbage in a large pot of boiling water. Let sit until the top few leaves become pliable and easily separated, about 5 minutes. Do not leave the cabbage in the water until it becomes too soft or the leaves will tear when you try to fill and roll. Remove the cabbage from the water, reserving the water. Separate as many leaves as come off easily. If you reach a point when the leaves no longer separate easily, return the cabbage to the water and repeat. Trim the heavy center rib off each leaf as if you were shaving it and reserve the shavings. Do not cut the leaf in half.

Shred the reserved ribs and any remaining cabbage to put in the bottom of the cooking pot with the sauerkraut.

Make the filling:
In a 12-inch stainless sauté pan, over medium heat, heat the oil. Add the onions and sauté until soft and translucent but not brown. Add the meat and brown for a few minutes, stirring and breaking into small pieces with the fork or spatula. When the meat is browned add the raw rice and seasonings. Stir to mix.

Stuff the cabbage:
Put a rounded tablespoonful of the filling in the center of each cabbage leaf. Roll the cabbage up around the filling starting with the rib end and toward the wider part of the leaf. Roll up and tuck in both sides. Repeat until all filling is used. Place cabbage rolls on a tray seam side down as they are rolled.

Alternatively, put a rounded tablespoonful of the filling in the center of each cabbage leaf. Fold each side of the cabbage leaf over the filling, as if you were folding the leaf in thirds. Then roll up from the bottom and place seam side down on the tray.

Cover the bottom of an 8-quart pot or large enameled cast iron Dutch oven with half of the shredded cabbage and half of the sauerkraut. Place the stuffed cabbage neatly in the pot seam side down. Cover with the remaining shredded cabbage and sauerkraut.

Mix the tomato sauce with the seasonings and pour over the cabbage rolls. If the sauce does not cover the cabbage add enough water just to cover.

Bring to a boil over high heat. Decrease heat to low, cover tightly and simmer for about 2 hours, checking to see if the rice is cooked through. Alternatively you can bake tightly covered in a 350°F oven for 3 hours.

Stuffed Peppers

 Makes 10 servings

Stuffed Peppers are a wonderful alternative to Stuffed Cabbage and easier to prepare because you don't need to roll the peppers. Any combination of orange, red and yellow peppers presents beautifully on a platter. We rarely use green peppers because we find them somewhat bitter. All nature's colors are spectacular.

For the filling:
2 tablespoons vegetable oil
1 medium onion, finely diced
1 pound ground beef, turkey, chicken or a mixture of these
½ cup of uncooked long grain white rice
¼ teaspoon salt
Pinch black pepper
4 mushrooms, finely chopped, optional

For the peppers:
10 medium bell peppers, yellow, red or orange
1 (12-ounce) bag shredded cabbage
or
1 small head cabbage, shredded
8 ounces refrigerated sauerkraut, well drained

For the sauce:
1 (15-ounce) can tomato sauce
or
2 cups tomato juice
1 scant teaspoon salt
2 tablespoons sugar
Dash Seasoned Salt (page 66)

Beef for Stuffed Cabbage and Peppers
During my mother's childhood, growing up in Vásárosnámeny, stuffed cabbage was a common dish, but preparing the stuffing was a labor of love because there was no preground meat. There was one kosher butcher shop located across the street from the Weisz family house. When my maternal grandmother wanted to cook stuffed cabbage, she first bought the meat from the butcher. There was no refrigeration, so everyone purchased precisely the amount needed. The shoichet (ritual kosher slaughterer) shected (slaughtered) the meat on Wednesday and/or Thursday and the butcher sold it on Wednesday through Friday. Everyone kashered (laborious process of kashering) the meat that they purchased at home within 72 hours of slaughter. After kashering, my grandmother prepared the meat for the stuffing, mincing it by hand using a knife.

Make the filling:

In a 12-inch sauté pan, over medium heat, heat the oil. Add the onions and sauté until soft and translucent but not brown. Add the meat and brown for a few minutes, stirring and breaking into small pieces with the fork or spatula. When the meat is browned, add the uncooked rice, the salt and pepper, and the mushrooms, if using. Stir to mix. Remove from heat. Reserve.

Stuff the peppers:

Cut the top with stem horizontally off the pepper and reserve. Remove core and seeds and discard. Divide the filling equally and stuff the peppers loosely. Top peppers with reserved caps.

Cook the peppers:

Layer the bottom of a large Dutch oven or 8-quart pot with half of the cabbage and half of the sauerkraut. Arrange peppers on the cabbage-kraut layer in a single layer. Cover peppers with remaining cabbage and sauerkraut.

Mix tomato sauce or juice with seasonings. Pour over peppers. Cover with a tight-fitting lid. Over high heat, bring to a boil. Decrease heat to low and simmer until cabbage and peppers are cooked through, about 2 hours.

Alternatively you can bake, covered, at 350°F for 3 hours. Serve peppers on a large platter, alternating colors.

Chulent

Ⓜ Makes 8 to 12 servings

Chulent is an Eastern European Jewish solution to the problem of how to prepare a hot meal on Shabbos. The laws of Shabbos prohibit cooking, but it is customary to eat a hot holiday meal. So the chulent is put in the oven before Shabbos and cooks unattended during the night. (You may also use a contemporary slow cooker.) Today, while hot plates provide simple solutions to warming food on Shabbos, chulent has survived at least four generations in our family, and remains one of my mother's signature recipes. Traditional Hungarian chulent does not use potatoes, but a Geknetinem Kugel (recipe follows) is optional. I first tasted chulent with potatoes at a friend's house when I was nine years old. I told my mother how much I liked it and she began to add potatoes in hers. This recipe includes both potatoes and Geknetinem Kugel; choose one or both.

3 pounds bone-in short ribs
(see Variation)
1½ cups dried beans: red kidney, baby lima, and pinto, rinsed and drained and ½ cup pearl barley
or
2 cups mixed dried beans of choice
2 medium onions, chopped
2 cloves garlic, minced
3 russet potatoes, cut into chunks, optional
2 teaspoons of salt, or to taste
½ teaspoon Seasoned Salt (page 66)
½ teaspoon sweet Hungarian paprika, or to taste
¼ teaspoon freshly ground pepper, or to taste
Geknetinem Kugel
(optional, recipe follows)
4 cups water

In a 6-quart slow cooker or Dutch oven, arrange one layer of half the meat, beans and barley, onions, garlic, and potatoes, if using. Sprinkle over half the seasonings. Repeat with remaining ingredients and seasonings.
Add *Geknetinem Kugel* in center of *Chulent* now, if using. Add the water.

If using a slow cooker, put on high and cook for at least 2 hours before Shabbos. After 2 hours of cooking on high, before Shabbos begins, turn to low and cook overnight.

If using a Dutch oven, cover tightly and bake at 350°F for about 1 hour. After 1 hour, before Shabbos begins, reduce heat to 225°F and cook overnight.

Serve at lunch the next day.

Geknetinem Kugel

 Makes 1

1 cup flour
½ teaspoon salt
¼ teaspoon pepper
¼ teaspoon sweet Hungarian paprika
½ cup vegetable oil
1 egg, beaten
1 onion grated
½ cup water

In a medium bowl whisk together flour and seasonings. Add oil, egg and onion and mix together. Then add the ½ cup of water using a large spoon or fork and mold into an oval or log shape. Place the kugel in the center of the *Chulent*.

Substitute chunks of fertiloff, Scottie roast or middle chuck for short ribs.

Place marrow or soup bones on the bottom of the pot to add richness of flavor.

Substitute a piece of kishke for the kugel.

Chulent

Margit Kirsche remembers: "At home, my mother prepared the Chulent on Friday in a large earthen pot with an earthen cover. We carried it to the bakery before Shabbos and paid (about 25 cents) for the use of the oven. Most of the Jewish families from our neighborhood took their Chulent to the bakery on Friday." There were about 70 pots of Chulent, each marked with the family name, that were placed into the preheated oven using a long-handled shovel. The oven floor was made of thick, heat-retaining clay that stayed hot through the night. "We picked it up on Shabbos before lunch", my mother says. "The Chulent pot had handles on both sides, and we children would carry it by holding it with a thick cloth. It was a five to 10-minute walk from the bakery to our home, and if we dropped it, well, there went our lunch."

Meatloaf with Beef or Veal

(M) Makes 4 to 6 servings

My mother first began making meatloaf when my brother and I were young children. She made it often because my brother loved it. This is not a recipe from "at home," but it is easy, tasty and appealing, and you can stretch the recipe to fit the number of guests.

For the meatloaf:

1 pound ground beef or veal
2 eggs
½ large onion, grated
½ cup dry breadcrumbs
¼ cup water
1 clove garlic, minced
¼ teaspoon Seasoned Salt (page 66)
Dash freshly ground black pepper
2 to 3 hard-boiled eggs, peeled, optional
¼ red bell pepper, thinly sliced lengthwise
1 small tomato, thinly sliced
2 to 3 russet potatoes, cut in large chunks
Oil as needed
Sweet Hungarian paprika, as needed
Pinch of salt

For the sauce:

8 ounces prepared tomato sauce
1 teaspoon sugar
½ teaspoon lemon juice
Dash freshly ground pepper
Dash salt
Dash garlic powder

Preheat oven to 350°F. In a medium bowl, mix together the ground beef or veal with the 2 eggs, onion, bread crumbs and water along with the garlic, Seasoned Salt and pepper.

Shape the mixture into a loaf and place it in a 9 by 13-inch pan. If using hard-boiled eggs, pat half the meat mixture into a loaf shape and lay 3 eggs vertically along the length. Top with the remainder of the meat mixture, sealing edges.

Top the loaf with sliced pepper and tomato. In a medium bowl, combine all sauce ingredients and stir to mix. Pour sauce over meatloaf. Add potatoes alongside, and drizzle with oil lightly and sprinkle lightly with salt and paprika. Cover and bake until potatoes and meat are cooked through, about 1 to 1¼ hours. Uncover and bake for an additional 15 minutes.

> If using a pan without a cover, spray aluminum foil with nonstick spray and cover pan, sprayed side down.
>
> Spray the bottom of a pan, just to cover with nonstick cooking spray and then sprinkle evenly with a thin layer of breadcrumbs to prevent loaf from sticking to the pan bottom.

Food, Family and Tradition

Omit tomato sauce entirely and bake meatloaf as directed.

To make meatballs, form 1-inch diameter meatballs from meatloaf mixture. Sauté in oil in a skillet until cooked through, or bake on a parchment paper-lined pan in a 350°F oven until cooked through.

Brisket

Ⓜ Makes up to 20 servings

This is an original recipe from my father, "Mr. Kirsche," as he was affectionately called by his customers. His brisket has been so well loved and so sought-after that through the years customers were constantly asking him for advice. Brisket is a great example of "no joy without meat and wine." While my father was meticulous about using a meat thermometer, he seasoned by instinct, and I encourage you to do the same. This recipe can be used also for any roast that you want to bake covered. If you want a tenderer roast, add ¼ cup wine before adding the seasonings.

1 whole brisket, 10 to 12 pounds
3 large carrots, cut in chunks
2 large onions, chopped
2 stalks celery, cut into 2-inch chunks
Sweet Hungarian paprika, to taste
Garlic powder, to taste
Freshly ground black pepper, to taste
2 bay leaves, optional
Water, as needed

Preheat the oven to 350°F. Lay the brisket in a roasting pan. Place the carrots, celery and onions around the roast. Season the brisket on all sides with paprika, garlic powder and pepper. Add bay leaves to the pan, if using. Pour a little water on the bottom of the pan.

Cover tightly and bake until the meat thermometer registers 180°F, and the meat is very tender, about 3 hours.

Rosh Hashana in Freising, 1946

"After the Holocaust, while I was living in Freising, Germany with my older brother, Morton, our apartment was a central gathering spot for the my brother's friends, all of whom were single and were now living alone," remembers Margit Kirsche. "There was no kosher meat available until a year after the War, when someone began shechting and selling kosher meat in Munich. There were about 10 young men who had been together during the Holocaust and the Death March, survivors as we all were with no family, and they all wanted to have kosher food for Rosh Hashana. So I traveled to Munich, about 30 kilometers (more than 18 miles) away to buy the meat, bring it home, and cook it in a soup and they all ate in our apartment."

Rib Eye Roast

(M) Makes 8 to 12 servings

This is my simple, easy way of preparing a rib or rib eye roast or any roast that can be roasted uncovered. I combined my father's use of a meat thermometer for timing, and my mother's addition of wine to tenderize and add flavor. Their roasts were always perfect. My recipe is foolproof; the only trick is buying the best possible cut of meat.

1 large onion, diced
1 (4- to 6-pound) rib eye roast
2 to 3 cloves garlic, minced
Seasoned Salt (page 66), to taste
Freshly ground black pepper, to taste
¼ cup wine

Preheat the oven to 350°F. Place half the onions in the bottom of a roasting pan, large enough to accommodate the roast. Season the bottom and sides of the roast generously with garlic, Seasoned Salt and pepper. Place the roast in the roasting pan. Pour the wine over the roast. Season the top of the roast. Put the rest of the onions on top and around the roast.

Roast uncovered 20 minutes per pound for medium-rare and 30 minutes per pound for well done. Use a meat thermometer to determine doneness: 140°F for medium-rare, 160°F for well done. Remember that it will continue cooking and reach a temperature of about 5° higher, even after removing from the oven. Let rest for 20 minutes before carving.

When grilling a roast, grill on high (direct heat for charcoal grill) for a few minutes on each side. This will seal in the juices. Then turn the temperature to medium-low (indirect heat for charcoal grill, charcoal arranged around not directly under roast) and baste often. Test for doneness with a meat thermometer. For any beef roast that can be roasted uncovered, estimate 20 minutes per pound for medium rare or 30 minutes per pound for well done. To be sure, always check with a meat thermometer.

Rib or Rib Eye Roasts:
Several methods exist for timing and temperature. Some recipes oven-roast at 350°F the entire time. Some indicate that if you want to seal in the juices roast at 500°F for 10 to 15 minutes and then decrease and roast at 300°F to 350°F. Some roast at 300°F to 350°F and then roast at 500°F for the last 10 minutes to brown the exterior.

Preparation of Roasts

Throughout the years many of our customers at Hungarian Kosher Foods have commented on how fresh and appealing the meats look in our fresh meat case, and how perfectly cooked and delicious the prepared meats from the deli case are to eat. They then often admit that they actually have no idea how to prepare the various cuts of meat.

Using a Meat Thermometer

In preparing meat, my father, Sandor Kirsche, always used an instant-read meat thermometer to test for doneness. I use a meat thermometer just as he did. While my father resisted using measuring cups, an expression of his more creative, and natural cooking style, he insisted on using a meat thermometer, a reflection of his discipline and precision. In contrast to my father's way of cooking meat, my mother never baked a roast uncovered at home. She always roasted it covered, or braised it covered on the range top. It was always melt-in-your-mouth soft and delicious.

This paradox between creativity and precision encapsulates the challenge that I tackled in formally formatting recipes that originated in instinctive, intuitive (rather than by-the-book) cooking.

Tips, Times and Temperatures For Roasts

When roasting or grilling use a meat thermometer, and follow the USDA temperature guide. Roasts will continue to cook after removing from oven, about an additional 5° to 10°; be aware of this and remove the roast to correspond to the desired degree of doneness. All roasts should rest after cooking is complete about 15 to 20 minutes before slicing.

Boiled Tongue

(M) Makes 8 servings

My cousin Ibi says, "My father, Leib Weinberger, gave me this recipe from his home in Czechoslovakia. He taught my mom how to make it. We made our own mayonnaise at home, as there was no mayonnaise to purchase. Tongue was very expensive and hard to obtain, so we cooked and served this for a special occasion such as a birthday or holiday. I often serve this as an appetizer."

For the tongue:
2 cloves garlic
3 bay leaves
4 whole black peppercorns
Pinch salt
1 beef tongue or 2 veal tongues

For the sauce:
½ cup light or regular mayonnaise
1 clove garlic, crushed

Chopped fresh dill, as needed,
for garnish
Fresh parsley sprigs, for garnish

Fill an 8-quart pot half full with water. Add all seasonings. Bring to a boil over high heat. Place tongue in the boiling water. Decrease heat to low, simmer, loosely covered, until tongue is tender when pierced with a fork, about 1½ to 2 hours for beef and 45 minutes to 1 hour for veal.

Meanwhile, in a small bowl, combine mayonnaise and garlic. Mix and refrigerate, covered.

Carefully remove tongue from water using tongs to lift and a large spatula to support. Place on a large plate to cool.

When cool enough to handle, make one or more slits in the skin at the large end of the tongue and peel off the skin in strips. It should come off easily. Discard skin. Trim fat and gristle at end and discard.

Slice diagonally ¼-inch thick and arrange slices on a platter. Spread sauce thinly over the tongue slices. Sprinkle lightly with dill and garnish platter with fresh parsley. Refrigerate covered. Serve cold or at room temperature.

Pickled Tongue and Roasted Tongue

In my parents' time, my grandmothers used to pickle tongues at home. Now we can buy already pickled tongues, ready to simmer in water, covered, until tender, about 1½ to 2 hours. It is good served hot or cold. And it makes a nice sandwich sliced on rye.

To intensify the flavor of tongue, prepare Boiled Tongue (page 174). Preheat oven to 350°F. Lay cooked, peeled tongue in a roasting pan. Brush lightly with vegetable oil. Rub surface with 1 clove minced garlic. Surround with chopped onions and mushrooms, to taste. Roast until tongue is nicely browned, about 30 minutes. Slice and serve as desired.

A Traditional Delicacy

Living in the Soviet Union after the Holocaust, the Jews in Munkács, as in some other communities under the oppressive Communist regime, remained firm in their religious observance. As my cousin, Irving Weinberger, tells it, his father was a cattle buyer for the Soviet Union, and had access to cattle. However, it was illegal to shecht (slaughter) kosher meat. Consequently, in order to obtain kosher meat, a few families would save up enough money to buy a cow and then the shoichet (ritual kosher slaughterer) would come to their back yard to shecht it, and the families would divide the meat. His father would sell the non-kosher cuts to butcher shops. Irving remembers putting the cuts of meat in his bicycle basket and delivering it to other Jewish families in the town. There was, of course, only one tongue per animal. We can understand their appreciation of tongue as a delicacy, difficult to obtain.

Sweet and Sour Tongue

Ⓜ Makes 8 to 10 servings

Sweet and Sour tongue is a delicacy that I associate with Purim, a festival that celebrates the victory of the Jewish people over Haman's decrees. (Haman, vizier to the Fifth-century B.C.E. Persian king Achashverush, wanted to annihilate the Jewish people.) You may follow the recipe using beef tongue as my mother's family did in Hungary. As an alternative, my mother enjoys veal tongue, now readily available, and it makes smaller slices for an attractive appetizer.

For the tongue:
½ teaspoon salt
⅛ teaspoon freshly ground black pepper
1 beef or 2 veal tongues

For the sauce:
1 tablespoon vegetable oil
1 medium onion, diced
4 mushrooms thinly sliced
1 cup prepared tomato sauce
¼ cup water
1 tablespoon lemon juice
½ tablespoon sugar
⅛ teaspoon freshly ground pepper, or to taste

Fill an 8-quart pot half full with water. Add salt and pepper. Bring to a boil over high heat. Place tongue in the boiling water. Decrease heat to low and, simmer, loosely covered, until tongue is tender when pierced with a fork, about 1½ to 2 hours for beef tongue and 45 minutes to 1 hour for veal. Carefully remove tongue from water using tongs to lift and a large spatula to support. Place on a large plate to cool.

Meanwhile, over medium heat, heat oil in a 12-inch sauté pan. Add onions and mushrooms and sauté, stirring, until onions are soft and translucent, about 10 minutes. Add tomato sauce, water, lemon juice, sugar and pepper. Stir to mix. Simmer on low.

When tongue is cool enough to handle, make 1 or more slits in the skin at the large end of the tongue and peel off the skin in strips. It should come off easily. Discard skin. Trim any fat or gristle from end and discard.

Slice diagonally ¼-inch thick. Add sliced tongue to the tomato-onion mixture. Bring to a boil, reduce heat and cover and simmer for 10 minutes.

Serve slices as desired on small plates drizzled with sauce for an appetizer. For an entrée, serve in a covered casserole.

Veal Breast

Ⓜ Makes 8 to 10 servings

Veal Breast can be made with or without "a pocket." To stuff the veal breast, ask the butcher to "make a pocket," then stuff with one-half the Bread Stuffing recipe (page 232). The circular stuffing in the center of each slice looks beautiful and makes the veal very moist and flavorful. You can also stuff it with Veal Meatloaf (page 168), or the filling for Stuffed Cabbage (page 162), or with any vegetable or fruit stuffing, or even mashed potatoes. I use wine to tenderize the meat and add flavor.

1 (4- to 5-pound) veal breast
½ recipe Bread Stuffing (page 232), optional
1 large onion, chopped
3 to 4 cloves garlic, minced
1 tablespoon sweet Hungarian paprika, or to taste
½ teaspoon freshly ground black pepper, or to taste
¼ cup wine
2 teaspoons Seasoned Salt (page 66) or to taste

> For any veal roasted covered, estimate 1 hour for the first pound or less and then an additional half hour for each pound. Test for doneness with a meat thermometer. The internal temperature must read at least 165°F.

Preheat oven to 350°F. If you are stuffing the veal breast, stuff it now, by spooning the stuffing into the pocket and mounding it more in the center. Either close the pocket opening with toothpicks or leave as is.

Place half of the onions and garlic on the bottom of a large roasting pan. Season the bottom of the veal breast (the side with the bones and not the meat) with paprika, Seasoned Salt and pepper. Lay the veal breast (stuffed or unstuffed) on top of the onions and garlic, meat side up.

Pour the wine over the veal. Then season with the remaining paprika, Seasoned Salt and pepper. Sprinkle the remainder of the onions and garlic on top.

Cover tightly with a lid or with foil and bake for about 3 hours. Baste every 20 to 30 minutes. Uncover the last 20 minutes for a brown crispy top. Remember, veal must be soft; do not make it rare, or it will be tough. Using a meat thermometer, we usually test for 165°F to 170°F.

Serve sliced on a platter garnished with orange slices, or accompanied by a fruit compote.

Veal *Paprikás*

Ⓜ Makes 6 to 8 servings

In Munkács under the communist regime during the 1950s to 1970s, my cousin Ibi tells me that the Jewish families were able to obtain kosher veal so infrequently that it was reserved for the Jewish holidays. One of the most memorable meals that my aunt, Goldie Weinberger, prepared was this recipe. Today, her daughter Ibi still prepares it the same way and it remains a family tradition for the Jewish holiday. Served over a plate of mashed potatoes or wide noodles, it is beautiful and tasty.

2 tablespoons oil
2 medium onions, chopped
2 pounds boneless veal stew meat,
cut into 1½ to 2-inch chunks
1 tablespoon sweet Hungarian paprika
¼ teaspoon freshly ground pepper
1 bay leaf
1 clove garlic, minced
1½ to 2 cups water
1 recipe Mashed Potatoes (page 207)
or
1 pound wide egg noodles, cooked

In a 6-quart Dutch oven or heavy pot over medium heat, heat oil. Add the onions and sauté over medium heat until soft, about 5 minutes. Add the veal and continue to sauté over medium heat until the veal is browned on all sides, stirring occasionally, about 15 minutes. Add the seasonings and mix.

Add 1½ to 2 cups of water. Bring to a boil over high heat. Decrease heat to low, simmer, half covered for about 1½ hours. As the veal becomes tender, near the end, uncover to reduce the liquid and cook for about 20 minutes longer, making sure the veal is tender. Remove bay leaf and discard.

Serve ladled over mashed potatoes or cooked noodles on a large platter.

Veal Schnitzel

M Makes 4 servings

Veal Schnitzel is a traditional Eastern European delicacy. Because kosher veal was rarely available in Vásárosnámeny before the War, my mother learned to cook veal in the States. The tricks to this recipe are: first, cover the veal to seal in juices, and second, uncover it for the last 15 minutes to make it crispy.

1 cup flour
1 teaspoon Seasoned Salt (page 66)
¼ teaspoon freshly ground pepper
¼ teaspoon garlic powder
1 to 1½ cups dry breadcrumbs
¼ teaspoon sweet Hungarian paprika
2 eggs, beaten, mixed with 1 tablespoon of water
Vegetable oil, as needed for frying
4 veal chops, preferably bone-in rib chops

Preheat oven to 350°F. In a shallow bowl mix together the flour with the Seasoned Salt, pepper, and garlic.

In second shallow bowl, place the egg-water mixture. In a third shallow bowl, mix together the crumbs, with paprika. Dip each veal chop on both sides in the flour then the egg, and then the crumbs to coat. Place chops on parchment paper-lined tray.

In a 12-inch skillet over medium-high heat, heat enough oil to the depth of ¼ inch. Fry chops until crispy on both sides, turning once.

Transfer chops to a large shallow roasting pan. Bake, in a single layer, covered, at 350°F for about 1 hour. Then uncover for 15 minutes if you like the veal chops to be crispy.

For a complete meal cut 2 russet potatoes into large chunks and place around edge of roasting pan, not touching chops. Drizzle potatoes with a little vegetable oil and sprinkle lightly with salt, pepper and paprika. Bake with chops.

To make breadcrumbs:
Dry leftover challah or rolls on a plate a room temperature or in a brown paper bag. When dry, grate by hand or in a food processor. Store, covered, and freeze for longer storage.

181

Chapter 7
Vegetables and Salads

Vegetables:
Candied Carrots
Cabbage with Noodles, *Káposztás Tészta*
Cauliflower with Bread Crumbs
Fried Cauliflower
Sautéed Vegetables, *Lecsó*
Sautéed Mushrooms with Onions
Roasted Vegetable Medley
Pineapple-Orange Sweet Potatoes
Tzimmes

Salads:
Beet Salad
Beets with Horseradish, *Chrain*
Chick Peas, *Zucher Bundlach*
Cucumber Salad, *Ugorkasaláta*
Israeli Salad
Pickled Vegetables

"Know that every single blade of grass has a unique song of its own — and from the songs of all the blades of grass together we will make a melody"
(Naomi Shemer adapted from the words of Rabbi Nachman MiBreslav)

Just as every blade of grass has a unique song of its own, every vegetable has a unique flavor and taste. Cooked together in combinations traditional to the Hungarian-Czechoslovakian region where my parents were raised created the unique style, the melody, of the traditional vegetable dishes in this chapter.

When my parents were children, vegetables were either home grown or grown on local farms and were bursting with flavor. The climate (cold in winter and warm in summer) favored hardy vegetables: carrots, potatoes, squash, and beets, as well as cauliflower and beans. Fresh vegetables were served in season, and the surplus canned or pickled or stored in the root cellar for the winter. Home canning and pickling vegetables, today a gourmet cook's pastime, were at that time a necessity.

My mother remembers canning including homemade tomato sauce and storing it in the cellar.

She says that her grandparents had "just a few stalks of corn" growing in their yard, just enough so their family would have corn during the season. While they lived modestly in other ways, they had the luxury of fresh-picked produce, from stem to stewpot. In the States today we import fruits and vegetables from all over the world at all seasons, but what we gain in variety we often lose in ripeness, freshness and flavor.

Today, when I recreate these recipes in my home kitchen I don't have the luxury of picking vegetables from my own backyard; however, I still have their unique recipes and traditions.

Candied Carrots

Ⓟ Makes 4 to 6 servings

Candied Carrots, traditionally served on Rosh Hashana, the Jewish New Year, when we pray for a "sweet year" has been a family favorite for generations. It can be a side dish for meat or poultry and also a dessert. My mother says her mother cooked it on Rosh Hashana and also for dessert on Friday, Shabbos, dinner. Her father, Samuel Weisz, explained his soft spot for the dish by saying "carrots are very healthy." Just as my mother remembers it as one of her father's favorites, I remember it as one of my father's favorites. Candied Carrots appealed to my father in so many ways: he loved to snack on vegetables and fruits and he loved sweets.

1 tablespoon oil
1 pound carrots, peeled and thinly sliced horizontally
½ cup sugar
2 teaspoons flour
1 cup water
Pinch salt

Place oil in a 2-quart saucepan. Add the carrots and the sugar. Cover and cook on very low heat, stirring frequently, until the liquid reduces, approximately 1 hour. Meanwhile, in a small separate bowl, stir flour into ¼ cup of the water, mixing until smooth. Add the remaining water, stirring to mix. Add flour-water mixture slowly to cooked carrots, stirring; add salt. Increase heat and bring to a boil. Decrease heat to low, stirring gently so as not to break carrots, and cook until sauce thickens. Remove from heat. Serve warm or at room temperature.

A Blessing
My father's father was a Spinka Chassid (a follower of the Spinka Rebbe, from the town of Spinka near the Hungarian border). My father remembered once when his father went on Rosh Hashana or Yom Kippur to pray with the Chassidic Rabbi, following the Chassidic custom. When my father was eight, his father took him to the Spinka Rebbe for a blessing. Throughout his life my father always believed in the power of a blessing and felt deeply that one reason he survived the Holocaust was just because of that blessing.

Cabbage with Noodles, *Kápozstás Tészta*

Ⓟ Makes 4 to 6 main dish servings

This dish is authentically Hungarian. Because of the climate, cabbage grew most of the year, making it readily available. This recipe is simple to prepare and yet flavorful and satisfying. It's the perfect dish to serve during the "Nine Days" when only dairy is eaten during this time. My parents ate it "at home" as an entrée, often with soup as a starter. Served on a platter or in a shallow bowl it makes a beautiful side dish with beef, poultry and even fish.

2 to 3 tablespoons oil, or as needed to film bottom of pot
1 large head cabbage, cored, coarsely chopped or shredded
1 medium onion, diced
1 teaspoon salt
12 ounces bow tie or broad noodles, cooked and drained

Serve cabbage without noodles for a less caloric dish.

In a 6- to 8-quart pot over medium heat, heat oil. Add cabbage, onion and salt in batches, stirring as cabbage wilts. Decrease heat to very low and cook, covered, stirring occasionally to prevent bottom from burning, until cabbage is soft, about 1 to 1½ hours.

To serve, place noodles in a large bowl, add cabbage and toss to mix. Alternatively, add noodles to pot with cooked cabbage, toss to mix and serve.

Cauliflower with Bread Crumbs

(P) Makes 4 to 6 servings

Cauliflower is a favorite in Hungary and this is an authentic Eastern European recipe for its preparation. The golden breadcrumbs that lightly coat the cauliflower florets and add flavor and texture are used in several recipes: Hungarian Shlishkes (page 211–212), Kreplach (page 112), and other dishes. It is quick and easy to prepare. If the cauliflower head is large use the larger amounts of margarine and breadcrumbs; if medium sized, the smaller amounts.

1 large head of cauliflower,
cut into florets
Water, as needed
1 teaspoon salt
3 to 4 tablespoons margarine
1½ to 2 cups dry breadcrumbs,
preferably homemade from challah,
(page 181)
1 teaspoon Seasoned Salt (page 66)

For a dairy dish, substitute butter for margarine.
For added flavor add 1 teaspoon powdered parve chicken-flavor soup base to cooking water.

In a 6-quart pot place cauliflower florets. Add water to cover and salt. Bring to a boil, cover and cook until soft and tender, about 15 to 20 minutes.

Meanwhile, in a 12-inch sauté pan over medium heat, place margarine and melt. Decrease heat. Add breadcrumbs and Seasoned Salt and fry, stirring, until lightly browned, about 5 to 7 minutes. Remove from heat and reserve.

Drain cauliflower and chop into bite-size pieces. Toss in sauté pan with breadcrumbs to coat and cook until hot, about 2 minutes.

Serve hot, at room temperature, or refrigerate, covered, and reheat.

186

Fried Cauliflower

P   Makes 8 servings

This is crispy and best prepared in a deep fryer. For a lighter, healthier choice, oven-bake it on a cookie sheet.

Oil, as needed, for deep frying
1 cup breadcrumbs, preferably from challah (pages 224, 226)
or
1 cup cornflake crumbs
¼ teaspoon salt
¼ teaspoon Sweet Hungarian paprika
⅛ teaspoon freshly ground black pepper
1 cup flour
2 eggs, beaten
1 large head cauliflower, separated into florets

> For extra crispness, before baking, first drizzle about 2 tablespoons of vegetable oil evenly over the florets.

If frying, pre-heat the oil to 350°F in a deep fryer or deep pot. Season breadcrumbs or cornflake crumbs with the salt, paprika and pepper. In three separate shallow dishes place flour, eggs and crumbs.

Dip the cauliflower florets first in the flour, next eggs, and then the breadcrumbs.
Fry in batches in the deep fryer, drain on paper towels.

Alternatively, preheat oven to 400°F. Place breaded cauliflower florets on a parchment paper-lined baking sheet sprayed with nonstick cooking spray, and bake until crisp and browned, about 20 minutes, turning pan once in oven.

The Limits of Expediency

The Arrow Cross, Nyilas Party, rose to power in Hungary in the early 1940s, defeating the government of Miklos Horthy, then prime minister of Hungary. Although the Hungarian government had imposed anti-semitic restrictions on the Jews, such as "numerus clausus", Horthy would not submit to Hitler and would not allow the Jews to be deported. However, in the spring of 1944, Hitler defeated Horthy and in a few months, Hitler quickly "cleaned out" most of Hungarian Jewry, sending the majority to the Death Camps. After the War, one of Horthy's bodyguards lived in Freising, Germany with his family. His daughter was a flower girl at my parents' wedding.

Sautéed Vegetables, *Lecsó*

P Makes 4 to 6 side dish servings, or 8 appetizer servings

Every culinary culture has its twist on mixed, braised seasonal vegetables. The French have ratatouille, the Italians have caponata, and the Hungarians have Lecsó. Sweet peppers are central to Hungarian cooking, and they are a main ingredient in Lecsó, which my mother often prepared. It can be served as an appetizer on toast, as a side dish to accompany meats, poultry or fish and, with scrambled eggs as an entrée. Use three or more colors of sweet peppers for variety.

2 tablespoons vegetable oil
2 medium onions, chopped small
3 bell peppers (red, green, yellow or orange), chopped small
Pinch salt
2 medium tomatoes, chopped

In a 12-inch stainless steel sauté pan over medium heat, heat oil. Add onions and peppers. Season with salt to taste and sauté, stirring, until vegetables crisp-tender, about 15 minutes. Add tomatoes and sauté, stirring, until vegetables are soft and translucent but not browned, about 20 to 30 minutes.

Serve as a side dish, or on top of toast as an appetizer.

My mother often adds 4 chopped mushrooms to the mixture. For a main dish: Beat 2 eggs well, place in preheated oiled skillet. Add ¼ cup of *Lecsó*, and cook, stirring constantly, until eggs are cooked through. Makes 1 serving.

Ibi's *Lecsó*: Ibi's *lecsó* is a bit crispier because of her special technique. Ibi says, "The secret to my *lecsó* is to sauté the vegetables separately, not together. Sauté the peppers in one pan and the onions separately in another pan. Then drain the peppers and the onions of excess cooking liquid. Add the tomatoes to the onions when they are almost ready, sauté for a few minutes and then mix it all together. The *lecsó* will retain the flavors and be crispy but tender."

Sautéed Mushrooms with Onions

(P) Makes 1 to 1½ cups

Many of our recipes call for sautéed mushrooms and onions—simple and basic, yet this combination enhances many dishes. Add it to rice, or as a topping for hummus or Bean Dip (page 98). My mother makes this into an open-face sandwich. You can sauté the onions and mushrooms in advance and refrigerate, covered.

2 to 3 tablespoons vegetable oil
1 extra large onion, about 1 pound, peeled and diced
8 ounces mushrooms, sliced

In a heavy 12–inch sauté pan over medium heat, heat oil. Add the onions and sauté on medium for about 10 minutes, stirring so that the onions do not burn. Add the mushrooms and continue to sauté until golden, about 10 more minutes, stirring often.

To serve, use to top cooked rice or mix with cooked rice. Top burgers or grilled chicken. Cool to room temperature and use as a topping for hummus, Bean Dip, or top toasted bread for an open-face sandwich.

Roasted Vegetable Medley

P Makes 8 servings

Our family often makes chicken or meat dishes in the oven surrounded by vegetables. We also love to make potatoes roasted in the oven. Through the years, we have developed this dish using those vegetables plentiful in Eastern Europe. It can easily be varied to any vegetables you have available. The onions and garlic add a wonderful, rich flavor. Roasted vegetables are soft on the inside but golden brown on the outside. You just need a hint of salt.

1 large or 2 medium carrots, cut into 1½ inch chunks

1 beet, cut into 1½ inch chunks

1 extra large onion, cut into 1½ inch wedges

1 celery root, cut into 1½ inch chunks

1 turnip, cut into 1½ inch chunks

1 kohlrabi, 1½ inch chunks

1 sweet potato, cut into 1½ inch chunks

2 small shallots, peeled and sliced

2 cloves garlic, peeled and sliced

3 tablespoons olive oil

½ teaspoon kosher salt, or to taste

⅛ teaspoon freshly ground black pepper, or to taste

Preheat oven to 375°F. In a 9 by 13-inch or similar shallow roasting pan, place carrots and beets and cover with foil and bake for 15 minutes.

After 15 minutes, add remaining vegetables to pan with carrots and beets, drizzle with the oil and sprinkle with the salt and pepper. Toss the vegetables to coat with the oil and seasonings.

Bake, covered, for 30 minutes, stirring once or twice. Halfway through the baking, taste and adjust seasoning, adding more if needed.

Uncover, stir and continue to bake for another 45 to 60 minutes, stirring every 10 to 15 minutes. The vegetables will become golden and crispy on the outside and softer on the inside. Test for doneness by piercing with a fork; the vegetables should still be firm, not falling apart.

Hyman Kane, a Survivor, born in Novydwor, Poland, was imprisoned in Bergen Belsen Concentration camp during the Holocaust. After the War he came to live in Minneapolis. Years later, visiting his son in Chicago for Succos, he went shopping at Hungarian Kosher Foods. He suddenly saw a man in one of the aisles and starting screaming: "Shloimie!" The man began screaming: "Hymie!" They had been in Bergen Belsen together but had not seen each other for 50 years, since the end of the War.

Pineapple-Orange Sweet Potatoes

Ⓟ Makes 8 to 12 servings

There seem to be as many recipes for sweet potato casseroles as there are families to eat them. They are traditional in the States for Thanksgiving dinner, and most recipes tend to be overly sweet for my taste. My mother preferred plain baked sweet potatoes. However, because my father liked things sweet, she sometimes peeled and boiled the potatoes in a light pineapple-orange sauce, using her cook-to-taste technique. I took this childhood memory and developed the recipe that follows.

3½ pounds sweet potatoes, peeled and cut into 2-inch chunks
1½ cups canned crushed pineapple or pineapple tidbits with juice
¾ cup brown sugar
½ cup orange juice
1 teaspoon cinnamon

Preheat oven to 350°F. Place sweet potatoes in a lightly sprayed 9 by 13-inch pan. Cover with foil and bake for 30 minutes.

Meanwhile place pineapple and juice, brown sugar, orange juice and cinnamon in a small saucepan over medium heat and heat, stirring, until sugar dissolves. Remove from heat. Reserve.

After 30 minutes, uncover baking pan and pour sauce over potatoes evenly. Continue baking, uncovered, until potatoes are soft but not mushy, 30 to 40 minutes.

Tzimmes

P Makes 20 servings

Tzimmes is a traditional side dish of carrots, sweet potatoes and dried fruits served on Rosh Hashana (for a sweet New Year), Succos, and Pesach. Prunes are essential to the dish and my father loved prunes, which reminded him of home. The longer tzimmes is baked and stirred, the deeper and richer the flavors. Tzimmes is sometimes served on Shabbos; however, it's a special dish most often reserved for the holidays. When we say "Don't make a tzimmes," it means "don't make a big deal out of it." My father added short ribs to tzimmes; however, many people today prefer the vegetarian version which follows.

2 cups pineapple juice
3 pounds carrots, cut into ½-inch slices
3 pounds peeled sweet potatoes, cut into 1-inch chunks
2 cups mixed dried pitted prunes and apricots
1 cup sugar
¼ cup honey
1 teaspoon cinnamon

In a 6-quart Dutch oven place pineapple juice and carrots and add water just to cover. Bring to a boil over medium heat. Decrease heat to low, cover, and simmer until carrots are tender, about 30 to 45 minutes.

Meanwhile, preheat oven to 350°F. Add remaining ingredients to Dutch oven and mix well. Uncover and bake for at least 2 hours, stirring to mix every 15 to 20 minutes.

Serve as a side with brisket or poultry.

"Preparing Passover with Mr. Kirsche"
For over 20 years Caryn Bean, who started at Hungarian Kosher Foods as a teenager, worked with my father. In 1992 she remembers her first "Pesach experience" and preparation for Seder. According to Caryn's memory, the first Seder was on Sunday evening. My father, his family, and some staff were working through the night to prepare the thousands of dinner orders (some orders numbering in the hundreds). Caryn remembers looking around in the middle of the night after most everyone had gone home, and wondering how everything was going to get cooked, assembled and packed, when my father said to her, "You go home, and get some rest!" She went home for an hour and when she came back, she remembers, "Mr. Kirsche, then 66 years old, was still working. He worried about others, but always had the energy to keep going. He worked, through the night, non-stop, until we closed on Sunday. All the orders were filled and all the customers could celebrate Pesach."

Beet Salad

Ⓟ Makes about 7 cups, serves 14

Beets are a traditional Eastern European vegetable used in Borscht (page 86), Chrain (page 195) and many other dishes. The flavor is best made with fresh beets, but beets stain (they were used as a dye in ancient times), so use gloves to peel the beets and an apron to protect your clothing. This salad makes a bright, piquant side dish that keeps well refrigerated. Made in advance, the beets sit in the marinade, and become more flavorful. Use only enough water to cover when cooking because it becomes the base of your marinade, a concentrated flavor.

3 pounds fresh beets, peeled
Water just to cover
1 teaspoon salt
¾ cup white vinegar
¾ cup sugar
1 large red onion, quartered lengthwise
and thinly sliced horizontally

> Substitute 2 (15-ounce) cans good quality sliced beets for fresh beets. Drain, reserving juice. Pour juice into 4-quart pot with the vinegar and sugar and bring to a boil. Add beets and onions, bring to a boil, cook for 2 minutes. Turn off heat and proceed with recipe.

If beet sizes range from small to very large, cut large beets in half. Place beets in a 6-quart pot and add water just to cover. (The water will be needed for the marinade.) Add salt, cover, and bring to a boil over high heat. Decrease heat to low, and simmer until the beets are tender, about 1 hour. Test for doneness by piercing with a fork; the beets should be soft but firm.

Remove the beets from the water with a slotted spoon. Reserve the cooking water. Quarter beets lengthwise and then slice horizontally about ¼-inch thick. Reserve.

In a separate 4-quart pot, pour 1½ to 2 cups of the reserved beet cooking water. Add the vinegar and the sugar. Bring to a boil. Add the sliced onions and the beets. Bring to a boil once more, and cook for about two minutes. Then turn off the heat and let rest for 30 minutes. Transfer to a large nonreactive container. Cool to room temperature. Cover and refrigerate overnight. Keeps, refrigerated, for one week.

To serve, place in a large bowl and pass as an accompaniment to meat or poultry.

Food, Family and Tradition

Beets with Horseradish, *Chrain*

P Makes 5 to 6 cups

My father, Sandor Kirsche, developed his recipe for Chrain which his mother made when he was a child in Hluboka, and he made it as he made everything—"to taste." Without a written recipe, I made this "to taste" exactly as I remember the Chrain my father made. Fresh Chrain seems like a lot of work, as the horseradish root is very hard and difficult to work with. However with the use of a food processor, this recipe is really quite simple and the taste of the fresh beets mixed with the fresh horseradish is definitely worth the effort. Use disposable gloves when working with beets as the beets easily stain. When grating the beets, you can grate fine or coarser. I like to mix textures, so I grate both fine and coarse. While Chrain is traditionally served with Gefilte Fish (page 78), my father loved to eat Chrain as a side dish with Falcse Fish (page 139), as well as fish, beef or poultry.

1 teaspoon salt
3 pounds fresh beets, peeled
½ of a fresh horseradish root,
peeled, finely grated
¼ cup sugar
¼ cup vinegar

Fill an 8-quart pot with water halfway. Add salt, and bring to a boil over high heat. If beets are not the same size, cut the large beets in half. Add the beets, and bring to a boil. Decrease heat to low, and simmer, covered until the beets are soft and tender but not mushy, about 1 hour. Do not overcook. Test for doneness by piercing with a fork; the beets should be soft but firm. Drain well. Reserve beets.

Meanwhile, peel the horseradish using a vegetable peeler. The horseradish root is very hard. You can either grate it by hand on the second finest side of a four-sided grater, which is very difficult. Or you can also use the food processor. Using a sharp knife cut the horseradish into 1-inch chunks and then process with the metal blade until finely grated. Measure out ½ cup and reserve. Store remainder covered, refrigerated.

Grate the beets on the second finest side of a four-sided grater for the traditional fine-textured *Chrain*. Or grate half of the beets on the second finest side and half on the medium side for a relish with varied texture. Transfer the grated beets and ½ cup grated horseradish to a medium bowl.

In a small separate bowl, mix together the sugar and vinegar. Add the mixture to the horseradish-beet mixture in the medium bowl. Stir to mix. Let sit for at least one hour before adjusting seasoning. I usually let it sit overnight in the refrigerator so the beets absorb the flavors. Taste and adjust seasoning by adding more salt, sugar, vinegar or horseradish as desired. Refrigerate covered for two weeks.

Chickpeas, *Zucher Bundlach*

(P) Makes a snack for a crowd

The first Friday night after a baby boy is born we welcome him with a Shalom Zachor, a festive meal, and wish him well before his Bris Milah. Traditionally, men (today women also) stop in after dinner and drink l'chaim, wish the family mazel tov, and partake of a light meal or snack which always includes beans or zucher bundlach. Chickpeas are round, symbolizing the cycle of life and the cycle of the soul. This recipe is easy to prepare and tasty enough to serve as a healthy snack on any occasion, festive or informal.

1 pound dried chickpeas, rinsed
and drained
1 teaspoon salt
Freshly ground pepper, to taste

Place chickpeas in a 3-quart pot with water to cover by 2 inches. Add salt and bring to a boil. Lower heat and cover loosely. Simmer until chickpeas are soft and tender but not mushy, and skins have begun to separate from the peas, about 1 hour and 15 minutes.

Drain and spread chickpeas on a clean towel, sprinkle with fresh ground pepper, cover with another towel. Let cool to room temperature.

To serve, transfer to a large bowl and serve as a snack, or in salads, or as a garnish.

The Bris of Yesteryear

Today a Bris is celebrated as a festive event in all Jewish families. In my parents' generation you did not "invite" anyone to a Bris, because it was considered to be such a great mitzvah that one could not refuse to come. A Bris is the ceremony that identifies a baby boy as a member of the Jewish nation. So rather than invite, you simply announced when the Bris would take place, and family and friends in the small community would naturally come. My father believed strongly that one should not miss a Bris or a wedding ceremony because "It is the future of our people." In December of 1978 my brother became the father of a baby boy, my father's first grandson. However, my father's cousin in Israel was getting married. My father flew to Israel and came back within 24 hours so he could attend the wedding and be home for his grandson's Bris.

Cucumber Salad, *Ugorkasaláta*

P Makes about 1 quart, 8 servings

Cucumbers were readily available in Hungary and Czechoslovakia from spring through summer, making Ugorkasaláta a classic salad during this season, light and refreshing, perfect for a summer meal. My husband, Irv, likes to serve it as an accompaniment to grilled steak; it balances the richness of the beef. The vinegar and the salt are preservatives, allowing the salad to keep, refrigerated, for a week. Of course, as my mother says, "'At home' we never worried about the refrigeration, because it never lasted too long — it was all eaten up quickly." It is best prepared in advance, so the cucumbers have a slightly pickled flavor.

2 large seedless cucumbers
(about 1½ pounds), skin on,
sliced paper thin
1 medium onion, sliced paper thin
1 heaping tablespoon salt
⅓ cup water
⅓ cup sugar
⅓ cup white vinegar

Place the cucumbers and the onions in a medium bowl and toss with the salt. Let stand for 1 hour. Transfer to a colander and drain. Lay plastic wrap on top and press down to extract the maximum liquid. Transfer drained cucumber-onion mixture to a non-reactive bowl. Reserve.

In a small bowl, place water, sugar and vinegar, and whisk to dissolve sugar. Pour this marinade over the cucumbers and onions. Cover and refrigerate, for up to 1 week.

> Peel cucumbers if you prefer, and add 1 tablespoon of chopped fresh dill and chop. Before serving, sprinkle lightly with paprika.

Israeli Salad

(P) Makes about 3 pounds, 10 servings

In 1963, on our first family trip to Israel, lettuce was not readily available. The traditional salad in Israel was made of the vegetables that were most readily available: cucumbers and tomatoes. This salad always tastes best fresh and in season. Authentic Israeli Salad uses vegetables that are finely diced, about ½-inch or smaller. The dressing is light and meant to enhance the flavors of the fresh vegetables. To prepare in advance, first dice the vegetables and refrigerate, then add the dressing just before serving so the vegetables will stay crisp.

For the salad:

3 large firm, red ripe tomatoes,
(about 1½ pounds) cut in ½-inch dice or smaller
2 seedless cucumbers, peeled or peel-on (about
1½ pounds), cut in ½-inch dice or smaller

Optional:

1 green or red or orange pepper,
or mixed, cut in ½-inch dice or smaller
(about 1 cup)
¼ cup finely diced onion or scallion
1 to 2 sour pickles, finely diced
(about ½ cup)
1 clove finely minced fresh garlic

For the dressing:

¼ cup olive oil
2 tablespoons lemon juice
1½ teaspoons salt, or to taste
¼ teaspoon freshly ground black pepper,
or to taste

Transfer vegetables to a large nonreactive bowl. In a separate small bowl, mix the dressing ingredients. Pour over vegetables and toss to mix. Adjust seasonings to taste.

Searching for Home

After the Holocaust, my father, as many Survivors, struggled with his emotions. It was strange, he thought, where did one come from? Where would one go? He was 19 years old with no parents, no grandparents, almost no family left. How was he to begin again? How could he hold on to the few family who had survived? My father had gone home to Czechoslovakia, but, realizing that the borders were going to close and it would be impossible to cross the borders to a free country, he left and traveled to Germany. He signed up for passage on a boat to Israel (at the time, Palestine), but his boat was canceled. After meeting my mother, who wanted to come to the States to be with her only surviving brother, he changed his plans.

However, much of his surviving family and some of hers did make their way to Israel and were living there. Even after my parents came to Chicago, my father wrote weekly to both his aunt and uncle who were living in Israel. So, in the early 1960s, despite having little money, they traveled to Israel to visit their family. It was their nourishment, their foundation and instilled within them a renewed sense of belonging. I was eight years old, and this was our very first of many trips to Israel. Because of my mother's insistence and determination, my father is now buried in Israel.

Pickled Vegetables

Ⓟ Makes about 12 servings

This recipe comes from Ibi's mother Goldie in Munkács, and Ibi still makes it today. "At home" vegetables in season were pickled to preserve them for the cold-weather months. Pickled Vegetables are good not only in winter but in spring and summer as well to add flavor to almost any meal. As with the Cucumber Salad, this is a great way to have a "salad" ready to serve for unexpected guests.

For the brine:

2 quarts water
1 cup white vinegar
3 tablespoons sugar
1 bunch dill, washed and drained
10 bay leaves
6 cloves garlic, halved
18 peppercorns
1 teaspoon pickling spice

For the vegetables:

6 small pickling cucumbers, peel-on, sliced ¼ inch thick
½ head cauliflower, cut into florets
1 medium red or green tomato, halved, seeded, coarsely chopped
1 red pepper, cored, seeded, cut into thin strips
1 medium yellow onion, halved vertically, sliced vertically into ¼-inch strips
1 scant tablespoon salt

Place 2 quarts water in a 6-quart pot. Add spices and seasonings and bring to a boil over high heat. Boil for 10 minutes. Turn off heat. Reserve.

Place all the vegetables in a large non-reactive bowl. Season with scant 1 tablespoon salt. Let the vegetables sit in the salt for about 15 minutes. Transfer to a colander. Place plastic wrap on top and press out excess liquid. Reserve the vegetables.

On the bottom of a 2-quart glass jar with a tight-fitting lid, place the dill from the brine. Place the vegetables on top of the dill. Remove all the spices from the brine (reserving brine) with a slotted spoon, and mix the spices into the vegetables. Now, pour the boiled brine over the vegetables to cover. Seal the jar.

Refrigerate and let cure for at least 3 days before eating. Will keep refrigerated for 2 weeks.

Chapter 8
Potatoes, Noodles and Grains

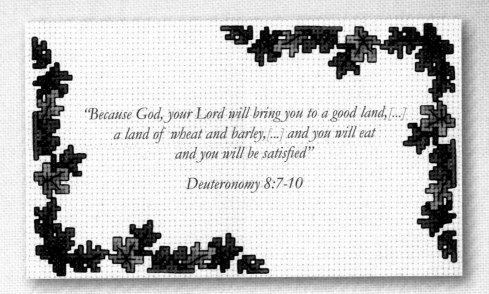

"Because God, your Lord will bring you to a good land, [...] a land of wheat and barley, [...] and you will eat and you will be satisfied"

Deuteronomy 8:7-10

This Biblical description of the land of Israel always made me feel that one of the abiding features of a bountiful land is the abundance of wheat and barley, those plentiful grains, which are the staple of man's diet.

Every regional culture has a pantry drawn from indigenous bounty. The recipes in this chapter describe dishes made from wheat and buckwheat, and also that abundant staple of Eastern Europe, potatoes. (Barley appears in recipes in chapters 2 and 6.) Noodles were homemade in my parents' childhood homes, and were therefore, fresh, light and had a flavor unlike the packaged products we buy today. Although rice was imported from China, my mother relates that it was easy to obtain at the open market, until 1942. Then the pressures of the War affected importing and rendered rice scarce.

Potatoes have been a basic food for centuries, and grew easily in the hardy climates of Hungary and Czechoslovakia. They were stored through the winter in the root cellar. Recipe examples in this chapter include: Latkes, Potato Kugel, *shlishkes*, *Geröstete* Potatoes, Potatoes *Paprikás*, and more. My mother has cooked potatoes almost every day. I am not sure if that was because they were so easy to obtain in the Europe of her childhood, or simply because my father loved potatoes.

Fresh noodles with additional ingredients became a main entrée for lunch or dinner or even a dessert dish. And rice, because at one time, it was a plentiful luxury, became the centerpiece for many traditional recipes.

In this chapter, I have included family recipes for potatoes, noodles, rice and kasha (buckwheat groats). Although my mother made all her noodles by hand, I have included only one homemade noodle recipe in this chapter. If you have never made your own noodles, I encourage you to give it a try.

Latkes

(P) Makes 8 to 10 Latkes

Of all the family recipes that I have attempted to translate to exact measurement, this is one of the most difficult. I learned to make latkes by cooking at the side of my mother, who, to this day, grates potatoes manually. Potatoes come in various sizes, so no two are exactly the same weight. Always fry latkes in enough hot oil so they will be crispy and not stick to the pan.

"At home," my parents traditionally ate latkes on Pesach, because they did not cook anything that contained matza or matza meal in water. American Jews added the custom of serving latkes on Chanukah as well. Each year on Chanukah, I prepare the latkes following my family's simple recipe and my husband follows his own created recipe (see variation below), and we wait to see whose latke was the "favorite." Every year all the latkes—mine and his—are always gone. I still believe my latkes are so simple that anyone can make them any time in no time flat.

4 medium russet potatoes
2 large eggs
½ teaspoon salt, or to taste
⅛ teaspoon freshly grated black pepper, optional
Vegetable oil, as needed for frying

> A medium russet potato is 2¼ by 3¼ inches. If the potatoes are very large, use 1 egg per potato.

Grate the potatoes into a medium bowl using the second finest side of a box grater. Or use the food processor fitted with the metal blade: Chop potatoes into chunks; grate finely by pulsing, but do not purée.

Transfer potatoes and their juices to a medium bowl. Add the eggs and salt. Mix very well. Add pepper if using.

In a 12-inch sauté pan over medium-high heat, heat ¼ inch of oil. When a drop of water sizzles and evaporates immediately, the pan is hot. Drop latke batter by ¼-cup ladles or large spoon carefully into the frying pan. Fry on one side until edges are crispy and golden about 3 minutes. Turn once and fry until cooked through and crispy on the other side.

Transfer latkes to a paper towel-lined plate and repeat using remaining batter, adding more oil if necessary.

My husband's latkes:
He does not grate the potatoes fine, but shreds them manually or by using the shredding disk in the food processor, then squeezes out all of the liquid and discards it. Then he adds eggs and salt and mixes. The cooking procedure is the same. His latkes are more like hash brown patties, but they are also delicious and crispy.

Latkes from Cooked Potatoes, *Chremslach*

(P) Makes 8 to 10 *Chremslach*

Here is a simple way to turn leftover cooked potatoes either whole, boiled, baked or mashed into a potato patty that is crispy on the outside and creamy on the inside. The recipe has guideline measurements because no leftover is ever the same amount. Feel free to adjust the eggs to the quantity of potatoes that you have.

3 medium cooked skinless potatoes, whole, pieces or mashed
2 large eggs, beaten
½ small finely shredded onion
Salt and pepper, to taste, optional
Vegetable oil, as needed for frying

Mash the cooked potatoes until smooth in a medium bowl using a potato masher.

Add the eggs and onion and mix well. If potatoes have been cooked in salted water do not add seasonings. If potatoes have been baked, unseasoned, add salt and pepper to taste. Mix well. In a 12-inch sauté pan over medium-high heat, heat ¼-inch oil until hot. If a drop of water sizzles and evaporates immediately, pan is hot.

> If you are using unseasoned baking potatoes, you may replace salt and pepper with sugar to taste for a sweet pancake. Serve it with cinnamon sugar or jam or applesauce for breakfast or dessert.

Ladle potato mixture into pan by ¼ cupful. Fry until golden and crisp on one side, 3 to 4 minutes, turn once and fry on the other side until golden, crisp and cooked through.

Transfer cooked patties to paper towel-lined plate and repeat with remaining batter.

Geröstete Potatoes

P Makes 6 servings

My father often ate Geröstete Potatoes when he was in Freising, Germany after the Holocaust. He loved this dish and ate it often at a restaurant there, using food stamps given to the survivors by the German government. The restaurant was owned by Frau Sperrer. Geröstete Potatoes was a specialty dish that she prepared fresh in large quantities, because everyone who entered the restaurant ordered it. My mother developed this recipe to duplicate the taste and flavors of this dish for my father.

Serve it fresh and hot, as a main entrée, as Frau Sperrer did, or as a side with poultry, beef or eggs.

12 small red potatoes, about
1¾ pounds, quartered
1 teaspoon salt
2 tablespoons oil
2 medium onions, diced
½ to 1 teaspoon sweet
Hungarian paprika

Place the potatoes in a 3-quart pot. Add enough water to cover and the salt. Bring to a boil on high heat. Decrease heat to low and simmer until the potatoes are soft, but still firm, not falling apart, about 15 to 20 minutes. Drain and reserve.

In a 12-inch frying pan over medium-high heat, heat the oil for 2 minutes. Sauté the onions in the oil for 5 minutes until the onions are translucent. Add the paprika and stir.

Add the reserved potatoes to the onions in the pan and fry together with the onions and paprika, stirring, until browned, 5 to 10 minutes. Taste and adjust seasonings.

For a dairy dish add a dollop of sour cream to the browned potatoes and onions and mix.

For a spicy version substitute half or all hot paprika for sweet.

Finding Faith in Freising 1945

After surviving the Death March from Buchenwald to Freising, Germany, my father Sandor (Sanyi) Kirschenbaum rented a room from a German woman. My father had no family, no job, and was alone at the age of 19. His "friends" were the men who had survived the Death March with him. He spent his days playing cards, going to visit DP Camps to find landsmen or people he had known before the War. He did a little business buying jewelry from Germans and selling it to American soldiers, and he took courses to learn to operate a movie projector. The Germans gave the Holocaust survivors food stamps plus a stipend for living every month. Using the food stamps, my father ate often, as did most of the survivors, at the restaurant, the Coliseum, owned by Frau Sperrer.

However, a few months after my father arrived in Freising, Jewish religious articles became available. He was able to obtain a set of tefillin, phylacteries, worn by men during weekday morning prayers. (The tefillin are two small leather boxes that contain verses from the Torah, worn on the head and on one arm and held in place by leather straps. Observant men and boys who have had their Bar Mitzvah wear tefillin during the morning prayers.) His original set of tefillin had been taken from him at Auschwitz. So that day in Freising, he resumed putting on tefillin as he had for all the years since he was a Bar Mitzvah. He continued every day until his death in April 2007.

Dairy Mashed Potatoes

(D) Makes 4 to 6 servings

These were a staple in our house and are known as the famous milchig mashed potatoes. For many years, my mother made these every Saturday night and served them with tomatoes cut in wedges and either smoked fish or tuna. The recipe calls for half-and-half, which my father used in place of milk. It reminded him of the rich fresh milk from the cows "at home."

2 pounds russet potatoes, cut into
1-inch chunks
2 teaspoons salt
¼ cup half-and-half
3 tablespoons butter, or to taste
¼ teaspoon Seasoned Salt (page 66)
Freshly ground pepper, to taste

Place potatoes in a 6-quart pot with water to cover. Add salt. Bring to a boil over medium-high heat. Decrease heat and simmer until potatoes are soft but still firm, about 15 to 20 minutes. Test by putting a fork into the potato. Drain.

Return potatoes to the pot, add the half-and-half, the butter and seasonings. Mash well using a potato masher, mix and fluff.

Potato Starch for Pesach

My mother and my aunt Goldie both made homemade potato starch. While today, it is available on the shelf of a supermarket, and makes recipes for Passover cooking very simple, "at home" they made their own potato starch and stored it for Passover. In addition to Pesach cooking, potato starch is excellent for gluten-free recipes, as a substitute for wheat flour in thickening soups and gravies, and for soufflés, cakes and for special Passover Lukshin or noodles.

To make potato starch: Peel one very large russet potato. Put a layer of cheesecloth in a colander over a large bowl. Using the finest grater possible, grate potato into cheesecloth. Pour 1 cup of water over the grated potato, gather up the cheesecloth, twist the top and squeeze. Repeat until no more starch comes out, at least three times. Discard cheesecloth and grated potato. Let starch settle into bottom of bowl. Pour water off top. Let starch dry overnight. You will have about 2 tablespoons of potato starch. How do I know? I made this. After I made my own potato starch my mother told me that her mother, my grandmother, had such a fine grater that no cheesecloth was necessary, the potato was completely processed in the grating leaving no pulp behind.

Parve Mashed Potatoes

P Makes 4 to 6 servings

My parents never made parve mashed potatoes "at home." Dishes were either dairy, made with butter, cream and milk, or meat, made with chicken schmaltz. There was no margarine or solid vegetable oil in my parents' hometowns. This version was developed in the States.

2 pounds russet potatoes, cut into
1-inch chunks
2 teaspoons salt
¼ cup margarine
¼ teaspoon Seasoned Salt (page 66)
Freshly ground pepper, to taste

Place the potatoes in a 6-quart pot with water to cover. Add the 2 teaspoons salt. Bring to a boil over high heat. Decrease heat to low and simmer until potatoes are soft but still firm, about 15 to 20 minutes. Test by putting a fork into the potato to see. Drain the potatoes.

Add the margarine immediately, so that it melts, and the Seasoned Salt and pepper. Mash well using a potato masher, mix and fluff.

> Sauté 1 small onion, diced, in vegetable oil until golden brown. Mix into finished potatoes or garnish on top.

About Potatoes

Idaho or white russet potatoes, which are fluffy, are best for mashing. These are also the best for latkes and potato kugel and for baking.

Red potatoes are waxy and better for soup, for roasting, and also for *paprikás* potatoes, because they don't fall apart in cooking as do the russet potatoes.

For potato salad, you can use either, depending on the flavor you desire. The red waxy potatoes do not fall apart during cooking, but they also have a very different flavor than the white potato. I make a skin-on red potato salad with an oil and vinegar dressing, but when I use a creamy dressing I always use russet potatoes. Please remember the Recipe Guidelines (page 66): all potatoes are peeled unless recipe states "peel on."

Potatoes with Paprika, *Paprikás Krumpli*

P Makes 4 to 6 servings

This is an Hungarian one-pot dish, simple to cook and full of flavor. It can be a side dish for meat, poultry or fish.

2 tablespoons vegetable oil
1 medium onion, diced
1 teaspoon sweet Hungarian paprika
4 to 5 medium red potatoes
½ teaspoon salt

In a 4-quart pot over medium heat, heat oil. Add onion and sauté, stirring, until translucent, about 2 minutes. Add paprika and continue to sauté, stirring, until onion is browned, about 5 minutes.

Meanwhile, slice potatoes in half vertically and then into ¼ inch-thick slices horizontally.

When the onion is browned, add the potatoes and the salt. Add just enough water to cook the potatoes, about 1½ inches deep. (If you add too much water, it will still be fine, but a bit liquid.)

Bring to a boil, cover, lower heat and cook on low until potatoes are soft, about 20 minutes.

The Cellar: Yesteryear's Fridge

For the convenience of today's cook, this cookbook provides tips on cooking in advance, refrigerating or freezing. However, originally, all the recipes were cooked fresh on a daily basis, a culinary tradition in which the family took great pride. One reason for this tradition was the limited availability in the 19th and early 20th century of refrigeration in my parents' hometowns. The childhood home of my mother, Margit Kirsche, was built four steps above ground level, with entrance steps on one side of the building. Right behind those steps, attached to the back of the house, was a short door. The door opened onto eight steps going down to their cellar, an underground room with a mud floor and no windows. This underground room kept hardy vegetables from freezing during the winter, and maintained a cooler temperature and steady humidity for storing food supplies during summer months. They used the cellar on a daily basis for storing dairy products as well as onions and potatoes.

My mother's cellar was small compared to the 30-foot-square, 8-feet-deep cellar used in Vásárosnamény for commercial meat storage. The cellar was filled with ice cut from the nearby Tisza River in winter. The ice was packed with straw and stayed cold throughout the summer.

Potato Kugel

Ⓟ Makes 12 servings (one 9 by 13-inch pan)

This easy potato kugel, baked in the oven, is familiar to most people today. Put it in the oven and you're done. In a second recipe for potato kugel (page 210), called a Kaizle, the kugel is cooked on the top of the range. The Kaizle is more traditional in Eastern Europe and while it cooks faster, it requires more attention. Potato Kugel is most commonly enjoyed on Shabbos and the holidays, but it is so delicious and easy, you can enjoy it any day for a meal, or even a snack.

10 medium russet potatoes,
about 3 pounds
5 eggs
1 teaspoon salt
¼ teaspoon Seasoned Salt (page 66),
optional
⅛ teaspoon freshly ground pepper
3 tablespoons vegetable oil, divided

Preheat oven to 375°F. Grate the potatoes into a medium bowl using the second finest side of a box grater. Or use the food processor, fitted with the metal blade, to grate finely by pulsing, but do not purée.

Transfer potatoes and their juices to a medium bowl. Add the eggs and salt. Mix very well. Add Seasoned Salt, if using, and pepper.

Using 2 tablespoons of the oil, oil the bottom of a 9 by 13-inch baking pan. Pour in the potato kugel mixture. Drizzle remaining oil on top.

Bake uncovered for 30 minutes. Lower heat to 350°F and bake for 1½ hours.

A Matter of Taste

Today I peel potatoes and toss the peels away without thinking. My mother tells me that in Auschwitz their daily diet consisted of breakfast coffee laced with bromides to keep them quiet and sedated. Their second and last meal of the day was a soup of unwashed vegetables gritty with dirt and a piece of bread. "When we were lucky, we found a potato peel lying on the ground, left from the guards' cooking their meal. We ate it and felt as if we struck gold," she says.

Traditional Potato Kugel, *Kaizle*

Ⓟ Makes 8 servings

A Kaizle is a potato kugel cooked on the range top, like a very large latke the size of a frying pan. It is simple to cook, but tricky to turn. Be careful it does not stick to the bottom, so you will be able to flip it without breaking. The aroma of the Kaizle frying on the stovetop will entice any guest to join you for Shabbos dinner. This dish is traditional in the Moskovics household, my father's mother's family. My cousin, Rachel Moskovics Grossman, daughter of Golda Moskovics, gave me her mother's recipe.

4 large russet potatoes,
about 1½ pounds
1 medium onion
2 eggs
1 teaspoon salt
½ teaspoon freshly ground pepper
½ cup oil plus 2 tablespoons for frying

Manually grate finely the potatoes and the onion using the second finest grate on a four-sided grater.

In a large mixing bowl, place the grated potatoes and onion. Add the eggs, salt and pepper. Taste and adjust the seasonings, adding salt as needed. Add the ½ cup oil and mix.

In a deep, nonstick 12-inch frying pan over high heat, heat the 2 tablespoons of oil. Make sure the pan is hot by testing with a drop of water. If the water sizzles and immediately evaporates, the pan is hot enough. Add the potato mixture.

Cook, uncovered, on medium heat, until bottom is brown and crisp, about 30 minutes. Using 2 long-handled, broad spatulas to slip underneath the kugel, flip it onto a large plate, then slide it back, browned side up, into the frying pan. Cook until brown on the bottom and cooked through in the center, about 30 minutes more.

> The potatoes are fluffier if you bring the ½ cup of oil to a boil before adding to the mixture. This is a trick that my father used; apparently he learned this from his mother. It is the same method that his aunt Golda, his mother's youngest sister also used. Golda's ratio is 2 potatoes to 1 egg.

Golda's Potato Dough *Shlishkes*

P Makes 8 servings

My cousin, Rachel Grossman gave me her mother's recipe. Potato dough is made into dumplings and the cooked dumplings are garnished with sautéed breadcrumbs. My father loved this dish, which his mother also cooked for him when he was a child.

4 large skin-on russet potatoes
about 2 pounds
1 teaspoon salt, plus a pinch
for the dough
2 eggs
1 cup flour
1 cup dried breadcrumbs, preferably
from challah
1 medium onion, diced
Vegetable oil, as needed

In a 6-quart pot, place potatoes. Add water to cover, and the teaspoon of salt. Bring to a boil over high heat. Decrease heat to low and simmer until potatoes are soft and cooked through, about 40 minutes. Drain.

Transfer the potatoes to a plate and let cool to room temperature. Peel the potatoes using your fingers and a paring knife where necessary for the eyes.

Transfer potatoes to a bowl. Using a potato masher, mash the potatoes well. Add the eggs, flour and the pinch of salt. If the dough is too loose, add a little more flour. The dough should be just thick enough so you can roll it out.

On a lightly floured board, roll of the dough ¼-inch thick. Cut in 1-inch squares or ½ by 1-inch rectangles.

Meanwhile, fill an 8-quart pot halfway with water and bring water to a boil over high heat. Drop the *shlishkes* into the boiling water and cook for about 10 minutes, stirring gently so that they do not stick together. *Shlishkes* are cooked when they rise to the surface. Remove with a slotted spoon into a colander.

While the *shlishkes* are cooking, sauté the breadcrumbs and the onions in two separate skillets with oil as needed. The bread crumbs should be browned, and the onions soft and golden.

Pour the breadcrumbs over the *shlishkes* and toss gently. Transfer *shliskhes* to a serving bowl and top with onions.

My Mother's Potato Dough *Shlishkes*

P Makes 10 servings

My mother used this potato dough to make both dumplings and lekvar-filled kreplach. She made the kreplach for my father who was enticed by anything with lekvar in it.

4 large peel-on russet potatoes
1 egg
About 3 cups flour
1 teaspoon salt
1 cup dried breadcrumbs, preferably from challah
Vegetable oil or butter as needed
1 cup *lekvar* (page 259), or as needed

> For the kreplach, roll out dough as above and cut into 2-inch squares. Place ½ to 1 teaspoon of *lekvar* or a fresh Italian plum half in the center of each, fold over like a triangle and pinch edges well to seal. Cook in boiling water as above. Sprinkle gently with sautéed breadcrumbs. Serve immediately.

In a 6-quart pot, place potatoes. Add water to cover, and the teaspoon of salt. Bring to a boil over high heat. Decrease heat to low and simmer until potatoes are soft and cooked through, but not mushy, about 40 minutes. Drain.

Transfer the potatoes to a plate and let cool to room temperature. Peel the potatoes using your fingers and a paring knife where necessary for the eyes.

Using a four-sided grater, grate on second finest side. Transfer grated potatoes to the work bowl of a heavy-duty mixer fitted with the dough hook. Add one egg. Mix well on low speed, scraping sides as necessary. Add flour, 1 cup at a time, until it is absorbed. Divide dough into four portions.

On a lightly floured board, roll out dough, one portion at a time, until it is about ¼-inch thick. Cut into 1-inch squares.

Bring an 8-quart pot filled with water and the salt to a boil over high heat. Add dumplings, one batch at a time, cook until done, about 10 minutes. When dumplings rise to the top they are done. Using a slotted spoon, transfer to a colander and repeat with remaining dumplings.

Meanwhile, sauté bread crumbs in a separate skillet in oil or butter until golden. Toss with cooked dumplings and serve in a large bowl.

Noodles with Walnuts, *Diós Tészta*

Ⓓ Makes 4 servings

Diós Tészta is a classically Hungarian dish. It serves equally well as a dessert and a main course. It is best served fresh and warm. Originally it was made with fresh homemade noodles, (page 216). Today, we have the convenience of packaged noodles. However, in order to retain the homemade, fresh flavor be sure to use the finest noodles and fresh walnuts, freshly ground.

8 ounces dried wide egg noodles, cooked and drained
2 tablespoons butter
1 cup finely ground walnuts
2 tablespoons sugar

Cook noodles in lightly salted water according to package directions. Drain and return to pot.

In a small separate pan, melt butter until it begins to bubble. Pour the bubbly hot butter over noodles. Toss the noodles immediately. Add the walnuts and sugar and toss again, while the noodles are still hot. Serve in a large bowl.

Keeping Kosher in 1943

It was the summer of 1943, during the "Nine Days" when it is customary to eat foods that are not meat. At this time, while the Hungarian Jews were not yet going to the Death Camps, there was religious persecution and laws against the Jews already enacted. Although the Jews could still run the business that they owned, they could not obtain a new license to own a business. There was a quota on the number of Jews who could attend higher education. Ritual slaughter of animals, shechting, was no longer allowed. And although the Jews were not yet required to wear a Jewish star, the young Jewish men were forced into slave labor instead of the Army.

A regiment of approximately 100 men in a slave labor unit were marching through the town of Vásárosnámeny, and camping in back of my mother's family house. A few of these conscripted young Jewish men, were attempting, even under these conditions, to eat only kosher.

Across the street from her home stood the shul, with an attached room that had a very large commercial size wood-burning oven. When my mother's family learned that some of the men wanted to eat only kosher, my grandmother asked my mother to make shlishkes. She needed a large enough room to make a sizeable quantity. So she crossed the street from her house and went to the back room of the shul, and prepared shlishkes for these men in the slave labor regiment. When she served them she realized not only how hungry they were and how they enjoyed this simple dish, but also how thankful they were to be able to eat kosher.

Sweet *Lukshin Kugel*

P   Makes 16 servings

Sweet Lukshin Kugel is traditionally served on Shabbos and Jewish holidays in the Ashkenazic, or Eastern European, Jewish homes. If made with cheese (page 117), it is served often on Shavuos, when it is traditional to eat dairy. But here is a parve version, that can be served either as a side with meat or poultry, or for Kiddush on Shabbos morning, or even for a dessert. It is equally good served hot or room temperature, which makes it a wonderful dish for Shabbos lunch, as it does not require heating. My father developed the recipe, "according to taste." The flavors of pineapple and cinnamon make a refreshing combination.

8 ounces medium dried egg noodles, cooked and drained
4 eggs
1 (8-ounce) can crushed pineapple, with juice
½ cup sugar
½ cup raisins
½ teaspoon cinnamon
2 tablespoons oil

Preheat oven to 350°F. In a large bowl, beat the eggs. Add the noodles, pineapple, eggs, cinnamon, sugar and raisins and mix well.

Oil the bottom and sides of a 9 by 9-inch non-reactive baking pan. Pour in the mixture. Bake until top is golden brown and crisp and kugel is firm, 1 hour.
Cut 4 by 4 for 16 servings.

Food, Family and Tradition

Noodles with *Lekvar, Mocskos Tészta*

P Makes 4 servings

To fully appreciate this dish, imagine fresh, homemade noodles (page 216) topped with fresh homemade lekvar (page 259), plum preserves made from plums picked fresh from your own plum trees. Light, fresh, simple, and so satisfying! This is how my father's family prepared and ate Mocskos Tészta "at home." Today, you can enjoy preparing this dish easily using packaged noodles and prepared jam. But for the best flavor, be sure to use good quality noodles and lekvar.

1 pound bow tie noodles, cooked and drained
2 tablespoons vegetable oil
1 cup *lekvar* (page 259)

Place warm noodles in a large serving bowl.
Toss the noodles with the oil.
Add the *lekvar* to taste and mix well.

Mocskos Tészta "at home"
In Vásárosnámeny when my mother was growing up, Mocskos Tészta was often served as an entrée with either a dairy or parve soup. There was no vegetable oil "at home." So if served with dairy it was made with butter, and if served with parve it was made with coconut oil. Both are delicious substitutes for vegetable oil even today. My cousin, Irving Weinberger, remembers his mother Goldie (my father's sister) used to cook potatoes on Shabbos for the family but would make Mochkos Tészta for herself. Perhaps, like my father, my aunt Goldie, tasted the plums of home through the lekvar in the Mochkos Tészta.

My Mother's Homemade Noodles

(P) Makes 1½ to 2 pounds

My mother has been making noodles from scratch since she was 10 years old. If you have never made noodles, give this a try. I believe you will find it easier than you imagined, and the taste and texture of homemade noodles are beyond compare. My mother said the flour in Europe was different and she never needed added oil there; however, in the States she adds oil for perfect consistency.

2½ cups unbleached all-purpose flour
4 eggs, beaten (to equal 1 cup)
¼ cup water
1 tablespoon oil

On a large wooden surface (at least 18 by 24 inches) heap 2 cups of the flour. Make a well in the middle. In a small bowl place eggs and water and whisk to mix. Pour the egg-water mixture into the well. Add the oil.

Mix together from the inside out using your hands to form a cohesive mass. Knead until smooth, at least 10 minutes. If dough is still sticky, add up to ½ cup more flour by the ¼ cup.

Divide dough into half. Keep unused portion covered with plastic wrap.

Roll out one portion at a time on floured board ⅛-inch thick into a rectangle. Using a sharp knife, or a pastry cutter, cut noodles lengthwise as thin or wide as needed, from 1/16 to ½ inch to 1 inch wide for soup, for kugel or for noodles with cabbage. Or cut into 3 by 1-inch rectangles or ½-inch diamonds. Transfer cut noodles to a lightly floured tray.

To cook noodles: Bring an 8-quart pot filled ⅔ full of water to a boil. Add 1 teaspoon salt. Add noodles and cook, stirring, until noodles float to surface and are tender, about 3 to 10 minutes depending on the width of the noodles.

Drain, return to pan and use in place of dried noodles for many recipes in this book.

Making Noodles

As the only daughter, and the second oldest child, my mother played a very important role in the daily responsibilities of her family life. She began cooking and baking at a very early age, proving her natural talents and expertise when she was only 10 years old. She always wanted to make noodles, but because she was very short and slight, her mother said no. Making the noodles meant preparing the dough, rolling out the dough, making the fire in the stove, boiling the water and cutting and cooking the noodles—quite a challenge for a little girl. But, one Thursday, which was the day for the open market in her hometown, an original farmer's market, her mother had gone to buy the fruits and vegetables. My mother, finding herself home alone, decided to prepare noodles. She made noodles, completely from scratch, which were ready when her mother arrived home. Her mother was delighted to have dinner ready and so, from that time on, my mother not only made noodles, but had defined her cooking skills and talents. And she moved on quickly to cooking and baking more complex recipes.

Passover Noodles, *Pesach Lukshin*

Ⓜ Makes 14 crepes, serves 20

"We did not eat gebrocht (broken) on Pesach at home," says Margit Kirsche, "so we did not make matza balls or cook with any matza in water. This is what we put into the chicken soup. It looks like noodles. My grandchildren love making the Lukshin, and it is a true tradition in our family." The flavor is best when made with schmaltz.

6 eggs
3 heaping tablespoons potato starch
1 cup water
1 teaspoon salt
Solid uncooked chicken fat from fresh chickens, as needed

In a 1-quart mixing bowl with spout, beat eggs together. In a separate bowl, place potato starch and ¼ cup of the water; mix. Add to egg mixture. Then add enough of the remaining water to measure 4 cups of mixture, adding water if necessary. Add salt and mix.

In a 12-inch frying pan over high heat, using a fork, rub pieces of the chicken fat so they melt and coat the bottom of the skillet.

Mix, then pour in about ¼ cup of the egg-potato starch mixture. Tilt the skillet to spread batter. Cook until brown on one side, about 2 to 3 minutes. Then turn and cook briefly on the other side. Transfer to a plate, cover with waxed paper and repeat, lifting waxed paper to top, until all batter is used, making sure to stir batter before each crepe (the potato starch settles) and to coat the bottom of the pan with the chicken fat in between.

When all crepes are cooked, roll each crepe into a cylinder. Slice crosswise into slices about ⅛-inch thick to make noodles. Refrigerate, covered, until needed, up to four days.

Use noodles in chicken soup.

Charoses without Ingber
My mother's maternal grandfather, who served the Jewish Kehilla (community) in Gergely as shoichet, mohel, and rabbinic advisor, made charoses each year for Pesach, giving everyone in the Kehilla just enough for the Seder. As a little girl, my mother watched her beloved grandfather, and she has prepared charoses every year for the Pesach Seder, for our family as well as for the customers at Hungarian Kosher Foods. My mother says, "He used apples, sugar, walnuts, cinnamon, and wine. And then he added ingber (ginger), which he grew in their yard. I make it exactly the same way, except that I never liked ingber, so I leave it out." And then my mother exclaimed, "See what a little girl can learn just from hanging around her grandfather?!"

Kasha

Ⓜ Makes 8 servings

Mark Levin, staff member at Hungarian Kosher Foods, has rich memories of kasha from his youth in the Soviet Union (see "Definition of Kasha," page 219). The following basic recipe, adapted from our recipe at Hungarian Kosher Foods can be used as a hearty, whole grain side dish, or as a main ingredient in Kasha Varnishkes. Kasha is sold as whole, coarse, medium or fine. We use coarse or medium.

2 cups coarse or medium
uncooked kasha
4 eggs
¼ cup vegetable oil,
plus 2 tablespoons
4 cups water
4 teaspoons powdered chicken soup
base, or 4 bouillon cubes
1 teaspoon Seasoned Salt (page 66)
¼ teaspoon freshly ground pepper
1 medium onion, diced
4 ounces mushrooms sliced

Make a pilaf by adding diced red bell peppers, toasted almonds and green peas to the skillet with onions and mushrooms. Sauté as directed and add to kasha.

Kasha Varnishkes is a traditional Eastern European dish. Make the basic Kasha recipe and toss to combine it with 1 pound of cooked noodles, usually bow tie.

Preheat the oven to 350°F. In a large bowl combine kasha, eggs and ¼ cup of oil. Mix well. Spread kasha mixture on a parchment paper-lined quarter sheet pan and bake until kasha is dry, brown and cohesive, but not burned, about 30 minutes.

Remove from oven and, using a meat mallet or the side of a potato masher, break up kasha into very small pieces.

Meanwhile, in a 6-quart pot over medium heat, add water, chicken base, salt and pepper and bring a boil. Add kasha, stir and cover. Decrease heat to low and simmer, covered, until kasha is tender and liquid is absorbed, about 20 minutes.

Meanwhile, in a 12-inch sauté pan over medium heat, heat the 2 tablespoons of oil. Add onions and mushrooms and sauté, stirring, until onions are translucent and mushrooms are tender, about 10 minutes. Stir onion mixture into kasha and serve warm as a side to meat or poultry.

Definition of Kasha
By Mark Levin

I finally looked at my new English-Russian dictionary for the word kasha. Now if you look at one of the grocery aisles in Hungarian Kosher Foods you will find colorful packages of kasha. But there was no "kasha" in my dictionary. Kasha is not an English word. In Yiddish, "to make a kasha" of something means to make a mess of things. In the Eastern European world kasha refers not just to buckwheat groats but to all kinds of grains: oats, farina, barley, farfel—even lentils, peas and beans.

These foods historically were for poor people and helped them survive terrible wars and times of starvation.

When I was growing up in Russia, we ate kasha every day—lentils, peas, beans, buckwheat. In the army we survived on kasha. If, during my youth, you asked what was for breakfast, we answered, "Kasha." If you asked what was for lunch or dinner? "Kasha." And if you asked what was for dessert; "Kasha." That is because kasha, as we knew it, could be breakfast porridge, midday soup, dinner Kasha Varnishkes, and dessert such as sweetened kasha puddings and kasha with dried fruits and nuts.

Rice With Prunes

(P) Makes 4 servings

My father loved all foods with fresh plums, dried plums or lekvar. This rice dish was among his favorites, and my mother cooked it often for him. His sister, my aunt Goldie, prepared this often for Shabbos, even in Munkács. I believe they both loved this dish because it reminded them of their childhood "at home."

1 tablespoon vegetable oil
1 cup uncooked rice
2 cups water
8 to 10 pitted prunes
2 to 3 tablespoons sugar, optional
½ teaspoon salt

In a 2-quart pot over medium heat, add the oil and the rice and cook, stirring, until rice is opaque, about 3 minutes.

Add 2 cups of water. Add the prunes, sugar if using, and salt. Bring to a boil, cover, decrease heat to low and simmer for 20 minutes.

Serve as an entrée or a side to meat, poultry, or fish.

Plums from Home

My father always regaled us with stories of the plum trees that grew in abundance on the family property at the back of his childhood home in Hluboka, Czechoslovakia. When he was hungry for lunch, his mother would say, "Go pick some fresh plums and have some fresh bread with butter and plums." And that is what he would do. (This habit continued through the years, as he picked an Italian or Freestone plum from the produce section at Hungarian Kosher Foods, for a quick snack). His mother also used the plums for pastries and plum preserves, lekvar. My father took his children and grandchildren on three different trips "back home" in the 1990s, and the very first thing we did when we reached his family home was to pick plums from the trees that had, as he had, survived the Holocaust.

Plum trees, Kirschenbaum orchard, Hluboka

Food, Family and Tradition

Rice With Wild Rice

P Makes 4 to 6 servings

I love the combination of white rice and wild rice. The mixture of the colors as well as the textures of the dish make it nutty and more interesting than plain white rice. Follow my mom's quick and easy preparation.

2 tablespoons vegetable oil
1 medium onion, diced
6 mushrooms, sliced
3 cups water
1 teaspoon salt
⅛ teaspoon freshly ground pepper
¼ cup uncooked wild rice
1 cup uncooked long grain white rice

In a 3-quart pot over medium heat, add oil. Add onion and mushrooms and sauté, stirring, until onions are translucent and mushrooms are soft, about 5 minutes.

Add water, seasonings, and wild rice. Bring to a boil, decrease heat to low, cover and simmer for 20 minutes.

Add white rice, return to a boil, cover, decrease heat to low and simmer for 20 minutes. Serve as a side dish with meat, poultry or fish.

Chapter 9
Bread, Pastries, Cakes and Cookies

Wine with Bread, Pastries, Cakes and Cookies

Traditionally challah follows the Kiddush that is recited on wine on Shabbos and Jewish holidays. The wine most traditional is sweet red Concord. Consider serving Concord wine mixed with sparkling water to add a kick to your meal.

Choose a gewürztraminer for a fruity, not too sweet, dessert wine. Another wonderful dessert wine is a late harvest white riesling, boasting crisp, refreshing fall flavors. For a light pastry or cookie, try a sweet, bright and effervescent moscato. And, of course, you can always choose a sparkling wine to go with your dessert and finish your meal the way you began it! *L'Chaim*!

"That's how the cookie crumbles!"

This universal saying expresses my parents' philosophy of life—fervent optimism under the most challenging situations, and adaptability in the face of life's twists and turns. As Holocaust survivors, they picked themselves up and, with barely any surviving family, built a new life in a new land and a completely different culture. Even though the culture in the States was new, my mother's homemade baking, recipes from "at home," created an inviting aroma that welcomed our childhood friends. These recipes also served both as a table centerpiece and a conversation starter as my parents told us stories of their happy childhoods, and the stark contrast of the Holocaust.

When I placed the recipe ingredients on the kitchen island for testing, I noticed their simplicity and economy. These basic ingredients cost a fraction of the bread, cake and cookie mixes and upscale baking materials available today. Most of my mother's ingredients are likely to already be in your pantry and kitchen: flour, sugar, eggs, butter, yeast, baking powder and soda, a few spices and jams. Although "at home" my parents lived without what we take for granted—indoor plumbing, refrigerators, gas or electric stoves—their baked goods reflect a refinement and elegance uncommon today.

The preparation methods of some of the recipes may be a challenge for the modern baker. Many begin with yeast dough.

If you have never baked with yeast do not be intimidated. The recipes will guide you through the process, and once you get the hang of it, yeast dough will become natural and easy. The amount of sugar in the recipes surprised me. Compared to other cookbooks in my collection, the ratio of sugar to flour is low. Yet the prepared recipes yield many servings and rarely make it from my table to my freezer. The flavor of the finished baked goods depends on so much more than sugar: the tartness of fruit, the lightness of the dough, the richness of honey, the complexity of spices, the texture of nuts.

For the presentation, take advantage of tradition: Enjoy *Lekvar* (page 259) or Quince Preserves (page 260) on a fresh slice of Challah (page 224). Serve a Tea Cookie (page 251) on the saucer alongside a cup of hot tea, a favorite of my great aunt Golda Moskovics. Have a coffee with a Cheese *Deltelach* (page 239) a favorite combination my aunt Goldie Weinberger, or place a slice of my mother's famous Chocolate Yeast Roll *Kakaós* (page 236) on a doily or serve it on a china platter.

The recipes here represent just a few of the intricate, beautiful breads and pastries which were baked "at home,"—my mother's home, my aunt Goldie's home and the homes of my grandmothers long ago.

223

My Mom's Crispy Challah

(P) Makes 3 large loaves

My mother makes her challah, crispy outside and tender inside, the way her mother did "at home" without too many eggs or too much oil. Braiding is an art. My mother easily braids from four to 15—for regular Shabbos challah, six braids, for special occasions, 15 braids. The starter gives the baked bread depth of flavor. "At home" the starter rested overnight, but because they got up at 3 a.m. to begin preparations for Shabbos, the overnight time was about 6 hours. Why bake challah at home when you can buy it? Baking challah gives the home a special fragrance, the bread itself has unparalleled flavor and texture, and it allows the woman an opportunity to say a special prayer (see below, "A Woman's Special Mitzvah").

For the starter:
1 cup lukewarm water
1 (2-ounce) cake of fresh yeast, crumbled (see Tip)
2 tablespoons sugar
½ cup all-purpose flour

For the bread dough:
2 eggs, beaten
1 cup lukewarm water
6½ cups of flour
1½ teaspoons salt
4 tablespoons sugar
¼ cup vegetable oil
1 egg beaten with
1 tablespoon of water for egg wash

If fresh yeast is unavailable, substitute 2 (¼-ounce, or 7-gram) packages of active dry yeast. Or use 5 level teaspoons of active dry yeast.

A Woman's Special Mitzvah

Every Jewish woman is endowed with three special mitzvos to perform, of which one is the special mitzvah of separating dough (the size of an olive) from the challah dough, and burning it, reciting the traditional blessing:

Blessed are You, Lord our God, King of the Universe,
who has sanctified us with his mitzvos
and commanded us to separate challah from the dough.

ברוך אתה ה' אלקינו מלך העולם
אשר קדשנו במצותיו וציונו להפריש חלה מן העסה

At this time she may add a special highly personal prayer of her own on behalf of someone in need. My mother, aunts, and the women of their Chassidic community have, for generations, been dedicated to this unique mitzvah, considering this a serious opportunity to pray on behalf of someone in need.

A Special Chesed, Kindness
The day after Passover, 1944, in Hluboka, my father's entire family was taken to the ghetto, where conditions were unbearable and they began to starve. Andre, the Czech husband of their former family housekeeper Hanya (see page 25), risked his life to smuggle bread for them through the barbed wire fence. Each piece of bread was the difference between life and death.

Make the starter: In a small bowl mix together the water, and yeast. Stir to mix well and dissolve the yeast. Add sugar and flour and stir well to mix. Cover with plastic wrap and let rest for 2 to 6 hours. Reserve.

Make the dough: In a small bowl mix the beaten eggs with the water; reserve. In a large 6-quart bowl, add 5 cups of the flour, the salt and sugar and mix well. Make a well in the center of the flour, add the oil., the reserved egg-water mixture, and the reserved starter.

With a large spoon stir to mix until a dough forms. Knead the dough in the bowl adding flour by ¼ cupful, kneading in between additions. Knead until the dough is smooth and satiny, about 10-15 minutes.

Remove dough from the bowl, oil the bowl lightly, return the dough to the bowl, turning once so that the oiled side is up.

Cover with plastic wrap, or a lint-free tea towel that has been wet and wrung almost dry, and let rise in a warm place until doubled, about 1½ hours.

Preheat the oven to 350°F. Turn dough out onto a lightly floured surface and cut into three equal portions.

Knead each portion briefly. Cut 1 portion into 3, 4 or 6 equal portions. Roll each into a 10- to 12-inch long rope. Braid the ropes into a loaf. Place loaf on a parchment paper-lined half-sheet pan. Alternatively oil a 9 by 5 by 3-inch loaf pan and place braided challah into pan. Repeat in 2 additional pans with remaining 2 dough portions. Brush the 3 braided loaves with egg wash, being careful to brush the loaves in the pan lightly on the top so they don't stick to the sides of the bread pan.

Bake until cooked through about 35 minutes. Let cool to room temperature before cutting. To freeze, place cooled loaf in a plastic bag, seal and freeze. To defrost, first remove from bag.

225

Mauer's Egg Challah

(P) Makes 4 (1-pound) challahs or 3 challahs and 4 rolls

This signature recipe comes from Joe Mauer, the son of Hyman and Sonia Mauer, who founded the original and the first kosher bakery in Chicago in 1954. Their challah was once rated the "best challah" by the Chicago Tribune. When using fresh yeast, or any yeast, do not use hot water; it will kill the yeast. In Israel, where the flour is sold by the kilo package, simply use 1 kilo flour, reserving about ¼ cup for the work surface.

1¾ cups water (14 ounces),
room temperature
2 ounces fresh yeast (see Tip)
6¼ cups high gluten flour (1 kilo)
(see Tip)
½ cup sugar
1½ teaspoons salt
4 large eggs, divided
5 tablespoons canola oil
Poppy seeds or sesame seeds,
as needed for garnish

If fresh yeast is unavailable, substitute 2 (¼-ounce, or 7-gram) packages of active dry yeast. Or use 5 level teaspoons of active dry yeast.

From Poland to Chicago: A Bakery is Born

Joe Mauer is the son of Hyman and Sonia Mauer, founder of the original Tel-Aviv Kosher Bakery in Chicago. Hyman, born in Lemberg, Poland in 1910, was the sole survivor of the Holocaust from his family, including his parents, grandmother, and nine brothers. Hyman was a frogman for Poland, fighting against the Nazis. When the Nazis finally invaded Poland, he became a Jewish Partisan, living in the forest, active in the Jewish Resistance Movement. He was captured by the Russians and, because he was fluent in six languages, he served as a translator. Sonia (nee Weisbrot) Mauer, born in Warsaw, Poland in 1919, survived Auschwitz. She was the only survivor of her large, religious family, including eight sisters and one brother, her parents and grandparents. The Mauers met in a DP camp after the War, married in 1946 and came to the States sponsored by Sonia's cousin, Hyman Mozak.

Hyman Mauer, who had learned to bake at home, got a job working for Rosen's bakery, eventually becoming a foreman. He also worked a second job, delivering flour. And when a customer, Mr Griese, who owned a traditional German bakery (which sold challah) on Kedzie Avenue south of Lawrence in Chicago, asked him to work, Hyman worked a third job, baking challah and rolls. In 1954, Mr. Griese asked Hyman to buy the bakery. Before purchasing the bakery, Hyman Mauer spoke to three local respected rabbis, who were all enthusiastic about opening a kosher bakery in Chicago, and agreed to be Mashgichim (religious supervisor). Hyman worked with the baking and Sonia worked with the customers (eventually they taught their sons and daughters-in-law, who continued running it). This was the first enduring all-kosher bakery under kosher supervision, fulfilling the mitzvah of "separating challah" (page 224), only parve baked goods, and closed on Shabbos and Jewish holidays.

In a small bowl, place water. Crumble fresh yeast and add to water. (If using active dry yeast, add to water.) Stir to mix, and let rest for about 10 to 30 minutes.

In the work bowl of a stand mixer, fitted with the dough hook, mix the flour, sugar and salt together. Add 2 of the eggs, oil and the water-yeast mixture and mix until the dough starts creeping up the dough hook, about 10 minutes. You must knead the dough for 10 minutes. The dough should be smooth and soft. If the dough is too stiff, add water by the tablespoon; if the dough is too soft, add flour by the tablespoon.

Transfer the dough into a lightly oiled 6-quart bowl and cover with a clean, lint-free towel that has been wet and wrung almost dry. Let rise in a warm place until the dough has doubled in size, about 1 to 1½ hours.

Turn dough out on a lightly floured work surface and shape into a large ball. Oil the top and cover with plastic wrap for 10 to 15 minutes. Break or cut with a bench knife into 4 balls.

Preheat oven to 350°F. Braid each challah, using 3, 4 or 6 braids. Place each in a greased and floured pan or parchment paper-lined pan. Let rise for about 45 to 60 minutes.

In a small bowl, beat the remaining 2 eggs to make an egg wash. Lightly brush with egg wash, and if desired, sprinkle with sesame or poppy seeds.

Bake until golden, 25 to 35 minutes.

Prepare and braid the challah on Thursday, but do not brush with egg wash. Place the loaves in the refrigerator, lightly covered with a sheet of parchment paper lightly sprayed with nonstick cooking spray, sprayed side down.
Remove from refrigerator Friday and let sit 20 to 30 minutes.
Then brush with egg wash and bake.

Commercial bakeries purchase high-gluten flour in bulk. Substitute bread flour for high-gluten flour. Bread flour is milled from hard wheat and has more protein than all-purpose flour, which is milled from soft and hard wheat.

Everyday Romanian Bread

(P) Makes 1 (1½ pound) loaf

Veronica Sporia, of Hungarian Kosher Foods, shared this recipe that her husband, Nicolae, prepares fresh for their family most every day. It is a fragrant reminder of his family's bakery in Romania. The Sporias bake a huge loaf in an oversized bread machine, which most kitchens lack. So I have adapted the recipe for a standard kitchen using a stand mixer, or a large capacity food processor, or a 2-pound bread machine. You can even mix it by hand in a 6-quart bowl. The recipe calls only for a few basic ingredients: flour, yeast, water, salt (and I add 1 tablespoon of sugar). But the result is greater than the sum of its parts: a light, flavorful bread perfect for toast or sandwiches.

3 to 4 cups unbleached all-purpose flour
1 (¼-ounce, or 7-gram) packet
or 2¼ teaspoons instant
or bread machine yeast
1 tablespoon sugar
1½ teaspoons salt
1¼ cups water

Bakeries in Vásárosnamény

In a town where the minority of the population was Jewish (about 200 families), three of the four bakeries were Jewish owned and operated. These three bakeries sold to everyone, Jews and non-Jews, even though they were closed on Saturdays and Jewish holidays. The bakery closest to my mother's home, owned by friends of my mother's family, was located near the town square. There were two large rooms: the front of the store for sales, and the back with kneading troughs and large ovens. They sold wholesale, including to non-Jewish stores in surrounding towns, as well as retail, assorted breads (brown, white, sourdough, pretzels, and more) and pastries. (For a vivid account of this bakery, see Eight Pieces of Silk, by Alex Zelczer, 8piecesofsilk@gmail.com.) Unlike today's bakeries you could also bring (or they would pick up) your own ready-to-bake challah or bread dough, marked with your family name, to be baked in the bakery ovens. (This is how my mother's family baked their weekly bread). The bakery charged by weight, by the kilo, to bake your bread. Also unlike today's bakeries everything was mixed and kneaded and shaped by hand.

To make in a stand mixer:

In the work bowl of a stand mixer fitted with the dough hook, place flour, yeast, sugar and salt. Mix on low for 30 seconds. With the machine running on low, slowly add the water. Let mix until a dough forms and pulls away from the sides of the bowl. Knead for 10 minutes.

Transfer dough to an oiled 6-quart bowl, turning dough over once so oiled side is up. Cover bowl with plastic wrap and let rise until doubled in a warm place, about 1½ hours.

On a lightly floured work surface, knead dough briefly to remove air pockets, and shape into a loaf. Place in an oiled loaf pan (8½ by 4½ by 2¾-inches is ideal), spray loaf top with nonstick cooking spray and cover lightly with parchment or a clean tea towel wet and wrung almost dry. Let rise in a warm place until doubled in size and an indentation made by pressing a finger into the dough remains and does not spring back.

While dough is rising, preheat oven to 375°F. Bake fully risen loaf until golden brown and cooked through, about 35 minutes. Remove from oven.

Transfer to a rack to cool. Do not slice bread until it has cooled to room temperature.

To mix in a food processor:

Place all dry ingredients in the work bowl of a large capacity food processor fitted with the plastic dough blade. Pulse briefly to mix. With machine running, pour water through the feed tube and process until dough forms and pulls away from the side of the work bowl.

Transfer dough to an oiled 6-quart bowl and follow directions for rising, shaping and baking.

To mix by hand:

Place all dry ingredients in a 6-quart bowl. Whisk to mix. Add water and with a sturdy spoon, stir until a dough forms. Turn dough out onto a lightly floured work surface and knead for 10 minutes. Wash, dry and oil bowl. Transfer dough to the bowl and follow directions for rising, shaping and baking.

To make in a bread machine:

Follow manufacturer's instruction for adding ingredients and baking.

Sweet Bread Kugel

(P) Makes 12 to 16 servings

A kugel is a casserole, and this one can be a dish for brunch with dairy, a side dish to serve with meats and poultry, or even for dessert, dusted with confectioner's sugar. The flavor changes according to the preserves you use, so pick your favorite flavor but use the very finest preserves you can find. My mother created this recipe because of her Survivor's dedication to not wasting a single morsel of edible food, particularly bread. This "leftover" is a gourmet treat.

1½ pounds challah,
broken into pieces, dried
5 eggs
¾ cup sugar
½ teaspoon salt
½ teaspoon cinnamon
1 to 1½ cups seedless preserves:
raspberry, apricot, strawberry or other
2 tablespoons vegetable oil

> To dry challah, break fresh challah into pieces or slice. Place in a large brown paper bag at room temperature until dry, about 3 days. Or, bake at 325°F on a baking tray for 15 to 20 minutes.

> Increase cinnamon to 1 teaspoon, and add ½ cup raisins.

Preheat oven to 350°F. Place bread in large bowl and cover with warm water Let soak until soft. Drain and squeeze out water. Dry bowl and return bread to bowl. Reserve.

In a medium bowl whisk together eggs, sugar salt and cinnamon, until eggs are well beaten. Pour over reserved bread, and mix well.

Oil the bottom and sides of a 9 by 13-inch pan. Film the bottom thinly with a little oil.

Pour half of the bread-egg mixture into the pan. Spread preserves over the entire surface. Pour the remaining bread mixture gently over the preserves, spreading carefully.

Bake until golden brown and firm, 1 hour.

Cut 3 by 4 for 12 dessert or brunch servings. Sprinkle with confectioner's sugar if desired. Cut 4 by 4 for 16 side dish servings. Serve warm, room temperature or cold.

Bread Stuffing

P Makes 12 servings

Moist and flavorful Bread Stuffing can be baked as a casserole (see Variation), used to stuff chicken or turkey, and in a wide variety of recipes in this cookbook. We added mushrooms, although they were not used "at home."

2 tablespoons vegetable oil
1 medium onion, diced
8 mushrooms, diced
1½ pounds challah,
broken into pieces, dried
6 eggs
½ teaspoon salt
½ teaspoon Seasoned Salt (page 66)
¼ teaspoon freshly ground pepper
½ teaspoon sweet Hungarian paprika,
optional

Preheat the oven to 350°F. In a 12-inch sauté pan over medium heat, heat oil until hot, about 2 minutes. Add the onion and the mushrooms and sauté until soft and translucent, but not brown. Reserve.

Meanwhile, place dried challah in a large bowl, cover with warm water and soak until soft. Drain and squeeze out. Dry bowl and return bread to bowl. Reserve.

Break eggs one by one, and add each to reserved challah, stirring to mix. Add the onions and mushrooms. Add seasonings. Mix well. Use immediately as a stuffing; do not refrigerate because of eggs in the mix.

To bake as a kugel: Oil the bottom and sides of a 9 by 13-inch baking pan. Pour in the stuffing mixture, and bake until golden brown and firm, 1 hour.

Clean and finely chop 3 *pupiks* (gizzards) and sauté together with onions and mushrooms.

Sweet Yeast Dough

(P) Makes 4 dough balls, rolled out to rectangles ⅛- to ¼-inch thick

This same dough is used for three pastries in this chapter: Golden Dumplings, Aranygaluska; Chocolate Yeast Roll, Kakaós; and Cheese Danish, Deltelach. All pastry chefs have their own dough recipes; this one developed from baking with my mother, who baked with her mother in Vásárosnamény. It is tender, airy and meltingly perfect. "At home" the dough was made with only fresh butter, milk and yeast. I offer a parve version because of its versatility; however, do try substituting butter and milk for margarine and nondairy milk, to fully recapture the flavor of "at home." I also have substituted active dry yeast for fresh.

2 (¼-ounce, or 7-gram) packages active dry yeast
(each package equals 2¼ teaspoons)
¾ cup sugar, divided
½ cup lukewarm water
1⅞ cups lukewarm nondairy milk such as soy, almond or parve creamer
1½ sticks (¾ cup) margarine, melted and cooled to room temperature
1 teaspoon salt
2 eggs
7 cups unbleached bread flour

> For a dairy version, substitute butter for margarine and milk for nondairy milk.

> To make the dough in a bread machine, place 1 cup nondairy milk or milk, ¼ cup water, 2 eggs, 6 tablespoons melted margarine or butter, ½ cup sugar, 3½ teaspoons dry yeast, 1 teaspoon salt and 3¾ cups flour. Program machine for dough cycle. Remove dough when finished. Makes 2 balls of dough. If you are using cake yeast, use 1-ounce cake for the full recipe and one .6-ounce cake for the bread machine recipe.

In a small bowl place yeast, 1 tablespoon of the sugar and ½ cup lukewarm water. Whisk to dissolve yeast and sugar. Reserve.

Place nondairy milk in a small separate bowl. Add the remaining sugar, the margarine, and salt and stir to dissolve sugar. Add the eggs and mix well.

In an 8-quart bowl place flour. Make a well in the center and pour in yeast mixture and nondairy milk mixture. Mix with a large sturdy spoon until a dough forms and pulls away from the side of the bowl.

Turn dough out onto a lightly floured board and knead until dough is smooth and satiny, adding more flour as necessary, 5 to 8 minutes.

Wash and dry the 8-quart bowl and oil lightly. Transfer dough to bowl, turn once so top is oiled. Cover with plastic wrap and let rise in a warm place (85°F) until doubled, 1½ hours. Punch dough down, knead briefly and let rise until doubled a second time.

Turn dough out on floured board and divide with a knife into 4 equal balls.

Golden Dumplings, *Aranygaluska*

Ⓟ Makes 24 *Aranygaluska*

Aranygaluska were traditionally baked for Shabbos or for a Jewish holiday. Served with coffee or tea, these golden fruit-filled dumplings make a perfect dessert. Because the shape is the same as traditional Hamantaschen (the three-cornered hat of Haman) Aranygaluska were often served on Purim. They are labor-intensive, but always worth the effort because everyone who eats them sits back and sighs with satisfaction. Aranygaluska freeze well, but you will never have any left to freeze. If you want to present these as a pull-apart cake (like monkey bread) then bake in an oven-to-table round or square baking dish. If you prefer to transfer to a serving platter in the kitchen, then use any regular baking pan.

1 Sweet Yeast Dough ball
(recipe, page 233)
Vegetable oil as needed for dipping

For the Filling:
½ cup *lekvar* (page 259) or apricot
or strawberry preserves or as needed

For the Topping:
1 cup sugar
1 cup finely chopped walnuts
1 teaspoon cinnamon

Roll out dough ball onto floured board into a 12 by 18-inch rectangle. Cut 4 by 6 for 24 3-inch squares.

Fill each square with 1 teaspoon *lekvar* or preserves. Fold into triangles. Moisten edges with water, and press to seal.

Place 1 cup of oil in a shallow bowl. Mix sugar, walnuts and cinnamon together in a separate shallow bowl.

Dip *Aranygaluska* in oil on both sides, then dredge in sugar-cinnamon-nut topping mixture.

Lightly spray with nonstick cooking spray an 8 by 8-inch square or 9-inch round baking pan, and dust with flour. Layer half of the *Aranygaluska* in one layer, fitting them together like a puzzle. Then top with a second layer. Let rise for approximately an hour.

Preheat oven to 350°F. Bake until golden brown, 30 to 40 minutes. Serve warm or let cool to room temperature. Separate gently with a spatula or pastry server and serve one piece per person.

Food, Family and Tradition

Purim in Vásárosnamény

The Jewish Kehilla (community) in Vásárosnamény owned a large acreage, paid for and maintained by community taxes. On that acreage stood the shul, the shecht shteible (slaughter house), the cheder (school), the mikvah (ritual pool), as well as the rabbi's house, a communal kitchen and other houses for Jewish community employees. My mother remembers that for Purim, Rabbi Cohen's wife in Vásárosnamény prepared her own recipe of Aranygaluska to serve everyone who was invited to the rabbi's house behind the shul for a Purim Shpiel. In the evening, after reading the Megillas Esther (the story of Esther), it is traditional to have a Purim Shpiel, a good-natured spoof of Jewish life. The following day, they sent shalach manos, gifts of food to friends and family, and the Yeshiva boys (teen agers) dressed in costumes and went from house to house entertaining everyone. "At home," for Purim my mother and her mother baked for hours on end, many of the recipes in this chapter such as kindle and meringue kisses. She still does this today.

Chocolate Yeast Roll, *Kakaós*

P Makes 1 (12 by 20-inch) cake roll, 20 pieces

Kakaós is authentically Hungarian and one of my mother's signature pastries. Her yeast dough makes it light and perfect. Use the best quality cocoa you can find. If you can roll the dough out to 12 by 20 inches that is the ideal thickness. However, if your work surface is smaller you can roll the dough out to 12 by 16 inches for a thicker but equally delicious cake.

1 Sweet Yeast Dough ball (page 233)
¼ cup unsweetened cocoa
½ cup sugar
1 egg beaten with 1 teaspoon water
1 teaspoon sugar

Roll out dough ball on a lightly floured work surface into a 12 by 20-inch rectangle.

In a small bowl mix together cocoa and the ½ cup sugar. Reserve. In a separate small bowl mix egg-water and remaining sugar to dissolve sugar. Reserve.

Spread cocoa mixture evenly over surface of dough. Roll as you would a jellyroll. Moisten edges with water and seal.

Transfer gently to a parchment paper-lined half sheet pan, seam side down, bending roll in horseshoe shape to fit, if needed. Let rise in a warm place until doubled, 30 to 60 minutes.

Preheat oven to 350°F. Brush top with egg wash. Bake until golden brown and cooked through, 20 to 30 minutes.

Let cool to room temperature and slice into 1-inch thick slices. Dust with powdered sugar if desired.

Food, Family and Tradition

Cheese Danish, *Deltelach*

D Makes 24 (3-inch) squares

Cheese Deltelach on Shabbos is traditional in my father's and mother's families for generations including today's. The cheese filling is not overly sweet, an example of a light sugar to flour ratio. "At home" it was made with fresh homemade farmer's cheese, but today we make it with store-bought farmer's cheese. Enjoy it any day of the week with a fresh, hot cup of coffee.

1 Sweet Yeast Dough ball (page 233)

For the Filling:
1 pound farmer's cheese
2 ounces cream cheese
½ teaspoon salt
½ teaspoon cinnamon
⅓ cup sugar, or to taste
1 egg

1 egg beaten with 1 tablespoon water
1 teaspoon sugar

> For a parve version, fill centers with 1 tablespoon of *lekvar* instead of cheese.
> If you want bigger pastries, roll out dough 12 by 16-inch and cut 3 by 4 for 12 (4-inch) squares.

Make the filling: In a large bowl, using a sturdy wooden spoon, mix the cheeses together until smooth. Add salt, cinnamon, sugar to taste, mixing well. Add the 1 egg and mix well. Cover and refrigerate for about 10 minutes, so the filling holds together. Reserve.

In a small bowl beat together the remaining egg with water. Add sugar and mix to dissolve sugar. Reserve.

On a lightly floured board roll out the dough ball into a 12 by 18-inch rectangle. Cut 4 by 6 into 24 (3-inch) squares.

Fill the center of each square with 1 tablespoon of the reserved cheese filling. Fold up the four corners, to meet in the middle, moistening each corner with water to seal. Do not seal sides, as you want the cheese filling to show through.

Line a half sheet pan with parchment paper. Place *deltelach* 2 inches apart to allow for rising. Let rest in a warm place until dough rises and looks puffy, for 30 to 45 minutes.

Meanwhile, preheat oven to 350°F. Using a pastry brush, brush the tops with the egg wash very lightly so as not to deflate pastries. Bake until golden, 20 to 30 minutes.

Kindle

Ⓟ Makes 2 (14- by 16-inch) rolls, or 1 (14- by 26-inch) roll

Kindle is the typical cake that was prepared for Kiddush on Shabbos after shul in the morning. My father recited the Kiddush on Shabbos with a drink of Schnapps, which he enjoyed while eating a piece of kindle. Kindle is also a wonderful accompaniment to a cup of hot tea. My mother's family customarily baked this for Purim and baked meringue kisses with the egg whites that were left. This custom continues in our family today. Unlike other yeast-based pastries, the characteristic texture of kindle depends on the dough not rising. This cake freezes well, and can be made in advance.

For the dough:
3 cups flour
½ cup sugar
1 teaspoon baking powder
⅛ teaspoon baking soda
pinch salt
½ lemon, juice (usually about 1 ounce)
and zest
3 egg yolks
Scant ½ cup oil
½ cup seltzer water
1 teaspoon active dry yeast

> Substitute 2 whole eggs
> for the 3 yolks.

For the filling:
½ cup preserves of choice, raspberry, apricot, or *lekvar*
1 cup finely chopped walnuts
¾ cup sugar
1 teaspoon cinnamon
⅓ cup dark raisins
2 tablespoons honey

1 egg beaten with 1 teaspoon water
¼ teaspoon sugar

Preheat oven to 350°F. In a large bowl, mix together all the dry ingredients flour, sugar, baking powder, baking soda, and the salt. Reserve.

In a medium bowl, mix together the lemon juice and zest, eggs and oil. Reserve. Pour the seltzer water into a small bowl. Dissolve the yeast in the seltzer water.

Immediately (the yeast is not set aside to rise) make an indentation in the middle of the flour. Add the egg mixture and the yeast-seltzer water mixture and mix. Knead the dough until it is smooth and comes off of your hands. Alternatively, you can do this in a stand mixer fitted with the dough hook. Mix until the dough is smooth and comes off the sides, making a ball. Do not let the dough rise.

Roll out the dough on a floured surface into a 12 by 24-inch or 14 by 26-inch rectangle. Spread the preserves in a thin layer on the dough. In a small bowl, mix the sugar and cinnamon together. Sprinkle evenly over the preserves with the nuts, the sugar mixed with the cinnamon, and then the raisins. Drizzle the honey evenly over the filling.

Starting with the long side, roll tightly. Moisten edge and pinch to seal. Place on a greased and floured cookie sheet, or on parchment paper-lined cookie sheet. Cut the cake in half and with your hands, spread the cake gently to make it a bit longer, around 15 to 16 inches. Pierce the top of each roll with a fork every 2 inches along the top.

In a small bowl, mix the egg, water and sugar to make the egg wash. With a pastry brush, brush the top and sides of the cake with the egg wash.

Bake at 350°F in the center of the oven for 50 to 60 minutes until golden brown. Cool to room temperature and cut into thin slices to serve.

Part II - Recipes: Bread, Pastries, Cakes and Cookies

Sponge Cake

(P) Makes 1 angel food cake tube pan

My mother has been baking sponge cakes, especially for Pesach, since she was a child. While she has made sponge cake without cake meal, I chose this cake meal recipe because we all love this cake's flavor and texture. Make sure that both the orange and lemon are juicy for a flavorful and moist cake. It is important that the cake meal and the potato starch are sifted for a light cake. This cake freezes well, and can be made in advance.

½ large orange
½ large lemon
10 eggs, separated
dash of salt
1¼ cups sugar
⅔ cup sifted matza cake meal
⅓ cup sifted potato starch

Preheat oven to 325°F. Rack should be in center or lower third of oven. Remove the seeds from the orange and lemon and discard. In the work bowl of a food processor fitted with the metal blade, process the orange and the lemon, together with the rind until finely puréed. Reserve.

In a large bowl, beat the egg whites until stiff. Add salt during beating when the egg whites foam, and continue beating until the whites are stiff. Reserve.

In a large bowl, beat the egg yolks, slowly adding the sugar, until they are light and fluffy. Add the orange and lemon to the egg yolk mixture and beat. Slowly add the sifted cake meal and the sifted potato starch to the egg yolk mixture and mix. Fold in the egg whites. Pour the mixture into a dry angel food cake tube pan.

Bake for 1 to 1½ hours, until the cake is golden.

Remove from the oven and immediately invert pan. Allow the cake to cool. After the cake has cooled, turn right side up and cut around and remove cake. Let cool to room temperature before slicing.

Mitzvah Matza

Among my mother's vivid memories of Pesach "at home," were some of her beloved maternal grandfather's customs. He followed the special Chassidic custom, rare today, of baking mitzvah matza on Erev Pesach (Passover Eve). On Erev Pesach, one is no longer allowed to even possess, much less eat, any chametz (leavened) food. So he perfectly timed and baked just enough matza for the Seder, careful that it did not rise and become chametz. When my mother was liberated from Torgau concentration camp in 1945 she traveled home to Vásárosnamény to see if anyone in her family had survived. She found no one (and did not yet know that one brother, Morton, had survived). Material objects meant nothing, but walking through the home her family had lived in, she found the wine glass that her grandfather had used for the Pesach Seder. She took it with her as she journeyed forward, and each year it holds a place of honor at our family Seder table.

Honey Cake, *Lekech*

Ⓟ Makes 2 (9 by 5 by 3-inch) loaf pans

Honey is traditionally eaten on Rosh Hashana, the Jewish New Year, for its sweet taste. As we pray to God for a "sweet New Year," we set our table with sweet foods. Either challah or apples dipped in honey begin the festive meal. Honey Cake, or Lekech, is a special recipe from my aunt Goldie for the Kiddush or dessert on Rosh Hashana.

1¼ cups vegetable oil
1¼ cups honey
1¼ cups sugar
1 cup strong brewed coffee
1 teaspoon baking soda
6 eggs, separated
3 cups flour
½ teaspoon baking powder
3 to 4 drops lemon juice

Preheat oven to 350°F. Spray loaf pans with nonstick cooking spray and line sides and bottom with parchment paper.

In a large bowl, place oil, honey, sugar, coffee, baking soda and egg yolks. Mix until smooth. Reserve.

In another medium bowl, mix flour with baking powder. Slowly add the flour mixture into the cake mixture, beating on a low speed.

In a large bowl, beat the egg whites on high, adding 3 to 4 drops of lemon juice, until whites are stiff. Carefully, fold the whites into the cake mixture.

Divide batter equally among the prepared baking pans. Bake in the center of the oven, until the top browns, about 10 to 15 minutes. When the top is brown, reduce the temperature to 325°F. Continue to bake until a toothpick inserted in center comes out clean or the cake springs back when pressed lightly, about 1 hour.

Cool to room temperature and slice into ½-inch slices.

Ceasar Ben Haim
by Margit Kirsche

"While I was in the prison camp, Torgau, I worked with a drill. A male prisoner, working in the room next to me, needed to use my drill so he often came over to borrow it. He asked some of the other female prisoners, "Why are you here?" They said that they did not know, but when he asked me, I said that I was there because I was Jewish. He told me that he was from Algiers, that he was with the French Legion and that the Nazis thought he was a French POW. When he was freed, just before leaving, he came over, whispered good-bye and handed me a scrap of paper. His name was Ceasar Ben Haim, he was married, and he said that if the Nazis had known he was Jewish, they would have killed him. He said that if I survived the War and had no one and no where to go, I should go to his mother, and I would be a child of his mother. The scrap of paper had his name and address on it. I have kept it with me all these years."

Chocolate Nut Cake

P   Makes 1 (9- or 10-inch) springform pan

Nuts were often used in making desserts in Europe, and they still are. My mother loved to make cakes from nuts and made this flourless cake for Pesach. It is delectable any time of year, and takes only four steps to prepare. Serve plain or with Fresh Raspberry Sauce (page 270) on the side.

10 eggs, separated
1 cup sugar
6 ounces dark chocolate, melted and cooled
2 cups walnuts, finely ground
Pinch of salt

Preheat oven to 350°F. Spray pan with nonstick cooking spray. Line bottom with parchment paper cut to fit.

In the work bowl of a stand mixer fitted with the whisk attachment, beat egg yolks with sugar until thick and light yellow. Using a silicone spatula, fold in the chocolate. Then fold in the nuts.

In a separate large bowl beat egg whites until stiff, adding a pinch of salt when almost done. Carefully fold the whites into the cake mixture.

Pour cake batter into prepared pan. Bake cake in the center of the oven for 1 hour, until a cake tester inserted in center of cake comes out clean. Remove pan to a rack to cool. Using a thin spatula, loosen sides, and remove from pan. Transfer to a serving platter. Slice and serve with fruit sauce on the side, if desired.

The Beginning of the End
by Margit Kirssche

"It was the last day of Pesach in 1944. My uncle Hersch Meilich came over to our house after shul. I was so happy to see him, because I loved my uncle and was always happy when he came over. Then he started to cry. He said that all the Jews would have to leave their homes. I was scared. In fact, I had been scared and could not sleep for most of the month prior, and I started to cry. My three younger brothers immediately went to pray — to say "Tehillim" (Psalms). We tried to escape. My uncle's family and my family each hired a non-Jew with a wagon to take us away, separately. We hoped we could hide out until the War was over, but the Nazis caught us after 30 kilometers and brought us back. That was the last time I saw anyone from my uncle's family. None of them survived."

Marble Cake

Ⓟ Makes 1 cake

After years of baking my own and eating other cooks' marble cakes, this is the best I have tasted. It was a favorite of my mother's cousin, Sara Muschel, known affectionately as Suri. Suri loved cooking and baking, especially for Shabbos and the Jewish holidays. This marble cake is light and perfect for a morning coffee, an afternoon tea, or dessert anytime. The layered batter marbleizes itself during baking. This cake takes about 10 minutes to mix. It freezes well, and can be made in advance.

¼ cup cocoa
¼ teaspoon baking soda
¼ cup hot water
2 cups flour
1½ cups sugar
3 teaspoons baking powder
1 teaspoon salt
½ cup oil
7 eggs, separated
¾ cup water
2 teaspoons vanilla

Preheat oven to 375°F. In a small bowl, mix cocoa and baking soda in the ¼ cup hot water until it is a thick paste. Reserve.

In a medium bowl, sift the flour, sugar, baking powder and salt. Reserve.

In the work bowl of stand mixer, pour oil, egg yolks, the ¾ cup water, and vanilla. Mix until smooth. Add dry ingredients and mix until smooth.

In a separate bowl, beat egg whites until white and fluffy, and soft peaks form when beaters are lifted. Do not beat stiff or dry. Carefully fold the whites into the cake batter. Divide the batter in half. Fold the cocoa paste into half the batter, mixing well so no streaks remain.

In an ungreased tube pan, pour half the white batter on the bottom, then half the cocoa batter, and repeat, first the white batter and then the cocoa batter.

Bake at 375°F for 55 minutes.

Remove from oven and let the cake cool. Cut out and serve.

Suri's Legacy

My mother's first cousin Suri, Sara Muschel, was born in a Chassidic family in Czechoslovakia, the youngest girl of eight siblings. As a young child, she was sent to my mother's to spend one summer vacation. She was so attached to her own mother, that her family thought she would want to come home immediately. Instead she had a wonderful time and was not homesick at all. It was during this vacation that my mother first became so attached to her. Suri survived Auschwitz (she was Number A7616) as a young teenager together with her older sister Freida Rifka. She lost both parents and two brothers and countless other relatives. Suri came to the States in the late 1940s with her older sister Piri and met and married her husband Rabbi Nachum Muschel. Despite not speaking English when she arrived in the States, Suri not only earned a high school diploma but also a master's degree while having four children, making a traditional home and supporting her husband's life's work as rabbi, Jewish educator and founder of a Jewish day school. Suri was a courageous, brilliant and capable woman, and passionate about everything she did in life. She was lovingly attached to everyone in her family and dedicated to the future generations of the Jewish people. And despite the hardships she endured throughout her life, she always maintained her sense of gratitude to God.

Her mother's last words to her as they entered Auschwitz were "Always remember, you are a Jewish daughter." She never forgot and dedicated her life as a Jewish woman, Jewish wife, Jewish mother and grandmother. This was the legacy Suri left to all of us who were privileged to know and love her.

Yeast Crescents, My Mom's *Kippilach*

Ⓟ Makes 4 dozen

For a dairy version, see "Variations," below. I always use fresh yeast for this because my mom always did; however, feel free to substitute 2 (¼-ounce, 7-gram) packages active dry yeast. Kippilach is a small, crescent-shaped pastry well known in Hungarian and Czech baking traditions. (You may have heard it called rugelach.) My mother's version is crisp and tender and soft at the same time. For nondairy I use soy milk.

For the dough:
1 (1-ounce) cake fresh yeast
or
2 (¼-ounce, 7-gram) packages
of active dry yeast
½ cup lukewarm non-dairy milk
or creamer
3 cups unbleached all-purpose flour
1 cup (2 sticks) margarine
2 tablespoons sugar
2 egg yolks

For the Filling:
1 cup finely chopped walnuts
¾ cup sugar
1 teaspoon cinnamon
4 tablespoons melted margarine

Substitute butter and milk for nondairy.

Spread with raspberry or apricot preserves either in addition to the mixture above or instead.

Crumble the yeast (or sprinkle the dry yeast if using) into a small bowl. Add milk and let soak until mixture foams, about 20 minutes.

Make the filling: In small bowl mix the nuts, sugar, and cinnamon. Reserve. Place the 4 tablespoons of melted margarine in a separate small bowl. Reserve.

Place flour in a medium bowl. Cut the cup of margarine into small pieces and add. Using a pastry blender or fork, cut margarine into flour until mixture is like fine meal. Add sugar and mix.

Add yolks and reserved milk-yeast mixture. Stir with a sturdy spoon until cohesive dough forms and pulls away from sides of bowl.

Turn dough out on a lightly floured board and divide into four balls. Roll out each ball into an 8-inch diameter circle, ⅛-inch thick. One at a time, covering unused dough balls to prevent drying out. Brush the circle lightly with melted margarine. Then sprinkle ¼ of the filling on the circle.

Cut each circle into 12 equal wedges (cut in half, then in quarters, then cut each quarter into thirds). Roll up each wedge, starting with the wide end, into a crescent.

Place crescents 1 inch apart on a parchment paper-lined half sheet pan. Repeat with remaining dough balls and filling.

Meanwhile, preheat oven to 375°F. Bake until cooked through and golden, 20 to 25 minutes.

249

Walnut Crescents, *Kippilach* Cookies

Ⓓ Ⓟ   Makes about 6 dozen

My cousin Ibi is known for these authentic Hungarian nut cookies, tender and crisp, that she prepares effortlessly. Ibi learned this recipe directly from her mother Goldie Weinberger. The ingredients were originally measured not by cups, because they didn't have measuring cups, but by a glezele, or a glass. They keep well stored in an airtight container.

3 cups unbleached flour
2 cups finely ground walnuts
1 cup sugar
1 teaspoon baking powder
1 cup (2 sticks) butter or margarine, softened
½ cup seltzer water
Vanilla Sugar (see Note), or confectioner's sugar, as needed, for dusting

Preheat oven to 350°F. In a large bowl, place all the dry ingredients. Whisk to mix. Add butter or margarine, and, using a pastry cutter or fork, mix until mixture resembles coarse corn meal. Add seltzer and mix to form a dough.

Scoop by the tablespoonful. Using your hands, roll into a log about 2 inches long, tapering ends and shaping into a crescent. Place 1 inch apart on parchment paper-lined cookie sheets.

Bake until cooked through and lightly brown on bottom, 25 to 30 minutes.

Remove from oven. Cool to room temperature. Before serving, sprinkle with vanilla or confectioners sugar.

Bittersweet

In 1944, when my mother's family was taken on the second transport from the Berekszasz ghetto in cattle cars on the train to an unknown destination (which was in fact, Auschwitz), her mother had baked some cookies to take with from the little flour she had left. On the train my mother's 12-year-old brother Yitzchak Isaac finished his cookies. As the train traveled for days, he was desperately hungry, so she gave him all of her cookies. And on the way, through the open slats in the cattle cars, her mother saw the Carpathian Mountains. "I remember traveling through the beautiful mountains when I was a child. I always wanted to see them again in my lifetime," her mother remarked. "But I never thought I would see them like this." Of all the family members on the train, only my mother survived.

Vanilla sugar, commonly sold in small packets, is familiar in Europe where it is used to top cookies and other desserts and often used in baking, like vanilla extract. There are several commercially prepared brands on the market. However, if you wish to make your own, place 2 cups of confectioner's sugar in a container with a tight-fitting lid, add 1 or 2 fresh vanilla beans, cover and seal for 2 weeks. Replenish jar with sugar as it is used, and occasionally add 1 more vanilla bean.

Tea Cookies, *Ugiot Shel Savta*

D **P**   Makes 4 dough balls

This original family sugar cookie recipe, so simple and yet so perfect, goes back to my father's maternal grandmother, the mother of his aunt, Golda Moskovics. The recipe calls for many egg yolks, not unusual in traditional European cooking where other recipes call for many egg whites. The cookie is golden brown, super crisp and crunchy and keeps well in an airtight container. See Tip below for original European (or Israeli) measurements, from this recipe as given to me by my cousin Rachel Grossman, daughter of Golda Moskovics.

3½ cups flour
1¼ cups sugar
⅞ cup (14 tablespoons) butter or margarine, softened
2½ teaspoons baking powder
4 teaspoons vanilla sugar (page 248)
8 egg yolks

> **The original measurements from the Israeli recipe:**
> ½ kilo flour
> 1¼ cups sugar
> 200 grams butter or margarine
> 12 grams (1 package) baking powder
> 20 grams (2 packages) vanilla sugar
> 8 egg yolks.

Preheat oven to 350°F. In the work bowl of stand mixer fitted with the flat paddle, place all ingredients and mix until a dough forms and cleans the sides of the bowl. Alternatively, use a medium bowl and hand-held mixer.

Divide dough into 4 equal balls. One by one, on a lightly floured work surface, roll out each ball to a 9 by 12-inch rectangle, ⅛-inch thick. Using a glass or a cookie cutter, cut into rounds or choice of shape, such as stars, squares, and hearts.

Place at least 1 inch apart on parchment paper-lined cookie sheets. Bake at 350°F for 20 minutes, until golden brown.

Early Life in Chibat Tzion: The Long Journey Home
In January 1949, my father's aunt, Golda Moskovics, left Opava, Czechoslovakia, together with her husband, Eliezer, and two-year-old young son, Moshe, and traveled to Italy, where they began the arduous journey to Israel, on the Abbazia, a freighter. They were among the Survivors who came to Israel and helped build the state. They arrived in the port city of Yafo, Israel. Within a few days, they moved to Kfar Haroeh, a small village in central Israel, and bought land and an orange orchard in Chibat Tzion (the neighboring village). While they were living in one rented room without inside plumbing and not even enough money for shoes, they built a house, brick by brick, with their own hands on the land they had bought. In 1952, they were finally able to move into the home they built in Chibat Tzion, and although they had no refrigerator, no electricity in the first years, and did all the laundry by hand, they did have inside plumbing. (By 2006 Chibat Tzion had a population of 492.) They earned a livelihood by selling oranges from their orchards and eggs from the chickens in their chicken coops. My father's aunt Golda and her family lived there, happy to be home in Israel, for the rest of their lives.

251

Meringue Kisses, *Habcsók*

Ⓟ Makes 54 kisses

Habcsók, traditionally baked for Purim "at home" in the Jewish Communities in Eastern Europe, were just one among a large variety of pastries specifically for Purim. Kindle, another Purim pastry, used only egg yolks, so they had the whites leftover for Habcsók. Although Meringue Kisses are sold throughout the year today, our family continues to bake them in preparation for Purim every year. They are simple to make, light and airy, and decorate any pastry platter beautifully.

3 egg whites
1 cup sugar
54 walnut or pecan halves, or as needed

Preheat oven to 275°F. In a medium bowl, beat whites on highest power. Once the whites begin to increase in volume and look fluffy, begin to add the sugar slowly. Continue beating until whites are stiff.

Using 2 spoons, wrap each nut half in a teaspoon of meringue. Or leave the meringues plain, if you prefer. Place each meringue not touching on a parchment paper-lined cookie sheet. Using a spoon, pull each meringue into a peak.

Bake until meringue is set and dry, about 30 minutes, checking to make sure the meringues are not browning on top. If they begin to brown, immediately reduce the oven temperature to 250°F. The meringues are done when the cookies look and feel dry but are not completely dried out. Remove from oven. Let cool and transfer to a serving platter.

Mandel Bread

(P)   Makes 2 (18-inch logs) about 50 to 60 pieces

Elsa Ickovic, a close friend of my mother, was born and raised in Czechoslovakia until the Holocaust. She survived in Budapest and today lives in Chicago. At this writing, Elsa bakes almost every day for her extended family and friends. Mandel bread, like biscotti, is a dime a dozen, but her mandel bread is a delicacy and yet easy to prepare. It freezes well, so you can bake it in advance, freeze, and then enjoy with a cup of coffee at your leisure.

For the Mandel Bread:
2½ cups sifted flour
½ teaspoon salt
1½ teaspoons baking powder
3 eggs
¾ cup sugar
¾ cup vegetable oil
1 teaspoon vanilla
½ cup chopped pecans
½ cup dark raisins

For the topping:
¼ cup sugar
2 teaspoons cinnamon

Preheat oven to 350°F. In medium bowl mix flour, salt and baking powder. Reserve. In large bowl, mix eggs, sugar, oil and vanilla, beating to mix well. Add flour mixture slowly and stir until well mixed. Add pecans and raisins. Mix.

In small bowl, combine the sugar and cinnamon for the topping. Reserve.

Line a half sheet pan with foil. Using foil, build walls on both sides of the length of the pan. Do the same three inches from each side of the pan, down the length of the pan. Divide the dough in half, and form two logs within the foil wall. Using your finger, make a shallow indentation down the middle of each log, end to end. Sprinkle with the topping.

Bake for 25 to 30 minutes. Remove from oven. Cut into ½ to 1-inch thick slices. Lay slices flat on a parchment paper-lined cookie sheet. Sprinkle with any remaining topping. Bake for 5 to 10 minutes longer. Remove pan from oven. Let cool completely. Store in an airtight container, or wrap and freeze.

Elsa's Story

Elsa grew up and lived in Velké Kapušany, Czechoslovakia, until she was a young adult. She was the ninth of 11 children in a large Chassidic family; seven of the children survived the War. Three had come to the States before the War; four survived the Holocaust. In 1939–1940, when the Hungarians invaded Czechoslovakia, it became impossible for the young Jewish girls to work. Elsa found a job in Budapest and went to work as a seamstress in a salon. There she received a letter from home warning her not to return. So until the end of the War she survived in Budapest, from crisis to crisis from peril to peril.

She survived with non-Jewish papers and with Jewish papers, and with the help of non-Jews and Jews: a non-Jew who devoted his life to helping Jews and was ultimately killed by the Nazis, a Jewish lawyer who worked on behalf of the Jews of Budapest with a non-Jewish assistant, and countless others. Elsa's experiences in and out of the ghetto, dodging Nazis who were shooting Jews into the Danube, looking for survivors amongst the dead and dying, would require a full-length book to recount. Her last job, which allowed her survival, was as a nurse in a hospital.

After the War she met and married her husband, came to the States with her two brothers (her husband followed later), worked as a professional seamstress, raised three children, and has been famous in her family for her baking throughout the years.

Chapter 10
Fruit Soups, Sauces, Compotes and Preserves

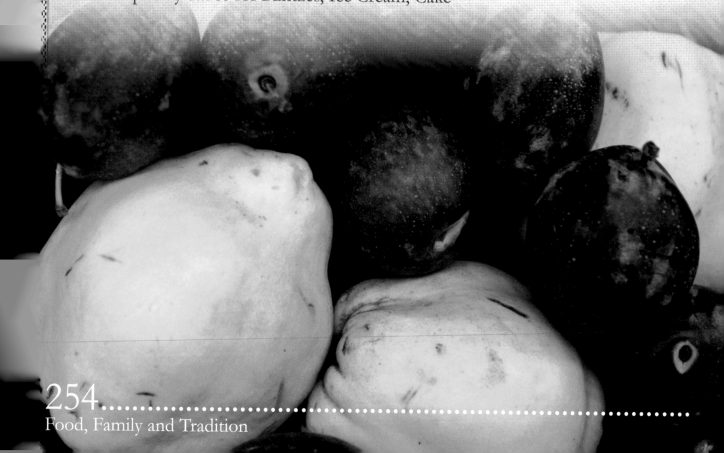

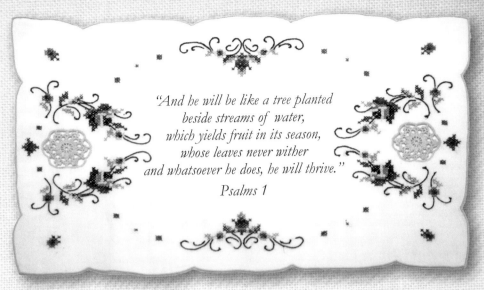

*"And he will be like a tree planted
beside streams of water,
which yields fruit in its season,
whose leaves never wither
and whatsoever he does, he will thrive."*

Psalms 1

The opening metaphor of the book of Psalms compares the perfect order of nature's cycles with the life of a good man. Central to the image that King David paints is "fruit in its season," a lesson that the good cook (like the good man) may take to heart. And from this metaphor the recipes in this chapter blossomed.

Just imagine cooking every day with perfectly ripe fruit just picked from the trees, vines or bushes in your garden! Of course that would mean constructing menus and recipes around the garden's seasonal bounty. My parents grew up in a time and place when their recipes relied exclusively on seasonal produce and methods of home preservation.

In the autumn, the tradition of dipping challah with a special prayer for a sweet New Year on Rosh Hashana has evolved into apples dipped in honey, because apples ripen in the fall. Their apple harvest became Baked Apples, Cooked Applesauce, and Sautéed Apple Relish.

The plum trees that grew in profusion on the back acreage of my father's childhood home bore fruit at the end of the summer. Plums were eaten fresh, out of hand, baked into pastries and stuffed into dumplings. The abundance that remained was turned into plum preserves, *lekvar*, which they preserved for use throughout the winter. The *lekvar* recipe in this chapter is as authentic in taste as that made by my grandparents; however, the updated method takes a fraction of the time to prepare.

My cousin Irving Weinberger recalls that "at home" his parents made slivovitz from the plums as well as wine from the grapes that grew in their yard in Munkács. My mother remembers picking berries from the banks of the Tisza River near her home in Vásárosnamény in the spring and summer. She loved them fresh but loved them even more in her mother's raspberry syrup and preserves. They are also delicious in my cousin Ibi's Fresh Berry Relish.

As the Hungarian cherries ripened in the summer, my parents' families cooked Sour Cherry Soup, wonderful served chilled on a summer day. My mother and my cousin still make it today. Quince had a brief fall season so my grandmothers made fresh compote for Rosh Hashana and Succos. Afterwards they used the surplus to make preserves for the winter.

While we appreciate the availability and convenience of frozen, canned and imported fruit, seasonal produce is still prized by home cooks and gifted chefs around the world. For this reason, I believe that farmer's markets, which offer seasonal produce at its peak, are growing in number. So when preparing the recipes in this chapter, please cook, as my grandparents and parents did "at home" with the freshest, ripest seasonal fruit.

Sour Cherry Soup, *Meggy Leves*

Ⓓ Makes 2 quarts, 12 (4-ounce) servings

This soup is made from the particular variety of cherries, sour cherries, which were abundant "at home." My mother's maternal grandparents had a sour cherry tree in their backyard in Gergely, Hungary. Her family cooked this soup during the months of July and August when the cherries ripened. A very fancy soup, it should be served in small portions and for special occasions. Many recipes call for adding a few cloves along with cinnamon, which adds a spicy fragrance to the soup. Sour cherry soup is light and refreshing and can be served hot or cold, as an appetizer, before the meal, or as a dairy dessert. Garnish it, as my cousin Ibi's mother Goldie did, with a fresh mint leaf on top.

1½ to 2 pounds sour cherries, pitted
6 cups water
½ cup sugar
1 teaspoon lemon juice
1 cinnamon stick or dash of cinnamon
Pinch of salt
1 cup sour cream
1 tablespoon flour, optional
Fresh mint leaves, as needed, optional garnish

Kosher Catering Munkács Style

My cousin Ibi Gelb remembers that her mother, Goldie Weinberger, served Sour Cherry Soup for company on Shabbos in the late afternoon in Munkács, for tea or a light meal (seudat shlishit), or at other special occasions. Since kosher catering did not exist in the Soviet Union, the women cooked and baked together, preparing as a community, in a private kitchen for social events. The Jewish community living in Munkács post–Holocaust had a strong bond and celebrated Jewish events, such as weddings, together. Although a wedding reception was either in a rented city hall or in a large yard attached to a private home, the wedding ceremony was always held on private property, in someone's yard within a fence, not in a public hall, because religious ceremonies were banned under communism.

In a 6 to 8-quart saucepan combine cherries, water, sugar, lemon juice, and cinnamon. Bring to a boil over medium-high heat

Decrease heat to low and simmer for about 20 minutes until the cherries are cooked and the soup becomes flavorful. Remove cinnamon stick and discard.

In a small bowl, combine the sour cream and salt. The flour will make a thicker, fuller soup, but it is not a necessity. If you want to add the flour, add it to the sour cream mixture and mix well, so that the sour cream is creamy.

Ladle out about 1 cup of liquid from the hot cherry soup. Add it very slowly to the sour cream mixture, beginning by adding one tablespoon at a time for about 6 tablespoons, and then ¼ cup at a time, mixing constantly after each addition to maintain the creamy consistency. Then add the sour cream mixture to the simmering soup, mixing constantly so it does not curdle. Heat through.

Serve hot in small bowls, or chill in an ice-water bath and refrigerate covered. Serve cold garnished with a fresh mint leaf. If you wish to reheat after refrigerating, reheat on very low heat to prevent curdling.

My mother originally added 1 egg yolk to the sour cream mixture, because she believed it made a richer soup. I have omitted it from the recipe, because we do not use uncooked eggs today. If you wish, beat 1 pasteurized egg yolk into the sour cream mixture and serve it immediately.

Add more cherries for a richer flavor. Add 4 cloves along with the cinnamon stick and discard them, after soup is cooked, along with the cinnamon stick.

Instead of using fresh sour cherries, you can make a quicker variation of this soup with canned or jarred sour cherries. Drain two (15-ounce) cans of sour cherries, reserving cherries and juice. Measure juice and add enough water to equal 6 cups total liquid. Add ⅓ cup sugar, a dash of cinnamon or 1 cinnamon stick and 1 teaspoon lemon juice. Bring the cherries and the liquid to a boil and cook for 5 minutes. Now prepare the sour cream mixture as above and add the sour cream mixture to the soup.

257

Strawberry Soup

P Makes 5½ cups, 8 to 10 servings

Sarah Muschel, Suri to the family, was my mother's beloved "baby cousin." Suri was always looking for new recipes. I found this in her recipe file just recently. I modernized the recipe somewhat, changing the wine from zinfandel to moscato for its effervescence of sweetness, and decreasing the grapefruit juice. Serve as a soup or a cocktail.

2 pounds fresh strawberries, stemmed and halved
3 tablespoons honey
Juice of 1 lime
¾ cup moscato wine
¾ cup grapefruit juice
Parve whipped topping, as needed
Honey, as needed

> Substitute frozen strawberries for fresh; adjust amount of honey if strawberries are sweetened.

In the work bowl of a food processor fitted with the metal blade, process the strawberries until puréed to desired consistency. Add the honey, lime juice, wine and grapefruit juice. Stir to mix.

Cover and refrigerate.

To serve:
Ladle into chilled bowls, top with 1 to 2 tablespoons of parve whipped topping and drizzle with a little honey. Or else pour into wine or Martini glasses, garnished with a slice of lime.

Food, Family and Tradition

Plum Preserves, *Lekvar*

Ⓟ Makes about 1 quart, 4 (8-ounce) jars

Homemade lekvar is fragrant, refreshing, in another culinary world from store-bought preserves. There is no exact formula for lekvar, but there is a traditional method: pit the plums, put them in a heavy pot on the lowest possible heat and stir for hours. "At home" they took turns stirring in a heavy copper cauldron. Sugar, if used, was added at the end of cooking. Added earlier, the preserve would have burned. When the preserve is thick and glossy (they knew from long experience), turn off the fire, and bottle the preserves. Today we have a shortcut—the food processor. Both methods are given below. My mother never started with less than 10 pounds of plums; I have good luck with 3 pounds. I do recommend a heavy, preferably enameled cast-iron pot.

3 pounds of ripe Italian plums
Sugar, as needed

Wash and drain the plums.
Halve and remove pits.

Traditional method:
Place pitted plums in a 4-quart heavy enameled pot over the lowest possible heat. Stir frequently until plums come to a simmer, then continue to stir constantly until plums become thick, heavy and glossy, the consistency of a thick preserve.
This will take 3 to 4 hours. When the preserves are ready, taste for sweetness and add 1 tablespoon sugar at a time, if needed.

Food processor method:
Place pitted plums in batches in food processor and pulse until plums are finely chopped but not puréed. Transfer to pot and proceed with recipe steps above, except shorten cooking time to 1 to 2 hours.

When *lekvar* is fully cooked and sweetened to taste, place in hot sterilized 8-ounce jars. Cool and refrigerate for up to 1 week. Or else can according to canning directions which can be found online: USDA Complete Guide to Home Canning.

Quince Preserves

P Makes about 1 quart, 4 (8-ounce) jars

Quince, hard and tasteless when raw, becomes fragrant and aromatic, soft and tender when cooked. My mother's grandparents had a quince tree in their yard, so quince preserves were prepared when the quinces were ripe and ready to be picked. In America quince is available in fall. It is easy to prepare and can be used as a side, for a pastry filling, or as you would use any other fruit preserve. Try it once, and you will fall in love with its unique, fragrant flavor, unlike any other fruit.

2 cups water
2 cups sugar
2½ pounds peel-on quince, about 4 to 5 quinces
½ peel-on lemon, seeded and finely chopped

In a 4-quart heavy pot over medium heat, cook the water and sugar, stirring occasionally, until the sugar has dissolved.

Meanwhile, core quinces. Reserve the cores with seeds intact. Tie cores in cheesecloth.

Coarsley dice quince. Add quince, reserved cores, and lemon to sugar-water in pot. Bring to a boil, decrease heat to low. Cover with a tight-fitting lid. Simmer very slowly for about 2 to 2½ hours, uncovering and stirring occasionally to prevent burning. As quince cooks, it begins to change color from white to pink.

Near the end of cooking, uncover and cook, stirring constantly, until preserves reach desired thickness. When preserves are rosy colored, aromatic and thick and glossy, they are fully cooked.

Transfer to hot, sterilized jars, seal and refrigerate for up to 1 week. Or else can according to canning directions, which can be found online: USDA Complete Guide to Home Canning.

Esrog Preserves and Candy

P Makes 1 cup

The esrog, a beautifully aromatic citrus fruit, is grown primarily in Israel for use on the Jewish holiday of Succos, the holiday of the harvest, taking place in the fall. After Succos the question always arises: what to do with the esrog? Many people stud it all over with whole cloves to use it for Besamim, the blessing on spices during Havdalah at the end of Shabbos. The esrog fruit, a variety of citron, is yellow, small to medium in size, ellipsoid or lemon shaped, with a long neck, and a rough and bumpy surface. Unlike a lemon, an esrog is quite seedy, not juicy, and inedible when raw. However, cooking transforms it into wonderful preserves, candy or compote.

1 esrog
1 cup sugar
1 cup water

For the candy:
Slice the esrog thinly and place in bowl covered with water. Cover and set aside for 1 day. The next day drain the water, and refill, cover and repeat soaking and draining for a total of 7 days. On the final day, drain the esrog.

Seed the esrog, reserving seeds. Tie the seeds in cheesecloth.

In a 2-quart pot, add the esrog and the cheesecloth-wrapped seeds, the sugar and water. Over medium-high heat, bring to a boil. Decrease heat and simmer, covered, stirring for about 45 minutes to 1 hour, until the esrog is cooked through. The consistency should be very thick and syrupy so, if needed, cook uncovered for the last 15 minutes.
Remove the esrog slice by slice with tongs and transfer to a platter. Pour the cooking syrup over the esrog slices. Let cool. When the slices are hardened and somewhat dry, transfer to an airtight container. It is similar to candied orange peel.

For the preserves:
cut the esrog into small pieces before cooking. Follow recipe directions. Immediately after cooking transfer esrog with syrup to a jar, cool to room temperature, cover and refrigerate.

Succos and Succah Decorations

A Succah as most Jewish people know, is a temporary hut built for Succos to commemorate the 40 years spent in the dessert. Margit Kirsche remembers, "Succos was a happy time, especially for the children. We were excited to build the succah, to decorate it, and we all looked to see who had the prettiest one. We made beautiful decorations, very different than the commercial ones today.
Our succah was made of cloth sheets attached to a wooden frame. On top we laid schach, or corn stalks.
We bought shiny papers, red, blue, green, purple, yellow, which we used to make the many decorations. We made interlocking stars of many colors.
We made birds of eggshells, using dough, beads and fancy paper. First we took the eggshells and used little tiny scissors to make pinholes on each of the four ends and blew out the egg. Then we mixed challah or dough with a little water, to form the head and added two beads for the eyes. Finally we folded shiny paper in accordion pleats to make them fan out and appear as the tail and the wings. The light at night was from the candles. We used our nice tablecloths and dishes; it was beautiful. We all ate in the succah, unless it was very cold."

Esrog-Quince Compote

P Makes 3 to 4 cups

If you are looking for a fresh alternative to using the esrog after Succos, this is a simple and refreshing recipe that takes advantage of the quince, which is ripe during the same season.

1 esrog
2 quince, peel-on, cored, thinly sliced
1½ cups water
1 cup sugar

Peel and seed the esrog. Discard seeds. Cut the esrog into thick pieces. Then follow the directions for soaking and draining the esrog for 7 days (page 262).

In a 2-quart pot, add the fruits, sugar and water. Over medium-high heat, bring to a boil. Decrease heat and simmer, covered, for 30 to 45 minutes, until the quince is pink and soft.

Remove from heat. Cool to room temperature. Transfer to bowl, cover and refrigerate.

The Four Species

On Succos, we hold the Arba Minim, the Four Species: the Lulav (palm branch) with Haddasim (myrtle branch) and Aravos (willow branch) in the right hand, and the esrog in the left to make a special blessing. The mitzvah is based on Leviticus 23:40: "And you shall take of yourselves on the first day the fruit of a goodly tree, a palm branch, the myrtle branch, and the willow of the brook; and you shall rejoice before the Lord your God seven days." Margit Kirsche remembers: "My grandfather always bought a lulav and esrog from Israel. They were expensive to bring in but we managed to obtain them. After Succos, we used the esrog for compote or preserves." Only 10 to 20 percent of the families in Vásárosnamény were able to afford the esrog. They were imported from Italy, Greece and Israel (Palestine). So, the shamas (rabbi's assistant) went from house to house carrying the lulav and esrog from the synagogue, knocking on each window, making sure that everyone, including those who could not afford to purchase the lulav and esrog was able to make the blessing.

Fresh Fruit Compote

(P) Makes 8 to 10 servings

There is no exact science to my mother's fresh fruit compote, except that the best compotes are made from slightly overripe fruit. Serve this either as a side dish or for dessert. My mother has always prepared and served this before Yom Kippur. After a filling meal this makes a light dessert before the fast.

3 pounds assorted fresh tree fruit, except for bananas and citrus fruit
¼ cup sugar, or to taste
Water, as needed, to just cover

Core and seed all fruit. You can peel apples and pears or not as you choose.

Slice fruit and place in a 3-quart heavy pot with sugar and water to barely cover. Bring to a boil over medium high heat. Decrease heat and simmer, uncovered, stirring frequently, until compote is reduced and soft, 15 to 20 minutes.

Serve warm or at room temperature. Or cover and refrigerate and serve cold.

Bananas

Since I was a young child, bananas and sour cream have been a simple and satisfying snack. As the years went by I have varied the dish my mother prepared for me.

She sliced one or 2 ripe firm bananas into a bowl and topped them with sour cream and sugar. Today, I have replaced the sour cream with yogurt or even frozen yogurt, reduced or eliminated the sugar and added berries to the bananas and maybe a touch of granola. Bananas did not grow in Hungary, and my mother tasted bananas only once as a child before coming to the States. Her father, who had been trying to find a way to get to the States with his family, had spent five years working as a watchmaker in Cuba, from 1923 to 1928. When he returned home, he brought my mother a necklace and a bunch of bananas for the family. My mother says that as a child she did not miss bananas, because the fruits that were available in Hungary were absolutely delicious: peaches, sour cherries, sweet cherries, plums, apples, pears, and my mother's favorite, quinces. My father, on the other hand, had at least one banana every day while working at Hungarian Kosher Foods. He loved bananas and when he was hungry, he would pick up a banana, peel it and eat it with great enjoyment. Because of his love of bananas, there was always a bunch on the kitchen counter in my parents' home. A bunch of bananas still has pride of place on my mother's kitchen counter today.

Dried Fruit Compote

P Makes 3 cups

"At home" dried fruit was available in stores, (such as my mother's Uncle Chaim's store) or else home-dried, as my aunt Goldie did, in the sun, outside her home. Dried fruit compote is a favorite for Succos. My mother made this frequently in the States with dried plums (prunes), apricots, pears and apples—whatever was available—but always dried plums, my father's favorites. Sometimes, in season, she added a cut-up fresh quince, an added special fragrance. She adds very little sugar, and she says that the water brings the fruit back to life.

1 pound mixed, dried fruit
1½ cups water
½ cup sugar or to taste

In a heavy 2-quart pot add fruit, water and sugar. Bring to a boil over high heat, stirring occasionally. Decrease heat, cover and simmer for 20 to 30 minutes, or until fruit is plump and liquid is reduced to a light syrup.

Cool, cover and refrigerate for up to 1 week.

Serve in a clear glass or a white china serving bowl as a side or dessert. Spoon over sliced plain cake or Honey Cake (page 244), or cinnamon ice cream.

Succos in Munkács

Religion was forbidden in the Soviet Union. My cousin, Sonia, who lived in an apartment in the center of town did not have a Succah; it was illegal. However, my cousins, Irving and Ibi remember well the Succah that their parents built in back of the house, which was located on the outskirts of the town. It was surrounded by a high fence and therefore not visible from the street. One had to be very careful, because even the neighbors could report you to the KGB, but regarding the Succah, Ibi remembers, "We could always claim it was a hut built for the children to play." My cousin, Irving, remembers their beautiful Succah, built every year and set for the holiday with his mother's candlesticks and his father's Kiddush cup.

> Add 1 cored, peel-on, diced fresh quince to the dried fruit.

> For extra spice, add a few cinnamon sticks, whole cloves, and some seeded, thin fresh lemon slices to the fruit compote at the beginning of cooking. Discard spices before serving.

265

Baked Apples

(P) Makes 4 servings

Baked apples were always one of my favorite desserts, both sweet and refreshing. Served warm or at room temperature they are like apple pie without the crust. Quick to prepare, they take an hour to bake. My mom made great baked apples with cinnamon and sugar. I have added a few bells and whistles.

4 Granny Smith, Jonathan, or Golden Delicious apples
4 tablespoons sugar
½ teaspoon cinnamon, or to taste
2 tablespoons chopped pecans, optional
2 tablespoons dark or golden raisins, optional
4 tablespoons *streusel* topping (recipe follows), optional

Preheat the oven to 375°F. Core apples leaving ½ inch at the bottom; do not cut through.

In a separate small bowl mix together sugar and cinnamon. If using pecans and raisins, mix with cinnamon-sugar.

Lightly spray an 8-inch-square glass baking dish with cooking spray. Place apples in baking dish. Spoon cinnamon-sugar, with pecans and raisins if using, equally among the hollowed apples. Cover with lightly sprayed foil. Bake one hour.

If using *streusel*, bake until apples are almost cooked through, 45 minutes. Remove from oven. Uncover, spoon on any pan juices, and sprinkle with 1 tablespoon *streusel* each. Return to oven and bake until apples are cooked through and *streusel* is golden, 15 to 20 minutes.

Streusel

Makes about 1 cup

⅔ cup flour
⅓ cup sugar
⅓ cup margarine

In a small bowl mix together flour and sugar. Cut margarine into small pieces and cut into flour-sugar mixture until the texture of a coarse meal.

Cooked Applesauce

P Makes 4 cups

"At home," without refrigeration, an abundance of fresh fruit was cooked both for a refreshing dessert and as a way to preserve it for future use. Applesauce is easy to prepare and wonderful as a side dish, a relish or a dessert, and it tastes entirely different from canned applesauce on supermarket shelves. I like tangy Granny Smith apples, so I have added sugar. My mom uses her favorite Jonathan. Feel free to use other apples, and adjust the sugar to your taste. Add cinnamon or cinnamon sticks to taste, or cook with a few drops of fresh lemon to enhance the flavor. A handful of raisins are also a nice addition.

3 pounds apples, cored and peeled
⅓ cup water, or as needed to cover the bottom of the pan
⅓ cup sugar, or to taste
½ cup raisins, optional
2 cinnamon sticks, optional
A few drops of fresh lemon juice, optional

Cut the apples into slices or chunks.

In a heavy 3-quart pot or Dutch oven, pour the water. Add the apples and the sugar, and the raisins, cinnamon and lemon juice if using.

Over medium heat, bring to a boil. Decrease heat and cover. Simmer, stirring occasionally to make sure the apples do not burn, for about 30 to 40 minutes, until the apples have reduced to a thick sauce. If it is too watery, uncover and cook, for another 5 minutes, stirring to make sure the apples do not burn. Remove cinnamon sticks and discard. Let cool to room temperature, cover and refrigerate for up to 5 days.

Just One Apple

Perhaps the following story explains why my mother has always believed in the healing power of apples. After she had been in Auschwitz for six months, my mother was transferred to Torgau, euphemistically called a "work camp" because it lacked gas chambers. A very dear childhood friend, Hindu, was also in Auschwitz with her own mother (the Rebbetzin or Rabbi's wife). In order to stay with my mother, Hindu and her mother had sneaked onto the train that was transferring my mother to Torgau, and were brutally beaten by the Nazis for doing so. While they were in Torgau, Hindu's mother became quite ill and thought that if only she could eat an apple, it would help her regain her strength. In Torgau, there was a German foreman, not a member of the Nazi party, who simply was kind to the Jewish prisoners. My mother had mended two of his torn shirts, and so he was especially nice to her. Sometimes, he brought her a bit of food. And one time, he even took my mother out to his house, and served her a dinner together with his family, a wife and four daughters. All of his daughters were married, and none of his sons-in-law were members of the Nazi party. On the day when Hindu's mother was sick, my mother asked this foreman for an apple and he brought it to her. My mother, who was herself starving, gave this apple to Hindu's mother. Both Hindu and her mother survived and were liberated together with my mother on April 27, 1945. About six months after the War, Hindu saw my mother's brother, Morton, walking across the street in Munich. She crossed the street and told him that my mother was alive.

Sautéed Apple Relish

P Makes about 2 cups

This variation of applesauce has more of the fruit texture in each bite and is easy and quick to prepare. Both Veronica Sporia and my cousin, Ibi, prepare and serve it often, because, as Ibi explains, everyone likes sides that are not starches. Serve it hot, cold or at room temperature. If you shred the apples by hand, do not core before grating, and use the coarsest grate. If you shred the apples in a food processor, core apples, slice into pieces and use the shredding blade.

3 pounds apples, a mixture of Red and Golden Delicious apples (about 6 to 7 apples), peeled but not cored
1 to 2 tablespoons vegetable oil, or as needed, to film the bottom of the pan
⅓ cup sugar
1 teaspoon cinnamon or to taste

> Ibi reduces the oil to 1 tablespoon, the cinnamon to a dash, and substitutes 2 tablespoons of brown sugar for ⅓ cup of white.
>
> For a less sweet relish, reduce white sugar to 3 tablespoons.

Peel apples and shred by hand on the coarsest side of a box grater into a colander. Reserve. Alternatively, core apples and slice and shred in a food processor using the shredder disk. Transfer to a colander.

Place oil in a 12-inch nonstick skillet. Add sugar. Over medium-high heat, dissolve sugar, stirring occasionally.

Press excess liquid from apples in colander. Add apples to sugar in pan. Let cook for 3 to 5 minutes. Then stir, and add cinnamon. Cook for 10 minutes, stirring occasionally, until apples are cooked through but not mushy.

Remove from heat and serve warm or at room temperature in a serving dish. Or else cover and refrigerate and serve cold.

Ibi's Fresh Berry Relish

P Makes 20 servings

Ibi has been making this relish for years, as her mother Goldie did "at home." Ibi says, "We served this with turkey and added little wild fresh strawberries, which gives a wonderful aroma and were abundant "at home", but are rare in the States." Ibi and her friends, who grew up in the Soviet Union, all celebrate Thanksgiving here and serve this as an accompaniment for the turkey. It is delicious and refreshing as well during fresh berry season.

½ cup chopped walnuts
1 pound strawberries, chopped fine
1 pint blueberries
1 pint raspberries, divided
1 tablespoon sugar

Omit sugar, add 1 (15-ounce) can whole berry cranberry sauce. Follow the recipe directions.

Cook the walnuts in an 8-inch nonstick skillet over medium-high heat, stirring often, until browned, 3 to 5 minutes. Reserve; let cool.

Meanwhile, in a large bowl mash all of the strawberries and half the raspberries with a fork or potato masher. Leave the remaining half of the raspberries whole.

Add the remaining berries to the bowl. Add sugar. Mix gently, cover and refrigerate for at least 30 minutes. Remove from the refrigerator, stir, transfer to a serving bowl and garnish the top with the walnuts.

Refrigerate leftovers covered for 2 to 3 days.

Fresh Raspberry Sauce for Blintzes, Ice Cream, and Cake

(P) Makes about 1 cup

"At home" the fruit sauces were not purchased in jars from the supermarket but made from fresh fruit. Try this and I believe you will never buy prepared fruit sauce again, especially if you use a food processor.

1 pint fresh raspberries
1½ tablespoons sugar

> Substitute one pint of fresh strawberries or blueberries for raspberries. Substitute blackberries, and strain out the seeds.

In a food processor fitted with the metal blade, purée berries. Add sugar and continue to purée until almost liquid. Transfer to a small bowl, cover and refrigerate. Or, before refrigerating, strain sauce through a very fine-mesh strainer to remove the seeds.

To serve:
Spoon sauce over blintzes, ice cream or cake.

Yesterday's Soft Drinks
Shabbos was always a special occasion, and there was always something extra. My mother and her brothers eagerly awaited their mother's special homemade Shabbos drink. Equal amounts of sugar and hand-picked raspberries were cooked until reduced to a syrup, and the seeds strained out. Then it was mixed with seltzer for a sweet, effervescent and much-anticipated treat.

Recipe Index

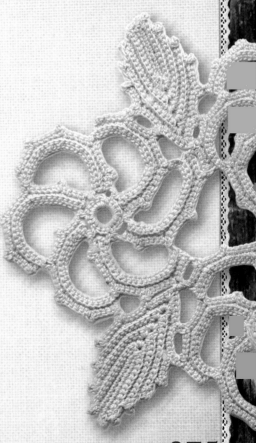

Metric Conversions and Equivalents

The following metric equivalents are approximate			
volume			
¼ teaspoon	1 milliliter	½ cup	120 milliliters
½ teaspoon	2.5 milliliters	⅔ cup	160 milliliters
¾ teaspoon	4 milliliters	¾ cup	180 milliliters
1 teaspoon	5 milliliters	1 cup	240 milliliters
1¼ teaspoons	6 milliliters	1¼ cups	300 milliliters
1½ teaspoons	7.5 milliliters	1½ cups	360 milliliters
1¾ teaspoons	8.5 milliliters	1⅔ cups	400 milliliters
2 teaspoons	10 milliliters	2 cups (1 pint)	460 milliliters
1 tablespoon	15 milliliters	3 cups	700 milliliters
2 tablespoons	30 milliliters	4 cups (1 quart)	0.95 liter
¼ cup	60 milliliters	1 quart plus ¼ cup	1 liter
⅓ cup	80 milliliters	4 quarts (1 gallon)	3.8 liters
weight			
¼ ounce	7 grams	3 ounces	85 grams
½ ounce	14 grams	4 ounces (¼ pound)	113 grams
¾ ounce	21 grams	5 ounces	142 grams
1 ounce	28 grams	6 ounces	170 grams
1¼ ounces	35 grams	7 ounces	198 grams
1½ ounces	42.5 grams	8 ounces (½ pound)	227 grams
1⅔ ounces	45 grams	16 ounces (1 pound)	454 grams
2 ounces	57 grams	35.25 ounces	1 kilogram
length			
⅛ inch	3 milliliters	2½ inches	6 centimeters
¼ inch	6 milliliters	4 inches	10 centimeters
½ inch	1¼ centimeters	5 inches	13 centimeters
1 inch	2½ centimeters	6 inches	15¼ centimeters
2 inches	5 centimeters	12 inches (1 foot)	30 centimeters

Familiar Ingredients with Approximate Equivalents

1 cup all-purpose flour	140 grams
1 cup uncooked white rice	185 grams
½ cup butter (4 ounces / 8 tablespoons / 1 stick)	110 grams
1 cup butter (8 ounces / 16 tablespoons / 2 sticks)	220 grams
1 cup granulated sugar	200 grams
1 cup brown sugar, firmly packed	225 grams

to convert	multiply
ounces to grams	ounces by 28.35
pounds to kilograms	pounds by .454
teaspoons to milliliters	teaspoons by 4.93
tablespoons to milliliters	tablespoons by 14.79
fluid ounces to milliliters	fluid ounces by 29.57
cups to milliliters	cups by 236.59
cups to liters	cups by .236
pints to liters	pints by .473
quarts to liters	quarts by .946
gallons to liters	gallons by 3.785
inches to centimeters	inches by 2.54

Oven Temperatures Conversions and Equivalents

To convert Fahrenheit to Celsius, first subtract 32 from Fahrenheit, next multiply the number by 5, lastly divide by 9

fahrenheit	celsius	british gas mark
200°	95°	0
225°	110°	¼
250°	120°	½
275°	135°	1
300°	150°	2
325°	165°	3
350°	175°	4
375°	190°	5
400°	200°	6
425°	220°	7
450°	230°	8
475°	245°	9

The capitalization and italicization of food names generally follows the recommendations in *Food Lover's Companion*, by Sharon Tyler Herbst (Barron's, 2007). The capitalization of wine names follows the recommendations in *The Wine Bible*, by Karen MacNeil (Workman, 2001).

My Recipes and Remembrances